A BOOK OF
MONSTERS

DAVID J. HOWE

BBC BOOKS

BBC DOCTOR WHO fiction novels include:

THE EIGHT DOCTORS by Terrance Dicks 0 563 40563 5
THE BODYSNATCHERS by Mark Morris 0 563 40568 6
GENOCIDE by Paul Leonard 0 563 40572 4
WAR OF THE DALEKS by John Peel 0 563 40573 2
THE DEVIL GOBLINS FROM NEPTUNE by Keith Topping and Martin Day 0 563 40564 3
THE MURDER GAME by Steve Lyons 0 563 40565 1
THE ULTIMATE TREASURE by Christopher Bulis 0 563 40571 6
BUSINESS UNUSUAL by Gary Russell 0 563 40575 9
ILLEGAL ALIEN by Mike Tucker and Robert Perry 0 563 40570 8

DOCTOR WHO titles on BBC Video include:

THE WAR MACHINES starring William Hartnell BBCV 6183
THE AWAKENING/FRONTIOS starring Peter Davison BBCV 6120
THE HAPPINESS PATROL starring Sylvester McCoy BBCV 5803

Other DOCTOR WHO titles available from BBC Worldwide Publishing:

POSTCARD BOOK 0 563 40561 9
THE NOVEL OF THE FILM on audio tape 0 563 38148 5/Z1998

Published by BBC Books, an imprint of BBC Worldwide Publishing
BBC Worldwide Ltd, Woodlands, 80 Wood Lane, London W12 0TT.
First published 1997.
© David J. Howe 1997. The moral right of the author has been asserted.

Original series broadcast on the BBC
Format © BBC 1963
Terry Nation is the creator of the Daleks.
Doctor Who, TARDIS and the Daleks are trademarks of the BBC.

ISBN O 563 40562 7

Imaging and design by **BLACK**SHEEP, © copyright BBC.

Printed in Great Britain by Cambus Litho Ltd, East Kilbride.
Bound in Great Britain by Hunter and Foulis Ltd, Edinburgh.
Colour operations by Dot Gradations, Wickford.
Jacket printed by Lawrence Allen Limited, Weston-Super-Mare.

ACKNOWLEDGEMENTS

As always I am indebted to numerous people who have taken the time to speak to me over the years about their work for *Doctor Who*, and also to several friends and colleagues for pointing me in the right direction.

First and foremost, this book was significantly improved by the input of Stephen James Walker and Andrew Pixley, to whom I owe, as always, a huge debt.

Thanks also this time around to Sophie Aldred, Robert Allsopp, Dee Baron, Bobi Bartlett, Martin Baugh, Paul Bernard, Lisa Bowerman, Allister Bowtell, David Brunt, Tony Clark, Raymond P. Cusick, Kevin Davies, Terrance Dicks, Sandra Exelby, Peter Griffiths, Patricia Holmes (for permission to reproduce Robert Holmes' original story outlines), Sylvia James, Barbara Kidd, James Macey (for a superb design job), Stephen Mansfield, Stan Mitchell, Susan Moore, Terry Nation (for permission to reproduce the *Daleks – Genesis of Terror* outline), Barry Newbery, John Peel, Marc Platt, Tim Robins and Gary Hopkins, Mark Stammers, Mike Tucker, Alexandra Tynan, Julian Vince, Martin Wiggins, Sue Willis, John Wood.

For archival interviews and other information, thanks must go to the following magazines, books and periodicals: *Doctor Who Magazine*, the *Radio Times, Dreamwatch Bulletin, TV Zone, Cybermen* by David Banks, *The Radiophonic Workshop: The First Twenty Five Years* by Roy Curtis-Bramwell and Desmond Briscoe, *Doctor Who: The Sixties, Doctor Who: The Seventies* and *Doctor Who: The Eighties* all by David J Howe, Mark Stammers and Stephen James Walker.

The following fan publications were also used to source selected quotes: *An Adventure in Space and Time* edited by Tim Robins, Gary Hopkins and Stephen James Walker, *Christopher Robbie: A Celebration* edited by Dominic May, *Cosmic Masque* edited by Ian McLachlan, *The Frame* edited by David J Howe, Mark Stammers and Stephen James Walker, *In-Vision* edited by Justin Richards, Peter Anghelides and Anthony Brown, *The MLG Megazine* edited by Graeme Wood, *Oracle* edited by David J Howe and Chris Dunk, *Shada* edited by Gary Russell, *TARDIS* edited by Stephen Payne and Richard Walter, *Wheel in Space* edited by Martin Wiggins and Chris Marton.

Some material included in chapters seven and eight originally appeared in the fan magazine *The Frame*, written and edited by David J Howe, Mark Stammers and Stephen James Walker.

Thanks to Keith Barnfather of Reeltime Pictures for making available all the original interview material recorded for their 1995 video release *I Was A Doctor Who Monster*, (which partially inspired this book in the first place) and to Gary Russell, who asked the questions for that release.

All script extracts remain © their respective authors.

Special thanks to Nuala, Margaret, Steve, Maritta, Sunita and, of course, Rosemary for believing in me. It means a lot, people.

DEDICATION

This book is for the monsters in my life: to James (chief monster),
Andrew (monster-in-training) and Rosemary (mummy monster).

AUTHOR'S NOTE

If there was one thing that brought me to watch *Doctor Who* week after week, it was the monsters. My earliest memories are of the Cybermen lurking in London's sewers and of the Yeti roaming the web-strewn Underground tunnels. My fascination for these unsung anti-heroes of the show has lasted to this day and, almost as soon as I was able, I delighted in seeking out and talking to all those men and women who were responsible for bringing my childhood nightmares to life. This book is foremost a celebration of the work of those people – the many creative talents that combined behind the scenes to bring monsters to viewers' television screens week after week.

According to the dictionary definition, a monster can be many things, and not just some shambling, drooling, multi-legged alien horror. In fact, in one of *Doctor Who*'s frequent early forays into history, a story called *The Aztecs*, one of the Doctor's companions rants at Autloc, an Aztec high priest: 'You're monsters, all of you, monsters!'

Whether this line was included in the scripts in order to point out that monsters come in all shapes and sizes is a subject for debate but this is not the focus of this book. The loose definition of 'monster' being used here is something that is generally non-humanoid and which involved a degree of costume and make-up skill to create. I therefore include such beings as the Voords (although they are visibly humanoid and are actually described as 'men'), because they are an early example of an alien life form created through the use of a fairly basic costume, and Davros (who is really nothing more than a crippled humanoid) because, as the creator of the Daleks, he holds a special place in *Doctor Who* mythology. We will not be meeting monsters of the human kind.

There are bound to be some favourite creatures that are not covered in detail in this book and this is because of the constraints of space and time. *Doctor Who* featured many different alien species, monsters, creatures, deformed humanoids, robots, exotic plants and other assorted life forms during its run on BBC television and the resources required to document them all fully are more than I have available for this volume. However, by way of compensation, there is an illustrated gazetteer to help identify many of the alien life forms that the Doctor faced during his televised adventures in time and space.

Over *Doctor Who*'s original 26 year span it was produced by no fewer than nine producers and the scripts for the show were commissioned and monitored by 15 different script editors (a post which was officially termed a 'story editor' for the first five seasons). The producer and script editor between them formulated the style and direction of the show and so, as people moved on and new faces arrived to take their place, *Doctor Who* changed. In addition, the actor playing the Doctor has changed seven times (from William Hartnell, through Patrick Troughton, Jon Pertwee, Tom Baker, Peter Davison, Colin Baker, Sylvester McCoy and, in the nineties, Paul McGann – although, as of writing, the eighth Doctor has yet to encounter any true monsters), and along the way he picked up and left behind numerous travelling companions. Because this book concentrates on the monsters, some of the chapters cross the boundaries between producers, script editors, Doctors and companions. In order to simplify the text, it will be assumed throughout that these personnel change from time to time and the text will refer to whoever was currently incumbent in the given role according to which period in the show's history is being discussed.

Throughout this book extracts from the original camera and rehearsal scripts have been used. Wherever possible, we have used the original grammar and spellings. In some cases, however, these have been corrected for reasons of clarity.

During the first two-and-a-half years of *Doctor Who*'s television life, each episode was given an individual on-screen title. Overall story titles did not start to be used on screen until *The Savages*, transmitted in May/June 1966. In this book, the overall titles as used internally by the BBC at the time of production are used for the stories prior to this, with individual episode titles specified to identify episodes within stories where appropriate.

One final comment. In many of my previous books about *Doctor Who*, a deliberate policy has been adopted of taking a totally impartial view of the show. Personal comment and criticism has, on the whole, been taboo. For this book, however, I have relaxed this 'rule' slightly to allow for some of my personal preferences and dislikes to be aired; for instance, in the choice of monsters covered.

I was brought up on *Doctor Who* and its monsters. Let's go meet them...

David J. Howe

CONTENTS

CHAPTER 1

THE MONSTERS ARE COMING

monster *(mon'ster) [O.F. monstre, L. Monstrum, a portent or omen, from monére, to warn],* **n.** *Something misshapen, abnormal, out of the ordinary course of nature; an abortion, a deformed creature; an imaginary animal, usually compounded of incongruous parts, such as a centaur, griffin, mermaid, gorgon etc.; an abominably cruel or depraved person; a person, animal, or thing of extraordinary size; a prodigy, a marvel, a portent.*

FROM THE CONCISE ENGLISH DICTIONARY, FOURTH EDITION, 1990, PUB. CASSELL.

Doctor Who would not be *Doctor Who* without the monsters.

It is almost impossible to think of the series without experiencing a heady rush of nostalgia at all those times when the programme scared viewers witless and sent thousands of children hurrying behind the sofa, out of the room or into the safety of their parents' arms.

Many people have many memories associated with the show, mostly tinged with a childlike fascination. I remember being wary of travelling by London Underground for years after I 'discovered', thanks to a 1968 *Doctor Who* story called *The Web of Fear*, that giant, furry, robot Yeti prowled down there, armed with deadly web-spewing guns. Even today, some thirty years after *The Web of Fear* was transmitted, I still feel a shiver of excitement when faced with the dark and somehow foreboding mouth of a beckoning London Underground railway tunnel. Others may remember the Cybermen and recall how childhood games were

perhaps played by wearing a knitted balaclava helmet on backwards to simulate the Cybermen's blank, expressionless faces. A Dalek was easier still for children to emulate. All you needed was a cardboard box, or a green metal school rubbish bin, and boys and girls across the country could be transformed into the Doctor's deadliest enemy.

Before we launch into a more detailed look at the monsters, perhaps some explanation of what *Doctor Who* is and how it all started is appropriate.

Doctor Who was, in 1989, the longest-running science fiction television series in the world, and one of the longest-running shows of any type. Its first episode was shown on Saturday 23 November 1963 and was billed in the BBC's television listings magazine *Radio Times* as consisting of 'adventures in time and space'. In a short article in the edition dated 21 November 1963 to accompany the transmission of the first episode, the basis for the serial was explained:

Dr Who? That is just the point. Nobody knows precisely who he is, this mysterious exile from another world and a distant future whose adventures begin today. But this much is known: he has a ship in which he can travel through space and time – although, owing to a defect in its instruments, he can never be sure where and when his 'landings' may take place. And he has a grand-daughter Susan, a strange amalgam of teenage normality and uncanny intelligence.

Playing the Doctor is the well-known film actor, William Hartnell, who has not appeared before on BBC-tv.

Each adventure in the series will cover several weekly episodes, and the first is by the Australian author Anthony Coburn. It begins by telling how the Doctor finds himself visiting the Britain of today: Susan (played by Carole Ann Ford) has become a pupil at an ordinary British school, where her incredible breadth of knowledge has whetted the curiosity of two of her teachers. These are the history teacher Barbara Wright (Jacqueline Hill), and the science master Ian Chesterton (William Russell), and their curiosity leads them to become inextricably involved in the Doctor's strange travels.

Because of the imperfections in the ship's navigation aids, the four travellers are liable in subsequent stories to find themselves absolutely anywhere in time – past, present, or future. They may visit a distant galaxy where civilisation has been devastated by the blast of a neutron bomb or they may find themselves journeying to far Cathay in the caravan of Marco Polo. The whole cosmos in fact is their oyster.

Doctor Who was initially transmitted on Saturday evenings, sandwiched between the popular sports show *Grandstand* and a puppet film series called *The Telegoons*. As time went on, the Saturday evening line-up of television programmes became more and more important as each TV channel attempted to come up with a formula which would ensure that viewers stayed tuned in to them. The BBC's line-up was, for many years, generally considered superior.

When *Doctor Who* started, following the News at 5.40 p.m. came *Juke Box Jury*, a popular pop-music show presented by David Jacobs. This was followed by *Dixon of Dock Green*, a long-running police show starring Jack Warner as PC George Dixon, *Wells Fargo*, an American-made Western series, and finally 'the Saturday Film'.

As time progressed so the schedule developed and in the seventies shows like *The Generation Game*, presented by Bruce Forsyth, became hugely popular with the public and, along with *The Basil Brush Show* and *Doctor Who*, kept viewers tuned to BBC1 in their millions. During the eighties, the BBC's programme schedulers decided to move *Doctor Who* from its traditional slot and the show found itself being transmitted on weekday evenings, for a time scheduled against the long-running soap opera *Emmerdale Farm* and finally against *Coronation Street*, one of the consistently top-rated shows of all time.

Until this time, for nearly two decades, *Doctor Who* was the reason why children and adults settled down by their television sets on Saturday evenings. This pattern was repeated in colleges and universities, with the show as much a part of student life as the scheduled lessons, lectures and bar opening times.

Doctor Who's first story was called *100,000 BC* and, while it did not feature any monsters, was a good example of how *Doctor Who* would work as a series. It would be partly educational, in this case explaining about prehistoric man (although the anachronism that they could speak was somewhat glossed over) and

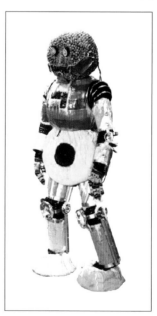

how fire was an important and vital tool for man's development; partly moralistic, in this instance showing how friends could turn into enemies and how enemies could be friends together; and partly adventurous with the Doctor and his companions getting themselves into difficult situations that they then had to work a way out of, for example being captured by a Stone Age tribe and sealed in a sacrificial 'cave of skulls'. There would also be fantastical elements, as in the opening episode of *100,000 BC* when the Doctor's and Susan's non-human origin is revealed and viewers are introduced to the Doctor's space-time machine called TARDIS – an acronym for Time And Relative Dimension In Space – a name invented by Susan to describe the Doctor's ship.

These historical escapades would alternate with tales set in the future, and a third type of story, the 'sideways move', was also developed. The drive to produce this mix was great enough for story editor David Whitaker to consider in April 1964 hiring writers as 'experts' in each area – Terry Nation was suggested as a senior writer to handle the futuristic stories, and another (unnamed) writer was suggested to handle the historical stories – in order to reduce the number of writers employed on the show and to try to ensure a degree of consistency and growth with the regular characters.

This mix of stories ensured that the show was constantly changing and one of the most exciting things about *Doctor Who* was its unpredictability. Every few weeks the TARDIS materialised somewhere new, and, almost without fail, the Doctor and his companions found themselves confronted by all manner of alien creatures, hostile monsters or megalomaniacal humanoids. Viewers knew that anything could, and probably would, happen. *Doctor Who* also made effective use of what was known as a 'cliffhanger ending'. This method of storytelling had been popularised in three *Flash Gordon* serial films made between 1936 and 1940 and starring Buster Crabbe as the eponymous hero. At the end of each episode, Gordon, his friends, or some other character was revealed to be in hideous danger – probably from Ming the Merciless – and the only way to find out how they escaped was to return to the cinema the following week.

Doctor Who operated in the same way with the added benefit of there being many more different adventures than Flash Gordon had enjoyed. The first episode of each story was especially key in this regard as, often, its ending revealed the first view of the monster. This may have been nothing more than a glimpse, a shadow or maybe a strange sucker on a stick, but the tradition of cliffhanger endings is one that no other television show has exploited so successfully.

The menaces that the Doctor came up against were legion but their inclusion in the plot tended to be for the same basic reasons: to show that good most often triumphed over evil (but not always) and that sometimes the line between 'good' and 'evil' was blurred. These themes provided the basis for the vast majority of the Doctor's adventures. As with all good drama series, where a structure was worked out in advance and a line was drawn which marked the apparent boundaries of the series, occasionally these boundaries were crossed and the Doctor would find himself up against demons from within. These adventures concerned no visible threat to the Doctor or his companions except that which they themselves had created. This type of story allowed for the all-important interplay between the main characters which, in turn, allowed for character development. *Doctor Who* mixed all these elements together and the result was an often potent brew of science fiction, adventure, horror, suspense and fantasy that managed to surpass the restrictions imposed by making a television show and presented imaginative stories told in a way which enthralled children and adults alike.

Doctor Who was also not afraid to moralise, or to use real-life events as the basis for the Doctor's adventures, but this aspect of the show was never thrust upon the viewers. Most often, the stories contained subtexts and layers and could be appreciated on many levels. For example, the fifth-Doctor story *Warriors of the Deep* is, on the surface, an action adventure tale about two species of reptile creatures called Silurians (land) and Sea Devils (aquatic) attacking an underwater military Sea Base in order to launch some nuclear missiles and trigger a war between human superpowers. There is intrigue aplenty in the plot with human spies and double-agents as well as the involvement of the reptiles.

There is, however, another level to the story, where the humans find themselves forced to use a gas lethal to all sea life in order to destroy the invading creatures. In the fighting that follows, almost everyone, human and reptile, on the Sea Base is killed. The Doctor just manages to prevent the nuclear missiles from firing and the Earth is saved, but at what cost? 'There should have been another way,' mutters the Doctor in exhausted exasperation at the story's conclusion, and this is perhaps the moral. The Sea Devils and Silurians – who are in the *Doctor Who* universe the original inhabitants of Earth – only wanted to reclaim their planet from the 'apes' who had risen to prominence while the reptiles hibernated, and the humans only wanted to live in peace (admittedly a peace enforced by a nuclear deterrent).

The Doctor advocated discussion and diplomacy all along but when one is being attacked, fighting back is the natural emotional response with the perhaps predictable result that death will follow. *Doctor Who* always tried to promote 'another way' and showed that peace and morals were something worth fighting for, but not in a manner that may result in the deaths of innocent creatures.

The monsters, aliens and other life forms encountered by the Doctor tended to be the focus through which the other important aspects of the series could be presented. With a nasty alien horror threatening a planet with slavery, destruction, or in some cases both, it was perhaps easier to create the moments of drama, tension and entertainment that form the bread and butter of a television series. There was always some area of conflict which the Doctor had to try to resolve. If there was no threat then there was no story and, the more the odds were stacked on the side of the oppressor, the more the Doctor had to use his intelligence and ingenuity to win out.

The life forms encountered by the Doctor have not all been intent on evil deeds. Some have no intelligence and simply react to situations around them (like the bell-plants on Tigella (*Meglos*) or the Dalek-spotting eye plants on Spiridon (*Planet of the Daleks*)) while others are nothing more than amoral, having no good or bad side and creating havoc simply because they can (like Azal (*The Dæmons*) or Sutekh (*Pyramids of Mars*)). There have been pacifist races (the Gonds (*The Krotons*), the Dulcians (*The Dominators*), the Thals (*The Mutants, Planet of the Daleks, Genesis of the Daleks*), the Xerons (*The Space Museum*) and the Rills (*Galaxy 4*)), militaristic races (the Sontarans, the Moroks (*The Space Museum*) and the Drahvins (*Galaxy 4*)), and races which have both good and bad sides represented (humans, Draconians (*Frontier in Space*), Kaleds (*Genesis of the Daleks*), Ice Warriors, Mentors (*Vengeance on Varos, The Trial of a Time Lord*) and Minorians (*Carnival of Monsters*)).

It is this mixture of motivation which makes *Doctor Who* so interesting, as it is a true reflection of real life. If a one-off monster or an alien race has been created with care, then its motives and motivations will have been well-defined. Many of the most enduring of the Doctor's alien friends and foes have had an established history and what might be termed a 'back story' developed for them. This, combined with some superb characterisation and acting from those artistes hired to bring the creatures to life, have ensured their place in *Doctor Who* history. Not all of these memorable monsters appeared on *Doctor Who* more than once but many of them did. Exceptional performances by talented actors like Bernard Bresslaw as the Ice Warrior Varga (in *The Ice Warriors*), Kevin Lindsay as the Sontaran Linx (in *The Time Warrior*), Michael Wisher as Davros (in *Genesis of the Daleks*) and Nabil Shaban as Sil (in *Vengeance on Varos*) won these creatures and races return matches against the Doctor. Other creatures were instantly popular because they were conceptually inspired. The Daleks and the Cybermen are both good examples of creatures which inspired the imagination and have gone on to earn their own chapters in *Doctor Who*'s history.

But just how did *Doctor Who* develop into a show that is remembered for its monsters? What were some of the key creations in its history and how did they come about? To find the answers, we must go back in time to 1963 and to the beginning of a legend.

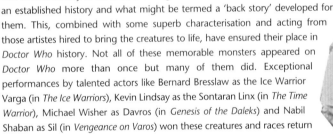

CHAPTER 2

THE SIXTIES

THE VOORDS

The Keys of Marinus (1964) 6 episodes
w. Terry Nation d. John Gorrie

The Doctor and his friends are forced
by Arbitan, who is holding the TARDIS
in a force field, to find and return four
of the five keys which operate the
Conscience Machine on Marinus,
which were hidden in different places
around the planet to prevent them
falling into the Voords' hands.

The intention was always to scare the children, but just to behind the sofa, not out of the room completely.

MARTIN BAUGH, COSTUME DESIGNER

During the setting up of *Doctor Who* during late 1962 and early 1963, everyone involved had been very keen that this new science fiction series should be educational and not pander to the sensationalist elements that had become typified by many American 'B' movies in the fifties. Aliens arriving in spacecraft to experiment on our women, giant mutant ants attacking Earth's cities and hostile alien blobs found on Mars would not form the basis for the Doctor's adventures.

Instead, *Doctor Who* would present human stories that contained elements of soap-opera-like drama, with problems being resolved in a rational and caring manner, without resorting to blowing up whatever threat had revealed itself. The Doctor relied on his wits and his intelligence to survive and his companions were, partly, expected to do the same.

While these wishes were all well intentioned, there was a wild card in the equation that no one could predict, and this was the viewers. The great British viewing public could be very choosy about what they liked and disliked. And if they disliked something then they had no hesitation in switching off their television sets or turning to the other channel in their millions. Likewise, if they liked something, then they were not slow to show their appreciation.

What happened in the case of *Doctor Who* was that a seemingly innocent story involving a race of humanoids mutated beyond all recognition and forced to live in metal life-support machines turned out to be one of the most influential pieces of fiction ever presented by the programme. *The Mutants* (to give the story its correct overall title, although it is also more commonly known as *The Daleks*) featured *Doctor Who*'s greatest success, the Daleks, and we will be taking a closer look at this particular race of monsters later in the book.

The Daleks, as well as being the most popular, were also the first living alien race presented by *Doctor Who*. Their impact and influence on *Doctor Who* did not really start to make itself known until the second season, although the public clamour for their return started almost as soon as the story that introduced them ended on television. The majority of the first season stayed within the format of alternating historical and science-fiction stories.

One result of the Daleks' popularity was that Terry Nation, the author of *The Mutants*, who had also been scheduled to write an historical story called *The Red Fort*, was asked instead to pen another science-fiction tale. This was *The Keys of Marinus* and, although it did not feature the Daleks, it did introduce another alien race, the Voords.

Nation recalled that on this occasion he was asked to produce a monster on a budget. His initial idea was that the creature be somehow eel-like, and the idea of using a wetsuit had been decided upon by the time he started his scripts.

In the camera scripts, the creatures were described as follows:

A HAND AND ARM ENCASED IN BLACK RUBBER, THE FINGERS WEBBED

And later on:

BIG CLOSEUP OF VOORD'S HEAD CASED IN A BLACK RUBBER MASK. RESPIRATOR TYPE. HUGE GLASS EYE PIECES. AS SINISTER AS POSSIBLE

'The main bodies were basically black rubber diving suits,' explained costume designer Daphne Dare in 1989. 'I designed the heads which were then produced, individually to scale for each actor to ensure, for example, that the eyes would be in proportion with everything else.' The masks and the webbed hands for the creatures were created by a firm of freelance prop-builders run by Jack Lovell who worked on a great many *Doctor Who* props and monsters during the sixties.

The Voords were the first in a long line of *Doctor Who* monsters the playing of which resulted in great discomfort for the actors. Martin Cort and Peter Stenson played two of the Voords in *The Keys of Marinus* and they both recalled that their experience was 'hot, sticky and, uncomfortable'. This comment has been echoed by actors and actresses throughout the entire history of *Doctor Who*. Playing a monster is not a easy task.

Left: A Voord (Peter Stenson) attacks Arbitan (George Couloris). Right: Barbara (Jacqueline Hill), the Doctor (William Hartnell) and Ian (William Russell) examine the remains of a Voord. *The Keys of Marinus.*

There were other problematic aspects as well. 'You couldn't see anything,' recalled Cort. 'Your vision was very restricted by the mask. Consequently I used to keep walking the wrong side of the camera. In the end someone had to lead me along the corridor and then push me to tell me which way to go.'

Stenson also recalled the problems of not being able to see in the costume. 'I had to drag Kathy Schofield [who was playing one of the human characters, Sabetha] along for reasons best known to the writer of the plot, and we had to go through a triangular doorway which was supposed to slide open as we approached it – there were two scene hands on either side to open the door. When we rehearsed it I said to them, "Now, you will remember to make sure that the door is properly open because I can't see." They told me to stop worrying. When we came to record the scene, they opened the top half of the door, but the bottom half got stuck and stayed closed. I went striding along the corridor and tripped over the bottom of the door. I swore audibly and waited for them to stop the shot but they didn't and so we just carried on with the rest of the scene.'

Yartek (Stephen Darthell) awaits the arrival of the Doctor and his friends, bringing with them the missing keys to the Conscience Machine on Marinus. *The Keys of Marinus.*

Cort's prevailing memory of making the story involved William Hartnell. 'One thing that I remember particularly about that story was that Bill Hartnell, as the Doctor, had to hit me on the head. I was pretty much in awe of Mr Hartnell at the time and when we recorded the scene, he hit me quite hard. I didn't like to ask him not to hit me quite so hard, so I had a word with the floor manager and asked him if he could ask Mr Hartnell not to hit me so hard. When we came to do the shot again, he hit me even harder. I wondered again if I should complain and I again spoke to the floor manager, yet on the third occasion Mr Hartnell hit me so hard I saw stars.'

After the success of the Daleks, the press were quick to recognise that *Doctor Who* was a potentially rich source of filler material featuring horrific monsters and pretty girls. As the costumes for the Voords consisted of little

A Zarbi on the surface of the planet Vortis. *The Web Planet.*

more than a rubber wetsuit, the press seemed more than happy to run photographs of one of the creatures hugging the attractive Carole Ann Ford in its arms.

John Wood's original design sketch of a Zarbi.

The various alien monsters and creatures encountered by the first Doctor tended to be a bit of a mixed bag. There were the mostly good (the Sensorites, the Rills), the bad (the Animus) and the ugly (the Rills again). On the whole, though, the threats faced by the Doctor tended to be more home-grown and humanoid, which was itself a reflection of the partly historical slant that the series as a whole seemed determined to stick to. In addition, the production team were striving to find another creation to become 'the next Daleks' – something that would repeat their success. This was, unfortunately for them, something that they were never to achieve.

One story, however, was significant in that it featured no humanoid characters other than the Doctor and his companions. This was *The Web Planet* by Australian writer Bill Strutton.

'I had to come up with something different from the robot-style Daleks,' Strutton said in 1965. 'Browsing through an encyclopedia, I thought of the giant ants and butterflies.'

'Then my wife stepped in with the "Zarbi" name. It's got a nice menacing sound. I think they look frightening but they are not intended to horrify.'

Strutton also claimed as inspiration seeing as a child a couple of bull-ants fighting in his garden and this, combined with seeing his two stepsons fighting together, led to the idea of a planet, Vortis, on which all the creatures were giant forms of insects found on Earth. There were the Menoptra, man-sized butterfly-like creatures, the Optera, wingless cousins to the Menoptra that lived in holes underground, the Larvae Guns, woodlouse creatures which could spit poison from their snouts, and, finally, the Zarbi, giant black ant creatures.

In the camera scripts, the Zarbi were introduced as follows, and it is interesting that no analogy to an ant was drawn at this point:

```
A TWO-PINCERED CLAW COMES INTO SIGHT, GRIPPING THE ROCK.

A SLEEK, SHINY HEAD APPEARS FROM BEHIND THE CRAG, ITS CYCLOPEAN EYE WATCHING
                        THE TELEPHONE BOX

              A CHIRRUPING SOUND EMANATES FROM IT.
```

As had become the norm with *Doctor Who*, the task of realising these creatures fell to the various designers allocated to work on the story. In the case of *The Web Planet*, these were primarily designer John Wood and costume designer Daphne Dare.

'I seem to recall that the production team hadn't initially decided what type of creatures they should be, or what shape the Zarbi should take,' commented Wood. 'Most of the people who worked on it were unhappy with the insect idea, as they felt it would be very difficult for the artists to operate these things. Verity Lambert, the producer, was very enthusiastic though.'

'Once it was settled that the Zarbi would be ants, I worked out a costume idea and did a sketch to show what I had in mind. The main thing was to disguise the human form as much as possible. Obviously I couldn't get the shape of an ant exactly, because at the end of the day the costume had to be worn by an actor. There was no way of avoiding the human legs. That didn't really matter, though, as the rest of the costume was sufficiently antlike that it drew the viewer's attention and created the right impression.

'The Zarbi were built by Shawcraft Models and were basically just fibreglass shells. Fibreglass was used as we didn't have the benefit of a lot of lightweight materials in those days. The Zarbi were quite easy to assemble: they were made up more or less like suits of armour – they came in various bits and pieces, which all strapped onto the actor.'

A Zarbi is prepared for the studio recording. *The Web Planet*.

One of the Zarbi props under construction at Shawcraft Models.

One of the actors to play a Zarbi was John Scott Martin, an actor who went on to appear in *Doctor Who* many more times playing monsters.

'The trouble with the Zarbi was that it was so heavy. You could not stand upright. If you can imagine, the body of the Zarbi was taller than I was, our hands controlled the head and the eyes. The tail of the Zarbi was longer than I was so once you were bolted into the costume, you couldn't stand upright, and in life, when you can't stand upright, that's what you want to do. The only way we could ease our bodies was to stand on a block with our tail tucked over the end.'

'On one occasion in the midst of rehearsal I just had to stand upright. I stood on the end of a ramp, flicked my tail over the edge, overbalanced and landed on my back six feet below, floundering like an overturned beetle. They thought I'd killed myself, but I was quite happy. I was comfortable for the first time.

One of a special sequence of photographs taken by the BBC Visual Effects Department showing the Mechanoid prop from different angles.

'The biggest problem was the lack of vision. You were looking out of a small hole about the size of a letterbox which had black net over it so that people couldn't see your face, and the Zarbis were quite useless because once we got mobile we were crashing into cameras and into scenery.'

Work on *The Web Planet* progressed far from smoothly, with numerous difficulties ranging from the sets not being ready on time, to having to allow longer breaks than usual

The Web Planet featured a menagerie of monsters: The Zarbi, the deadly larvae guns and the graceful Menoptra.

between scenes to allow the actors playing the Zarbi to get into position. Although there had again been significant press interest in the creatures, they were not deemed to be a major success in the studio and were not to return. However, they did feature, along with the Menoptra and the Voords, in the first ever *Doctor Who* annual, published in 1965 by World Distributors.

As well as the humanoid creatures, there were several robotic life forms encountered by the Doctor during the sixties. Aside from possibly the Ice Soldiers in *The Keys of Marinus* (it is never stated quite what these creatures are in the series but as they are discovered encased in ice it is unlikely they are flesh and blood), an android replica of himself, and robot versions of Count Dracula and Frankenstein's monster, beings called the Mechanoids were the first totally robotic race encountered by the Doctor and his friends.

The Mechanoids appeared in a story called *The Chase*, again scripted by Nation and once more featuring the Daleks. Nation's original story outline was called *The Pursuers* and in this he introduced the Mechanoids as follows: 'On the planet Mechanus, [the Doctor and his friends] find a society of machines. Machines built by a man-like creature a thousand years before, who was destroyed by his own invention. With all life ended, the machines created new versions of themselves. Hideous mechanical monsters, with, built into the memory cells, the order "kill".'

THE MECHANOIDS

The Chase (1965) 6 episodes
w. Terry Nation d. Richard Martin

After being chased across time and space by the Daleks, the Doctor ends up on the planet Mechanus, where another threat awaits.

CHARACTER

The Mechanoids originated on Earth and had been sent out as an advance guard to prepare a planet for colonisation. The problem was that the follow-up ships of humans were never sent and so the Mechanoids were waiting patiently for their masters to arrive. When a lone astronaut named Steven Taylor crashed on the planet fifty years later, the Mechanoids took care of him, but as he did not know their codes, he became a prisoner.

The Mechanoids are equipped with flame-thrower weapons and inhabit a fantastic city, raised on stilts above the surface of the planet Mechanus, access to which is achieved through lift shafts to the surface. They can speak and have a limited vocabulary. They have also been programmed with a complex series of moves and signals with which they communicate with other Mechanoids.

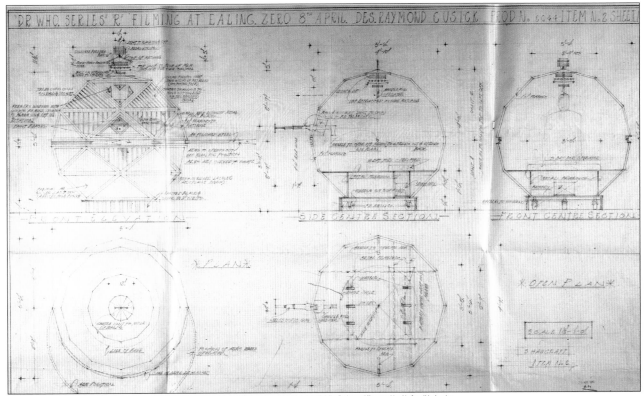

A detailed construction plan for the Mechanoid prop drawn by Nigel Curzon from Raymond P. Cusick's original specifications. Note that the final prop differs considerably from this drawing.

In the rehearsal script for the story's fifth episode (*The Death of Doctor Who*), in which a Mechanoid is seen for the first time, Nation described it as it emerged from a lift entrance:

ADVANCING FROM IT, A MECHON. (SAY MECK-ON) IT IS A MECHANICAL ROBOT THAT MOVES ON THE SAME PRINCIPAL AS THE DALEK. THAT IS TO SAY, LEGLESS. HERE, THE SIMILARITY ENDS, FOR THE MECHON IS SHAPED LIKE A LARGE SPINNING TOP. SLIGHTLY CONVEX AT THE TOP. WIDE AT THE 'SHOULDERS', THEN TAPERING AS IT NEARS THE GROUND. THE TAPER THEN SPREADS INTO THE BASE UNIT. IMAGINE A CAPSTAN WITH A PRONOUNCED TOP.

SPROUTING FROM THE MECHON ARE ANTENNAE, NO SUGGESTION OF HEAD, ARMS OR ANY HUMAN FEATURE. HOWEVER THERE ARE A NUMBER OF FLASHING DISCS BUILT INTO THE SURFACE OF THE MECHON...

THE MECHON VOICE MIGHT BE PRODUCED IN THE SAME WAY AS THE VOICE IN THE RECORDING OF 'SPARKY AND HIS MAGIC PIANO'.

Although Nation called the creatures Mechons in the script, and the Daleks had dialogue which referred to the creatures as this, all the other characters, including the Mechanoids themselves, referred to the robots as 'Mechanoids'.

The Mechanoids were designed by Raymond P. Cusick. 'They were robots, of course,' he explained, 'and in designing them I was inspired by the work of an American architect named Buckminster Fuller. It was he who devised the principle of geodesic construction, in which dome shaped structures are assembled from a configuration of small triangular elements. Geodesic structures are noted for their great strength: in the Second World War, for instance, they were used in the design of aircraft such as the Wellington bomber, which could be virtually shot to pieces and still hang together. So I was inspired by that.'

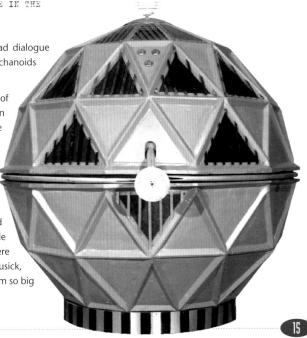

The Mechanoid casings were constructed in two halves, top and bottom, and featured extendable arms which could be used to grab and hold, and also a single flame-thrower gun which pointed from the middle-front of the casing. They were also very large indeed, being over six feet wide. 'I've heard it said,' commented Cusick, 'that the Mechanoids might have been reused in another story if I hadn't made them so big and unwieldy. There wasn't any mention of that at the time, though, and everyone seemed very pleased with them. I mean, I designed them to suit the requirements of this particular story, which as far as I knew was going to be their one and only appearance. They were going to be used on a very large set at Ealing, so I could afford to make them quite big. I had real flame-throwers built into them to make the battle scene as spectacular as possible.'

Nation was reportedly upset at their eventual appearance, as he had hoped to create another monster like the Daleks that would reappear again and again and would lend itself to many merchandisable spin-offs. Unfortunately the size of the props caused numerous problems in the studio and Nation quickly realised that his hopes of another success along the same lines as the Daleks were over. The Mechanoids did go on to

A Dalek meets a Mechanoid in the final episode of *The Chase*.

appear in several instalments of the Dalek comic strip which was running in *TV Century 21* magazine and there were two plastic models made available in the shops: one produced by Cherilee, which was around three inches tall, and one manufactured by Hertz Plastic Moulders, which stood around six inches high.

Although monsters had always been a large part of *Doctor Who*'s mix, they had always been on a more or less equal footing to the historical stories. During the sixties, several behind-the-scenes factors led to a gradual shift away from the historical/science fiction split.

Primary among these was the departure of producer Verity Lambert. She had steered the show through its formative years and, with the support of Sydney Newman, the BBC's Head of Drama, had fulfilled the original brief to keep *Doctor Who* as a semi-educational series. David Whitaker, the original story editor, had, during Lambert's tenure, handed over to Dennis Spooner, and Spooner passed on the reigns to Donald Tosh shortly before Lambert left.

Between them, the producer and the story or script editor define the look and direction of any television show, and *Doctor Who* was no exception. Under Spooner's guiding hand, the scripts became slightly more whimsical and comedic, eschewing real historical drama for light-hearted farce, in which the characters could be used to greater effect without the constraints of having to depict a historically well-defined period.

Tosh and incoming producer John Wiles introduced a more fantasy-based element into the show, being perhaps more experimental with the stories. The next changes in behind-the-scenes staff were the ones that had the most impact on the future of *Doctor Who*. Wiles' approach to *Doctor Who* was very much opposed by William Hartnell, who had the support of the BBC's Head of Serials, Gerald Savory. This conflict was one of the factors ultimately leading to Wiles resigning as producer in January 1966, followed shortly afterwards by Tosh. Sydney Newman appointed Innes Lloyd as the new producer and Gerry Davis came in to handle the role of story editor.

Lloyd and Davis had their own view as to what direction *Doctor Who* should take, and this was down the path of science fiction adventure rather than historical romps. There was one final change that occurred, and this was the introduction of a concept – later to be called 'regeneration'– which enabled the production team to change the actor playing the Doctor.

William Hartnell suffered from arteriosclerosis – a gradual hardening of the arteries – and one of the symptoms of this disease was a slow loss of memory. It was becoming apparent to everyone involved that he could not carry on with the rigours of weekly recording and so Lloyd decided to replace him and introduce a new actor as the Doctor. This was Patrick Troughton and, with the change over, it seemed that the fiction/fact mix of the Hartnell years truly had given way to a new era for the show, one in which the stories themselves were more firmly geared towards terrifying the young viewers rather than educating them. However Lloyd was still keen to use 'real science' stories in the mix.

Alongside the Daleks and the Cybermen (who were introduced in Hartnell's final story as the Doctor), several other monsters were featured, leading many observers to later label the show's fifth season (the first full season in which Troughton played the Doctor) 'The Monster Season'. Indeed, this sequence of seven stories, which started transmission in September 1967 and ended in June 1968, introduced two of the most memorable of the Doctors adversaries. The furry robot Yeti and the Ice Warriors from Mars.

Many of the classic Earth legends and mysteries have been featured in *Doctor Who*, whether they are being

A Yeti, robot servant of the Great Intelligence. *The Abominable Snowmen*.

Patrick Troughton and two 'topless' Yeti on location in Snowdonia. *The Abominable Snowmen.*

explained as the work of some alien being or a human scientist – or even as being true! One of the most enduring Earth mysteries involves the Yeti of the Himalayas. These reclusive creatures are supposed to inhabit the caves and ravines of the mountainsides, and are only occasionally glimpsed by civilised man. Other explorers find nothing but trails of apparently giant footprints in the snow.

Mervyn Haisman, the writer who, together with Henry Lincoln, brought the Yeti to *Doctor Who,* commented to an interviewer in 1989 that the idea of featuring these mysterious creatures in a story came out of a chance remark by Patrick Troughton. 'Henry knew Troughton as a fellow actor, and Pat had casually remarked that he was looking for something different. So we thought of an idea that is recognisable yet turns out to be different. That's when we hit upon the idea of the Yeti.'

Haisman remembers that he and Lincoln made numerous suggestions regarding the look of the story called, perhaps unsurprisingly, *The Abominable Snowmen.* 'Henry and I, having both stemmed from a mutual theatre background, actually drew the sets and did drawings of the Yeti ourselves. We didn't quite envisage them with such baggy legs. We were after something that looked fairly cuddly but had this surprising ferociousness about it. We also did a lot of the design work for the monastery and so on because we felt, certainly in those days, actually suggesting ways of doing it showed that you'd done a lot of homework on the subject.'

The camera scripts, however, were vague as to what the Yeti should look like, with perhaps the most detailed description appearing in the script for episode one:

> TRACKING SHOT FOLLOWING LARGE FOOTPRINTS. TRACKS LEAD INTO TREES. FOLLOW THEM UNTIL
> WE PICK UP AND SEE THE FOOT OF A YETI HIDING BEHIND A TREE. SLOWLY, THE CAMERA
> STARTS TO PAN UP THE SIDE OF THE BODY. A LARGE HAND COMES INTO VIEW.

The Yeti were revealed in the story as being robots and this was a logical extension of the story's basic concept, that of people being controlled and manipulated. 'We knew from our first thoughts that the Yeti would have to be the pawn of some other intelligence, which gave us the name, I suppose,' commented Haisman in 1986, talking about the fact that the power behind the Yeti was called the Great Intelligence.

'You couldn't have these Yeti talking, could you? Visually they were tremendous, and they looked very powerful on screen, but that was as far as they could go.' This idea of the Yeti and other characters as being pawns was further reinforced on screen by the idea of the robots being controlled and given instructions via the means of a chessboard upon which Yeti-shaped chess pieces were placed.

'Our first thought was, "what on Earth is a Yeti?,"' said Martin Baugh, the story's costume designer. 'The costume ended up being a kind of bird-owl creature, or a bear. The costume had an owl-like

Filming a Yeti on location. *The Abominable Snowmen.*

A Yeti meets its public. *The Abominable Snowmen.*

beak and eyes rather like a motorbike rider's goggles. We knew the story was set in Tibet, which is a cold place, and so, logically, the Yeti either had to have feathers or fur and we chose fur because it was easier to realise than feathers. The shape of the head and body was meant to be slightly owl-like.

'The problem with designing any monster is trying to alter the shape of the human that is inside it. With

THE YETI

The Abominable Snowmen (1967)
6 episodes
w. Mervyn Haisman and Henry Lincoln
d. Gerald Blake

The Doctor arrives in Tibet and becomes involved in a plot by the Great Intelligence to conquer the Earth.

The Web of Fear (1968) 6 episodes
w. Mervyn Haisman and Henry Lincoln
d. Douglas Camfield

The Intelligence returns and brings the TARDIS to Earth where it hopes to drain the Doctor's brain power.

CHARACTER

The Yeti are a timid race of creatures well known to the monks who live in the Detsen monastery in Tibet. However, when the creatures suddenly turn hostile, there seems to be no explanation. Also in Tibet is Professor Travers, an anthropologist who is trying to capture and study the reclusive creatures. He has also been attacked and seeks refuge in the monastery.

In fact, the abbot of the monastery, Padmasambhava, has been taken over by a formless intelligence from space – the Great Intelligence. The Intelligence intends to establish a bridgehead on Earth in order to invade and to this end has created robot Yeti creatures which are controlled through a silver control sphere situated in their chests. These spheres carry the Intelligence and can move about independently.

Luckily, the Doctor arrives in Tibet and manages to prevent the Intelligence from fully manifesting on Earth and sends it back into space. The Yeti robots become inanimate, Padmasambhava is freed and Travers continues his hunt for the 'real' Yeti. ➡

the Yeti, we attempted to hide the shape of the actor by giving it padded arms and legs so that it was not obvious where the crotch was.

'The costumes were basically bell shapes made on cane frames. All the actors playing them were about six and a half feet tall and whenever they got anywhere out in the open on location they would just blow over. Once

Captain Knight (Ralph Watson), Jamie (Frazer Hines) and friends encounter two Yeti in the Underground. *The Web of Fear.*

they fell over, they couldn't get up. I had not worked with fur before because "fun fur" was a new material – it was just coming in. We couldn't have used real fur because the costs would have been extraordinary and also it would have been far more identifiable. Fun fur was very cheap – something like sixty-three shillings (£3.15) a yard in those days – and was simple to use, but not terribly effective when seen in the cold light of day. I always felt that the *Doctor Who* monsters should not be seen until the end of the first episode and before that maybe just glimpses of a shadow or a silhouette. In the context that they were seen, I felt that they worked well.

'To give the Yeti a "face" I simply sprayed the fur with a black car spray. I started doing it in the wardrobe department at the BBC but was soon banished out to the scene dock to spray them because of the smell of the paint. I generally sprayed over all the costume to give them a little more texture.'

The costumes were constructed from bamboo frames, padded with foam rubber and then covered with fur. The framework was needed to give the bodies some defining shape, as one of the problems with working with a soft substance like fur is that, inevitably, something is required to provide the basic form, over which the soft outer covering can be placed. Their hands and feet were moulded from rubber. At the end of the story, a 'real' Yeti was briefly seen and for this the framework was removed from one of the Yeti costumes making the resultant creature far less bulky and intimidating.

The Yeti were deemed by the production team to be very successful, so much so that Haisman and Lincoln were commissioned to write a second story featuring the creatures, even before the first had been transmitted. The Yeti in this second story, called *The Web of Fear*, were of a slightly different design from those in the first.

'There was some feeling, I gather,' said Haisman, 'that after the first one went out, they decided that original design of the Yeti looked too cuddly and was having the wrong effect on children, who wanted to have a Yeti as a pet!'

To try to overcome this problem, the costumes were made slightly slimmer and smaller, and were equipped with glowing eyes and fangs. 'We lit the eyes up in that one,' recalled Baugh, 'because we knew that the story was taking place in the London Underground, where it is dark, and we wanted the creatures to be able to register their presence on the viewers. I redesigned the eyes and then someone from special effects supervised putting in the lights. We wanted them to look sinister in a dark environment and also, by putting the light in, it slightly blinded the camera so that you didn't see as much of the rest of the costume.'

When the Yeti was first seen in the first episode, it was presented as one of the original costumes, but once the Intelligence gained control of the robot, the creature transformed into one of the new breed of Yeti before attacking a helpless victim. This unscripted transformation was acheived using a simple technique whereby one image was mixed across to a second image.

The combination of images presented by *The Web of Fear* – darkly lit, cobweb-strewn underground tunnels, Yeti patrolling with their web-firing guns, silent, apart from the persistent beeping trill of their control spheres – resulted in one of the most frightening and memorable *Doctor Who* adventures from this decade. *Doctor Who* had always set out to frighten the children, but stories like *The Tomb of the Cybermen*, *The Web of Fear* and *Fury from the Deep*, all from the fifth season,

Around forty years later in London, Travers succeeds in reactivating one of the Yeti control spheres and the Intelligence is once more summoned to Earth. It manages to locate one of the original Yeti robots on display in a private museum and, once the sphere manipulates itself into the creature, the robot changes form into a sleeker and more vicious version of the original Yeti.

The Intelligence takes over the London Underground system, using the Yeti and a suffocating weblike substance to kill anyone who stands in the way. London is evacuated and the army is called in to try to clear the tunnels.

The Intelligence traps the TARDIS in space and forces it to materialise in London as it wants to drain the Doctor's brain power. The Doctor turns the tables on the Intelligence, however, and nearly succeeds in draining it instead. At the last minute, the Doctor's friends mistakenly 'rescue' the Doctor, allowing the Intelligence to escape back into space.

took that one stage further and presented almost out-and-out horror.

'The intention,' asserted Baugh, 'was always to scare the children, but just to behind the sofa, not out of the room completely. We were trying to scare people up to the age of about twelve and one expects the older children to suspend their disbelief and go along with the story.'

John Levene, who was to go on to play the regular character of Sergeant Benton in *Doctor Who,* started out playing monsters. His first role was as a Cyberman in *The Moonbase,* but he also played one of the Yeti in *The Web of Fear.* 'As a Yeti, when you fell over, it was like being in a theme park. Because of the foam, you simply bounced. I loved it. The difficulty was when you wanted to go to the toilet. Putting your hand up as a Yeti doesn't quite have the required effect.

'One day, we were down in the Underground at Covent Garden. Frazer [Hines, who played the Doctor's young Scottish companion Jamie] and I got on like a house on fire and one of the first things that happened was that Frazer pinned a number on my back and then we did a ballroom dance around Covent Garden, with me dressed up as a Yeti.'

Following *The Web of Fear,* the Yeti and the Great Intelligence would have made one further appearance in *Doctor Who* in a story set in the Scottish Highlands with the working title *The Laird of McCrimmon* (McCrimmon being Jamie's clan name). Unfortunately, Haisman and Lincoln suffered severe creative differences with the production team over their third story for the series (which did not feature the Yeti), *The Dominators.* These differences resulted in the latter story being transmitted under the pseudonym of Norman Ashby and Haisman and Lincoln vowing never to work for the show again.

With the Cybermen, Yeti and Ice Warriors gaining *Doctor Who* much attention in the fifth season, it was logical for the production team to try to repeat the formula with the following year's stories. Thus the Cybermen made a further appearance and the Ice Warriors returned. However, the remaining stories featured mainly robotic menaces. *The Mind Robber,* a story set entirely in a land of fantasy and fiction, made use of several already-existing robot costumes from an episode from a series called *Out of the Unknown* called *The Prophet,* as well as some new costumes for a squad of giant clockwork soldiers and other 'guest' appearances from mythological creatures such as the Medusa and the Minotaur, not to mention a unicorn. *The Dominators,* on the other hand, featured an eponymous race of humanoid aliens who were served by the robotic Quarks, small spiky-headed boxlike automata with high-pitched, almost unintelligible voices, and a devastating weapons system.

By far the most complex creations, however, were the Krotons, a crystalline life form which appeared in the final Troughton season in a story of the same name.

The Krotons started life as an idea submitted by writer Robert Holmes to story editor Donald Tosh on 25 April 1965. It was not followed up by Tosh because at that time scripts would have been required very quickly and Holmes was busy on another series, but in May 1968, Holmes discovered his original outline while clearing out some old files. Considering that the idea still seemed valid, Holmes again sent it in to the *Doctor Who* production office.

In his letter, Holmes commented, 'If you don't like it, please chuck it away – I don't want it back in the files!'

A Kroton (Miles Northover) unsuccessfully attempts to destroy the Doctor's TARDIS. *The Krotons.*

The basic outline for the story was contained in the original letter to Tosh and read as follows:

On an uninhabited planet, the travellers find a great space craft. They approach it cautiously but can detect no sign of life within. Vegetation has grown up around it in a way that indicates it may have lain there for centuries.

Growing bolder, they move still nearer, start searching for the entrance hatch. Inside the space ship a dynamo purrs into life. A robot-figure in the control room moves a switch and Dr Who and his companions flicker into vision on the television scanners etc …

Anyway, after a bit of this sort of thing, the travellers find themselves briefly surrounded by a thin, clammy

THE KROTONS

The Krotons (1968/9) 4 episodes
w. Robert Holmes d. David Maloney

The Doctor arrives on the planet of the Gonds, where the inhabitants live in fear of the unseen Krotons.

CHARACTER

The Krotons are a crystalline life form which can convert themselves back into a slurry when inactive. A Kroton spacecraft, called the Dynatrope, was discovered on the unnamed planet of the Gonds. It had been there for many, many years and the Gonds had become enslaved to the Krotons, who remained within their ship and were never seen.

Information and learning were strictly controlled by the Krotons and the Gonds were forced to learn through the Krotons' 'teaching machines', which measured intelligence. Each year, two of the most intelligent Gonds were sent into the Dynatrope to become 'companions of the Krotons'. In fact, the Krotons were in hibernation and their automatic systems were draining the mental power from the chosen Gonds in order to amass sufficient energy for the Krotons to reactivate themselves.

When the Doctor and his companions arrive on the planet, the Doctor and Zoe deliberately take the tests set by the Kroton teaching machines. Their intelligence triggers the reactivation process and the Krotons are re-formed.

They start to ready the Dynatrope for take-off, but its departure will destroy the Gonds and so the Doctor introduces some sulphuric acid into the Krotons' vat of nutrient and the Krotons and their ship are destroyed.

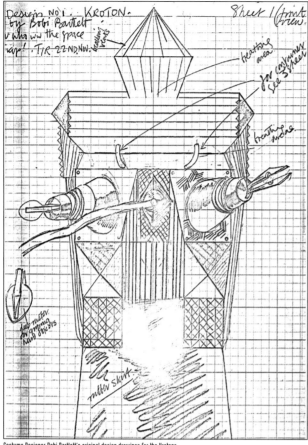

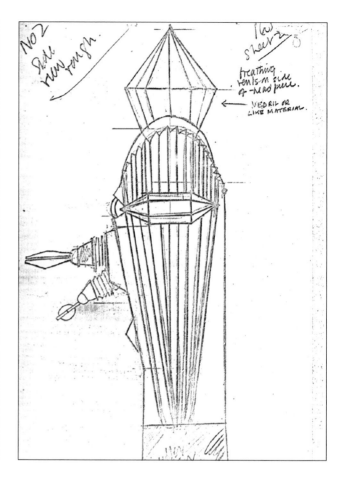

Costume Designer Bobi Bartlett's original design drawings for the Krotons.

mist which seems to come from nowhere and disperses as mysteriously as it appears. At first, they feel no ill effects and press on in their search for the entrance.

Actually, they have been enveloped in amnesia gas which progressively anaesthetises their memory cells. They forget their most recently acquired skills and knowledge first, then their purpose, what they are supposed to be doing, who they are, where they have come from – gradually it all goes until they are reduced to a state of almost infantile helplessness.

Then they are collected by two Robots and taken into the ship.

In the next episode they find themselves weighed and measured and scientifically examined in a variety of ways. The temporary effects of the gas are wearing off. The Robots offer no explanation of what is happening. They make two or three attempts to escape but their actions always seem to have been anticipated. When they need food and drink they have to 'win' it through intelligence and manual dexterity; they realise they are being treated like chimpanzees in London Zoo.

In the third episode the human controllers of the space ship wake from their state of suspended animation and we get an explanation of the set up.

Thousands of years earlier the ship had been cruising through space when it had run into a galactic ionisation belt – or whatever. The brutal deceleration involved had split the ship's thermal shield, killing five of the eight man (woman or mixed) crew. They had made an emergency landing on this deserted planet to carry out the necessary repairs.

When these had been completed, however, they faced the problem of handling a fresh blast-off with only three crew members – a complicated operation physically possible only for a crew of twice their number. The Robots, pre-tracked to perform only a certain number of functions, could not be utilised; in any case, they had built-in governors precluding them from being adapted to carry out humanoid tasks.

The solution had been that the humanoids had put themselves into suspended animation, prepared to wait for thousands or millions of years, while the Robots maintained a lonely sentinel duty – pre-tracked to catch any sentient creature that might stray near the space craft during the rest of time.

The Robots are charged to obtain three such captives, possessing a certain minimum level of manual and *mental ability, enough to fit them for training in crew duties, before re-animating their humanoid masters.*

In a word, Dr Who and his companions have been press-ganged and now find themselves facing the prospect of a long trip to a distant planet and with no hope of ever returning to the TARDIS.

Before the ship can take-off, however, they have first to be trained in their flight duties. As there are four of them (and the humanoids only require the services of three) they discover that at the end of the training period the least proficient of them will be bumped off. The humanoids are quite without sentiment.

In the end, of course, they manage to sabotage the ship and make their escape. There are two or three ways that occur to me in which this might be done but I don't want to go into too much great detail at this preliminary stage.

The best point of the idea, to my mind, is that it gets away from the usual pattern up to now – in part, at any rate – so that Dr Who & Co have only themselves to worry about.'

This concept was liked by *Doctor Who*'s producer, Peter Bryant, and he passed it on to assistant script editor Terrance Dicks who commissioned Holmes on 4 June 1968 to develop it further, taking into account that the Doctor was now played by Patrick Troughton and that there were only two companions with him in the TARDIS.

The outline returned by Holmes was called *The Trap* (although it had been commissioned under the title *The Space Trap* and this was also the title used on the rehearsal scripts) and presented a somewhat altered version of the original outline, in which the Doctor and his companions arrive on a planet inhabited by the humanoid Gonds who are slaves to a massive machine. Inside the machine are the Krotons, beings awaiting sufficient mental power in order to revive themselves. The Doctor and his companion Zoe provide the required power and the Krotons are reanimated.

The camera script described the creatures as follows:

THE PATTERN OF DOTS HAS NOW SOLIDIFIED INTO A RECOGNISABLE HUMANOID SHAPE, LYING SUPINE INSIDE THE TANK. THE BODY MOVES AS THOUGH AWAKENING...

A SILVER HAND AND ARM, COVERED IN METAL PYRITES, COMES OUT OF THE LIQUID AND GRIPS THE SIDE OF THE TANK.

Several images of the Krotons on board their space ship.
The Krotons.

and later:

KROTON ONE IS CLIMBING SHAKILY OUT OF THE TANK. IT IS BIG, SILVER, AND HAS A SCABROUS, CRYSTALLINE SURFACE. ONCE OUT OF THE TANK THE KROTON STANDS SWAYING DIZZILY. THEN IT GROPES FOR ONE OF THE TANK PIPES AND CLIPS IT INTO A SOCKET AT ITS WAIST. IMMEDIATELY THE KROTON SEEMS TO BECOME ALERT.

IT STOPS SWAYING AND STRAIGHTENS UP, SCANNING THE CONTROL ROOM LIKE A HUNGRY LION EXPECTING DINNER.

There was a long-running rumour among *Doctor Who* fans that the design of the Krotons originated from a 'design a monster to beat the Daleks' competition run the previous year by the BBC children's programme *Blue Peter*. Although there was a vague resemblance between the Kroton and the 'Aqua-Man', one of the winning entries in the *Blue Peter* competition, this rumour was perhaps borne out more by the fact that the Kroton looked as though it might have had its origins in a cardboard egg-box than on any factual basis. In fact, the Krotons were designed by the BBC costume designer allocated to work on *The Krotons*, Bobi Bartlett.

'I based their shape on crystalline structures in keeping with the plot,' she explained. 'I was pleased with the design and the fact that they had rotating heads, which worked effectively and appeared quite sinister as they had no defined face or features.'

The basis for the costumes was that the creatures were crystalline and had formed themselves from a liquid slurry. Therefore the creatures were given crystal-like 'heads' and their bodies also reflected the notion that they had been grown. To hide the operators' feet, a black rubber skirt was placed around the base, and they were connected via large tubes to the vat of crystal slurry that powered them.

Having designed the costumes, Bartlett handed her designs over to Jack Lovell Ltd for construction, and the overall cost was agreed to be handled by the effects department.

Bartlett was disappointed with the final result. 'They were perhaps a little bit too large and bulky for my liking, due to the overlarge men cast to wear them.' A further problem had been that the props had been constructed to the wrong scale and had ended up far larger than had been intended. 'As I remember,' said Holmes, 'they were a pretty impractical design. Once imprisoned in the costumes, the actors had a very

limited field of vision and had to be led around the studio.'

As the sixties drew to a close, *Doctor Who*'s producers, Peter Bryant and Derrick Sherwin, realised that the cost of creating new monsters for *Doctor Who* was increasing. In addition, there was a general expectation from viewers and from within the BBC that *Doctor Who* had to deliver the goods.

As an indirect result of their experiences with the Daleks, the BBC had expanded their group responsible for the marketing and licensing of programmes so that they were more able and more active in seeking out potential avenues which might be used to exploit the properties that they owned – in fact, the department was initially called BBC Exploitation before it was merged with BBC Radio Enterprises and renamed BBC Licensing. Bryant and Sherwin were well aware that *Doctor Who* was an important and lucrative source of revenue for the BBC and were upset that none of this money was channelled back into the show itself. Aside from the Daleks, which had resulted in a quite phenomenal boom in merchandise and income, the BBC also actively tried to generate interest in other properties: the Cybermen, Cybermats and Quarks amongst them. However, the Daleks seemed to have exhausted the market and, when Dalek merchandise started to tail off in 1967, the manufacturers and publishers seemed unwilling to try other *Doctor Who* lines. Despite this, the feeling was that *Doctor Who* had to continue to develop and present new ideas which might have the potential to become the 'next Daleks'.

A Kroton. *The Krotons.*

This feeling led to Bryant's writing on 21 January 1969 to the BBC's Head of Merchandising stating that, because the cost of making monsters for *Doctor Who* was so high, the production team had planned for the next six months without any. He went on to note that the monsters were deemed a popular draw, citing the recent audience figures of 9 million for *The Krotons* by way of example. The six-month period he referred to covered the production of the final two stories of the sixth season – *The Space Pirates* and *The War Games* – which between them accounted for 16 episodes, none of which featured any monsters – aside from brief glimpses of some of the Doctor's adversaries during his trial by the Time Lords at the conclusion of *The War Games*.

The adversaries conjured by the Doctor during this sequence were intended to remind viewers of some of the past successes of the show. Thus the Daleks were an obvious choice to be featured, as were the Ice Warriors and Yeti, both of which had appeared twice to that date. The Quarks were also included – the only creature in this sequence that never returned to the show – and so too were the Cybermen, the second most popular monster to be originated by *Doctor Who*.

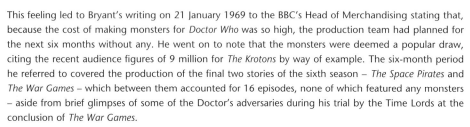

Two Krotons [Miles Northover, Robert Grant] inside their spaceship. *The Krotons.*

CHAPTER 3

CYBERMEN

> We had no idea that the Cybermen would turn out to be so successful and popular. It's nice to have been in at the birth of something like that.

DIRECTOR DEREK MARTINUS SPEAKING IN 1992

Alongside the Daleks, the Cybermen are one of the staple ingredients of *Doctor Who* that viewers tend to remember. For some, the Cybermen were far more terrifying and effective than the Daleks. With the Daleks, there were certain limitations: the creatures could apparently not negotiate stairs (although this shortcoming was rectified in a 1988 story), could not move very fast, and looked like robots, even though they were not.

The Cybermen, on the other hand, looked like people. They had legs and could walk up and down stairs with ease. They could run and hurry (although, like many monsters, they seemed to prefer a slow and ominous striding walk) and it was obvious that there was nowhere you could hide from them.

A further aspect of their character that touched a nerve was the idea that they could take a human being and physically turn them, against their will, into a Cyberman. This chilling concept made the Cybermen more than just an enemy to be defeated. They were really frightening, and if they caught you, then you wouldn't just be killed: you would become like them.

These very adult concepts came about because story editor Gerry Davis and producer Innes Lloyd decided that the show needed a scientific adviser. 'I was trying to get someone who might provide ideas and vet

APPEARANCES

The Tenth Planet (1966) 4 episodes
w. Kit Pedler (1-4) and Gerry Davis (3-4)
d. Derek Martinus

Earth is threatened by the appearance in space of its mirror image, a planet called Mondas. Cybermen arrive from Mondas intent on draining energy from Earth but are eventually repelled.

The Moonbase (1967) 4 episodes
w. Kit Pedler d. Morris Barry

The Cybermen invade a weather control station on the Moon and intend to use its resources to attack Earth in order to replenish supplies after the destruction of Mondas. The Doctor is on hand to stop them

The Tomb of the Cybermen (1967) 4 episodes w. Kit Pedler & Gerry Davis d. Morris Barry

The Doctor and his friends join an expedition of archaeologists to excavate the lost tombs of the Cybermen on the planet Telos. ➡

programmes, hardening the science,' explained Davis. He considered several notable scientists, including the astronomer Patrick Moore and Dr Alex Comfort – better known as the author of several good-sex manuals – before one of Innes Lloyd's former colleagues in the BBC's Outside Broadcast Unit recommended Dr Kit Pedler.

Davis and Pedler found that they enjoyed a good working relationship and this resulted in Davis commissioning Pedler on 17 May 1966 to write the storyline for what was to become the first Cyberman adventure.

Pedler had long been fascinated by computers and the human brain. 'I was thinking,' he explained in 1979, 'that although I could imagine a logical machine reasoning to itself and manipulating events outside it, by no stretch of the imagination could I envisage a machine producing a poem by Dylan Thomas.' It was from these initial thoughts that Pedler developed the idea of the Cybermen, a race of humanoid creatures who had replaced almost all their body parts with machines and had as a result lost their humanity.

Speaking in 1968, Pedler commented that he had been discussing the idea of spare-part surgery with his wife, who was also a doctor. 'We conceived the idea of someone with so many mechanical replacements that he didn't know whether he was a human or a machine.'

The original costume design for the Cybermen by designer Peter Kindred. This was developed further by costume designer Sandra Reid.

The first draft scripts for *The Tenth Planet*, the story that was to introduce the Cybermen and, coincidentally, to write out the first Doctor, were completed by Pedler. However, when Davis requested some rewrites in June 1966, Pedler was able to complete the work only for episodes one and two before he fell ill. Due to the pressure of time, Davis stepped in and completed the final two episodes.

In Pedler's final script for episode one, when the Cybermen first appeared, the following description was given:

```
    WE NOW SEE THEM AS TALL, THIN, CLAD IN A SILVER LINK ONE PIECE SUIT.

THE TWO SILVER CLAD FIGURES START TO TAKE OFF THE SOLDIERS' PARKAS. AS THEY DO SO,
     THE SLEEVE ON THE ARM OF ONE OF THEM SLIPS BACK. INSTEAD OF FLESH THERE IS A
   TRANSPARENT 'ARM SHAPED' FOREARM CONTAINING SHINING RODS AND LIGHTS. THERE IS A
                          NORMAL HAND AT THE END OF IT.

   A CLOSE UP OF ONE OF THEIR HANDS REVEALS A METAL PLATE RUNNING BETWEEN CENTRE HAIR
                           LINE FRONT AND OCCIPUT.
```

Although the script clearly uses the word 'hands' in this paragraph, the text is actually describing one of their heads. Later, in the camera script for episode two, the Cybermen were described in more detail:

```
   THEY ARE TALL, SLIM WITH ONE-PIECE, CLOSE-FITTING SILVER MESH UNIFORM, THEIR FACES
    AND HANDS ARE NORMAL BUT UNDER THE HAIR ON THE HEAD IS A LONG SHINING METAL PLATE
  STRETCHING FROM CENTRE HAIR LINE FRONT TO OCCIPUT. (THIS COULD BE DISGUISED BY A HAT)

   THEIR FACES ARE ALL RATHER ALIKE, ANGULAR AND BY NORMAL DEFINITIONS GOOD-LOOKING. ON
  THE FRONT OF THEIR TRUNKS IS A MECHANICAL COMPUTER-LIKE UNIT CONSISTING OF SWITCHES,
  TWO ROWS OF LIGHTS AND A SHORT, MOVEABLE PROBOSCIS. THEY ALL CARRY EXOTIC SIDE ARMS.
    AT THE SHOULDER JOINTS THERE ARE SMALL, RAM-LIKE CYLINDERS ACTING OVER THE JOINTS
    THEMSELVES. INSTEAD OF FLESH THERE IS A TRANSPARENT, "ARM-SHAPED" FOREARM COVERING
   CONTAINING SHINING RODS AND LIGHTS, BUT THERE IS A NORMAL HAND AT THE END OF IT.
```

The story's director, Derek Martinus, recalls the creation of the Cybermen. 'Kit Pedler, the writer, was a very interesting guy. He was a brilliant research doctor and was working on this sort of thing himself. That made it fascinating, the fact that this fantasy of cybernetic men was just an extension of what he was working towards as a researcher in real life.

'The perennial problem with *Doctor Who* is that inside the monster there's always got to be a human being. You've got to try and make a costume that can be worn by an actor, yet at the same time change the shape so that it looks less humanoid. The development of the look of the Cybermen came from discussions between myself, Kit Pedler, Sandra Reid [the costume designer] and Gerry Davis. Gerry and Kit would put their four pennyworth in, but Sandra and I evolved it between us.'

The original Cybermen reflected their origins as humanoids who had replaced their bodies with steel and

---

The Wheel in Space (1968) 6 episodes w. David Whitaker from a story by Kit Pedler d. Tristan de Vere Cole

The Cybermen hatch a complex plot to attack Earth using a space wheel as a base.

The Invasion (1968) 8 episodes w. Derrick Sherwin from a story by Kit Pedler d. Douglas Camfield

The Cybermen, in league with Tobias Vaughn, head of the powerful electronics company International Electromatics, plan an invasion of Earth.

The War Games (1969) 10 episodes w. Malcolm Hulke & Terrance Dicks d. David Maloney

During the Doctor's trial at the end of the story, a Cyberman is seen on a monitor screen as one of a number of examples of the evils the Doctor has fought.

The Mind of Evil (1971) 6 episodes w. Don Houghton d. Tim Combe

During an attack by the mind parasite within the Keller Machine, the Doctor is subjected to the things he fears most. A still picture of a Cyberman is seen.

Carnival of Monsters (1973) 4 episodes w. Robert Holmes d. Barry Letts

A Cyberman is one of the creatures held within Vorg's Miniscope.

Revenge of the Cybermen (1975) 4 episodes w. Gerry Davis d. Michael E. Briant

A group of Cybermen plan to destroy Voga, the planet of gold, as that metal is fatal to their systems.

Earthshock (1982) 4 episodes w. Eric Saward d. Peter Grimwade

The Cybermen plan to destroy a peace conference on Earth that will ally races against them. ➡

Two views of one of the original Cybermen. *The Tenth Planet.*

plastic. Their bodies and limbs were covered in a transparent plastic material through which could be seen various coloured tubes. The head was encased in a grey material with eye and mouth holes cut in. When the creatures spoke, their mouths opened but, although the lips quivered, they did not move in sync with the speech that emerged. They also had a vestigial nose visible on their faces. Their hands were still human with bare flesh visible, but their feet were encased in shoes. On their chests they carried a large and complex technical unit which supposedly replaced the function of their heart, lungs and other organs. Hung underneath this unit was a gun. This was a large, rectangular device which was held in both hands.

'We made the basic suit from a sort of plain knitted cotton jersey fabric,' Reid explained. 'On top of this was a clear plastic which made it very hot to wear – it was a marvellous way of slimming. In between the jersey and the plastic we used coloured strips made from a nylon tubing material. This was painted with a special spirit based paint which we used in the theatre for painting fabrics because it doesn't flake off.

'The jersey head mask was separate so that the actors could take it off when they got too hot. We placed strips of silver vinyl around the eyes and the mouth, stuck on to the fabric. The black earpiece was made from foam rubber and the lamp-like device on the top of the head was made from fibreglass.'

Working alongside Reid on the story was make-up assistant Sandra Exelby. 'The costumes were very funny in those days,' laughed Exelby. 'It was just made from grey jersey and we would poke our finger into the actor's face and ask, "Is your eye there?" and then cut a hole in the cloth when we had the position correct. We did the same for the mouth. We then had to paint round the actors' eyes and mouth with silver. The pieces on the costume covering the eyes looked like holes but we painted silver in the background so that if the camera caught a glimpse through, then you didn't see the flesh. We did this even though *Doctor Who* was made and transmitted in black and white in those days.

'That one had a lot of polystyrene "snow" blowing about and the poor Cybermen kept getting mouthfuls of this polystyrene. I think they used a kind of salt on the floor, and they used light polystyrene chips when they wanted to blow it about. They couldn't sit down very well either because hanging from their front was a metal computer, so we used to have to lean them against things.'

'I remember filming the scenes in the polystyrene snow at Ealing,' said Martinus. 'We used lovely great fans, with six stagehands chucking polystyrene around, and everyone got dry throats. I seem to remember we had an AFM [assistant floor manager] with contact lenses as well who had some problems.'

With the look of the Cybermen decided upon, what they would sound like was another priority. As with the Daleks, everyone working on *The Tenth Planet* knew that the Cybermen's voices had to be something special. They also had to be different as the last thing they wanted was to have the sound too close to that of the Daleks. 'There was endless discussion about the Cybermen's voices,' confirmed Martinus. 'I wanted something that had an eerie feeling to try to get away from the human voice but we didn't want to repeat the Dalek voice. So we came up with the idea of them opening their mouths and then not closing them again. We hoped that would add an other-worldly feel to it. We also developed the Cybermen's elliptical speech patterns which worked quite well.'

Roy Skelton, who had previously worked on *Doctor Who* providing the voices for the Monoids in *The Ark*,

The Cybermen prepare to attack the Antarctic base.
The Tenth Planet.

was contracted to provide the Cybermen's voices. They were intoned in a sing-song fashion which, when combined with the visual of the open mouth, brought the required alien feel to the creatures. In the final episode of the story, Peter Hawkins, who had been voicing the Daleks since their first appearance, also provided some of the voices.

The Cybermen were deemed to be very successful and on 18 November, less than a month after the story completed transmission, Davis commissioned Pedler to write an outline for *The Return of the Cybermen* which was retitled *The Moonbase* for production. Once again Pedler was assisted during the writing by Davis, but this time Davis was to receive no on-screen credit for his work.

For this second appearance, the Cybermen were completely redesigned by Reid. Part of the problem in their debut story had been that the suits were very bulky and the actors were literally fixed in with nuts and bolts. For *The Moonbase*, Reid attempted to address all the problems found in the original design.

'We had a bit more time and money, which allowed us to do more of what we really wanted,' she explained. 'They were simplified in style but they still retained the essential elements of the first lot like the piano accordion on their chests, and this time their hands were covered.'

The costumes used in *The Moonbase* consisted primarily of a silver boiler suit which covered the actor's entire body except his head. The hands had only a 'thumb' and two 'fingers'. The head was constructed from fibreglass with two thin clear perspex tubes leading from the sides of the head to a small light mounted in the metal casing at the top. The eyes and mouth were outlined in black tape and there was no visible nose. The chest unit was far more compact than before, consisting of three rectangular units arranged vertically down the chest, the centre one thicker and longer than the other two. The arms and legs had long ribbed tubes (rather like those used as the flexible hose on a vacuum cleaner) with a small plastic ball punched with holes situated at the shoulder, elbow, wrist, thigh, knee and ankle. The two balls at the shoulders had thin black piping leading to the top of the chest unit. A cyber-gun was situated at the base of the chest unit and was a small hand-held device, rather than the bulky arrangement of *The Tenth Planet*.

Although designed by Reid, the costumes were constructed by Jack Lovell Ltd. In a 1989 interview, John Lovell, Jack Lovell's son, explained: 'I think they wanted to make them more horrendous because the first ones were a fudge-up. We did the whole lot on the Mark II Cybermen: the tubing, the costumes, the toy plastic balls – the whole lot. If you look carefully at a photo of a Mark II Cyberman you can see the small holes we drilled into the side of the neck to let air in.'

The director of *The Moonbase* was Morris Barry. 'I knew that Cyberman actors had to be well over six foot two tall as a minimum,' he explained. 'Once we had the actors then their boots were blocked up by about four or six inches, which made them about six foot eight. On top were the helmets which made them very nearly seven foot tall. They were huge, really horrific.'

One of the actors hired to play a Cyberman in *The Moonbase* was Peter Greene, and he recalled the moment when 'his' Cyberman had to die after being sprayed with a cocktail of solvents by the Doctor's companions. 'That death was quite extraordinary – a bit like death by custard! The costumes had pipes coming from the back, and when we started the shot, what looked like custard came spurting out of the chest units at the front. The director shouted, "Right, you're dying. Do jerky movements." I had to fall over, jerking all the time as this stuff pumped out of the front. We looked like badly iced cakes afterwards.'

Continuing the theme from *The Tenth Planet* – of the Cybermen keeping open their mouths while speaking – for *The Moonbase*, the helmets were

CHARACTER

The Cybermen originated on the planet Mondas, which was Earth's twin. Aeons ago the two planets drifted apart in space, and Mondas undertook a journey across the solar system. Eventually it returned to Earth. The inhabitants of Mondas, who had originally been just like humans, had, when their scientists had realised that the species was getting weak as life-spans grew shorter, steadily replaced all their human organs with machines, creating a new race of powerful creatures, the Cybermen.

During the process of rebuilding themselves, the Cybermen realised that the concept of survival was paramount to their race and so made every effort to achieve that end. They recognised that emotional behaviour was a weakness and not to the good of the race as a whole and so eliminated it from their brains, turning themselves into coldly logical creatures who would take only those actions which related to their survival.

They have taken several steps to try to ensure this survival. They have conquered other planets, like Telos, the home of the Cryons, which is where they arranged for a honeycomb of tombs to be constructed deep in the planet's frozen centre. As well as the tombs, they also created a complex logic-puzzle system which anyone venturing into the tombs would have to solve. The idea was that any race logical enough to work out how to revive the Cybermen could themselves easily be turned into new Cybermen. ➡

Top: The Cybermen on the lunar surface prepare to attack. *The Moonbase.* Bottom: A group of Cybermen pose for the press during a photocall for *The Moonbase.*

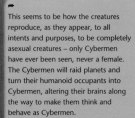
equipped with a small metal cover which the actor inside the costume could operate to uncover the mouth slot when the creature was speaking, and then to push the cover back down again when it had finished.

'The most extraordinary thing was having to learn the lines,' remembered Greene. 'Peter Hawkins did the voices and so we had to be able to give him a cue as to when to start talking. We had a piece of felt, I think it was, looped underneath our chins with a bit of elastic, so at the right moment, you'd drop your chin and that would open the mouth. Peter would then speak the lines, and we had to know what they were in order to know when to close the mouth again.'

A Cyberman attacks Ralph Adebayo (Mark Heath) in the store room. *The Moonbase.*

Along with the redesign of the look of the creatures, a decision was also made to change the voices. 'I was sent to a good dentist who was a specialist in speech defects and he made a false palate for me,' recalled Hawkins. 'In this palate was a small aperture into which they placed a small vibrator – similar to the ones used by people who are unable to speak because they have lost the use of their larynx – connected to a switch and a battery. By pressing the switch, the vibrator started buzzing, and when I spoke I mouthed the words around the buzz and my voice came out sounding very alien.

'The problem was that having something like that in your mouth, it made you salivate an awful lot – it was like having a big boiled sweet in your mouth! The buzzer became clogged up quite quickly and we often had to stop to free it up.'

Morris Barry was very pleased with Hawkins' work and, in a letter to the actor dated 2 March 1967, said, 'You may like to know that our four episodes have been considered highly successful – so much so that I believe they are planning to bring the Cybermen back for yet another go. It may even happen that I shall be directing it so, if you still have your palate, please refrain from jumping on it.'

Barry's information was totally accurate and on 3 March, the day before the final episode of *The Moonbase* was transmitted, Pedler and Davis, who had by this time moved on from his story editing duties, were together commissioned to provide the storyline for *Dr Who and the Cyberman Planet*. During its production, the story underwent a name change to *The Ice Tombs of Telos* but was retitled *The Tomb of the Cybermen* for transmission.

The Cybermen costumes, aside from the addition of three more black tubes leading from the chest unit to the ribbed tubing on their legs, were identical to those seen in *The Moonbase*. However, there was an addition to the ranks of the Cybermen in this story: the massive Cybercontroller, leader of the Cybermen.

The Cybercontroller's costume was, like the standard Cybermen, basically a silver boiler suit. However, the creature did not have a chest unit; there were no tubes and balls on its arms and legs; and its head, instead of having the two 'handles' leading from the sides to the top, was highly domed. The head was again constructed from fibreglass but the dome was left untinted and clear, although a fine tracery of red lines was painted on it, so that a light could be fixed inside, powered from a battery concealed in the back of the helmet. This gave the effect of the Cybercontroller's head glowing with power, but it was ultimately unused in the transmitted story.

The Cybercontroller was played by Michael Kilgarriff. 'It was very uncomfortable and claustrophobic,' he recalled. 'I remember during filming when I had been electrocuted, and I had to lie on the floor with smoke

This seems to be how the creatures reproduce, as they appear, to all intents and purposes, to be completely asexual creatures – only Cybermen have ever been seen, never a female. The Cybermen will raid planets and turn their humanoid occupants into Cybermen, altering their brains along the way to make them think and behave as Cybermen.

As well as the humanoid creatures (which retain the organic brain of the original creature, albeit in an 'altered' form) there is also a non-humanoid Cyber-Planner. This creature has no recognisable features although it is able to speak. Its function seems to be simply as a brain used to plan and coordinate the Cybermen's attacks, predicting the actions of others and directing the Cyberforces accordingly.

The Cybermen also have the technology to create small creatures called Cybermats. It is unclear whether they, like the Cybermen, were once organic, or have been built. The Cybermats act as the eyes and ears of the Cybermen, infiltrating an enemy encampment and sending back intelligence reports. The Cybermats can also be specifically tailored to a task: they have been seen to have the ability to home in on human brainwaves and to attack; they have also been given the ability to destroy a metal called bernalium and also to inject a deadly poison into humans (a similar neural poison was also used to weaken human resistance at a lunar base, but on that occasion was delivered through tampering with the sugar supply). ➡

A Cyberman emerges from his frozen sleep. *The Tomb of the Cybermen.*

pouring from every joint. As I lay there with plastic tubes attached to me all over, tea break occurred. Suddenly the lights were turned out and everyone vanished. I couldn't move without assistance, let alone get up, so I shouted and yelled until someone came and helped me up, unscrewed the helmet and gave me a cup of tea.'

'Michael was six foot four to start with!' commented Barry. 'He was, quite rightly so, a little bit concerned about playing the part because he didn't have any lines to say – the voice was again dubbed on by Peter

The Cybermats, deadly rodent-like creatures. *The Tomb of the Cybermen.*

Hawkins. Michael still had to know the lines because he had to make the mouth of the helmet open, but he didn't actually speak himself.'

Another aspect of Cyber culture was revealed in this story. The Cybermen were trapped underground while the humans stayed above ground in the control room of the Cybermen's complex on Telos, and the silver giants used small metallic rodent-like creatures to attack them. These were called Cybermats.

'Some of the Cybermats were radio controlled and some were pulled along on wires,' recalled Barry. 'Do you remember when they brought out the little toy Daleks which were battery operated? The mechanics of the Cybermats were rather based on that in that they had batteries and a motor to make them roll along, but to control the position and the direction they used radio control. It was the early days of using these sort of things in the studio, and I remember there was a problem with them. The floor manager has a radio link with the gallery so that he can talk to the director and vice versa, and the next studio has the same thing but on a different wavelength. I remember that when we tried the Cybermats they were an absolute headache, because they went out of control. They suddenly went round and round in circles, then they stopped or went shooting off in a totally different direction. Nobody could control them. What had happened, so they said, was that they had got on to the next studio's wavelength, and whatever the studio was transmitting in the form of verbal messages was making the Cybermats go crazy; the operators weren't controlling them at all. That was a big worry because we had a very short time to get the Cybermats to do the things that the script required.'

The Cybermats were constructed by the BBC's Visual Effects Department and the designer in charge of the story was Michealjohn Harris. Harris recalled that, in order to make the Cybermats move, several techniques were used all at once. As well as the radio control, another method was employed: 'Our heroes had gone to sleep and the Cybermats were crawling up to them ready to pounce, and obviously there is no way in which you can do it forward, so we did it in reverse and it was very, very effective because, curiously enough, when you do a thing in reverse like that it starts slowly and darts forward as though it's made an effort, creeps forward and jumps, and the effect is very good.'

As well as the radio-controlled and pull-along Cybermats there were also a number other props created, including one with meshing 'teeth' on its underside, and other, smaller model Cybermats.

The BBC was very keen to market the Cybermen and the Cybermats and in August 1967, they agreed a deal with Pedler that any royalties would be equally split between him and the BBC. As it happened, nothing came of this and no Cyberman or Cybermat products were produced in the sixties, although the creatures did make several appearances in the *Doctor Who* comic strip running in *TV Comic.*

The following Cyberman story, *The Wheel-In Space*, was not written by Pedler and Davis. David Whitaker, *Doctor Who*'s first story editor, was instead commissioned on 14 December 1967 to write a set of six scripts based on an initial idea by Pedler. Primarily, the story featured only two Cybermen, and their costumes were redesigned once more, the basis now being a silver-painted diver's wetsuit.

The redesign was carried out by costume designer Martin Baugh. 'It was the beginning of cybernetics: aiding human movement by robotic means,' he explained. 'The tubes on the sides of their arms and legs were meant to be cybernetic enhancements to their own limbs. I wanted to get the idea of some sort of hydraulic system. I moved away from the loose silver suits which the Cybermen had worn previously

The Cybermen have also created powerful blank-faced androids to protect a bomb hidden on Earth, intended to wipe out a conference which would ally races against the their own. These androids had a constant video link to their Cybermen masters and were equipped with a devastating flesh-dissolving ray which was fired from the palm of their hands.

In terms of rank, although all Cybermen simply obey orders, the Cybermats appear to have little or no intelligence other than the instinct to attack. Then there are the Cybermen troops, which are directed by a Cyberleader and, sometimes, a Cyberlieutenant. Other types of Cybermen appear to have been developed for specific functions; for example the Cyberscout, used to map out terrain and keep watch, and some black-painted Cybermen used as camouflaged troops in the London sewers. Above the Cyberleader is the Cybercontroller. This creature appears to be in overall charge and it is possible that there is only one Cybercontroller in existence at any one time. ➡

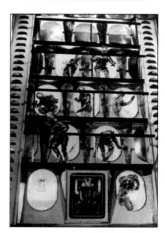

Top: The Cybermen awake. *The Tomb of the Cybermen.*
Bottom: The Cybercontroller's helmet from *The Tomb of the Cybermen.*

The Cybermats in *The Wheel in Space* were of a slightly different design.

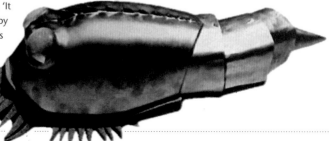

because I felt they looked a bit floppy. If something's baggy, it tends to indicate that the character is cuddly and floppy and in some way comic. If you want to make a character in a suit slightly comical then you put

him in a suit that is baggy. I wanted to make the Cybermen much harder as they are nasty things and that was the basis of all the changes I made.

'I desperately tried to find a way of attaching the rods to the upper legs rather than placing them on to what looks like a suspender belt, but attaching them straight into the rubber wetsuit just tore the rubber. We didn't really have the material to attach them properly.'

The by now traditional chest unit was still present, but was the same prop from the previous two stories worn upside down. Reflecting the idea of a hydraulic system, the hose-and-ball arrangements on the

Zoe (Wendy Padbury) is unaware that she has company in the form of two Cybermen (Gordon Stothard, Jerry Holmes) in a publicity photograph from The Wheel in Space.

arms and legs were replaced with a system of metal rods connected by small rectangular boxes. Black tubing came from the base of the chest unit and disappeared up behind the unit and a further length of back tube crossed the shoulders at collarbone level, connecting the rods at the top of the arms together. This tube also helped to mask the join at the bottom of the helmet. The hands had only three fingers as before, but each finger was capped by a thimble-like arrangement.

The helmet also underwent some restyling. Small holes were added to either side of the eye holes (in a position similar to that of the tear duct on a human eye) and the mouth slot also had a hole cut in the bottom centre. The black edging around the eyes and mouth was absent.

'I never quite understood whether the Cybermen were meant to be robots or whether they were humanoid creatures wearing spacesuits,' said Baugh. 'People tend to assume that you as a designer know the history of these creatures, but this wasn't the case.'

At the conclusion of the story there was a short scene featuring a group of Cybermen walking in space. For this scene, the costumes were a mixture of those as previously used in The Tomb of the Cybermen, with the chest unit positioned correctly as for that story, and the two new costumes created for The Wheel in Space.

The Cybermen invade London. The Invasion.

The Cybermats appeared once more and were also redesigned. According to the script they attacked by using blasts of energy which could paralyse and kill their victim, presumably when that paralysis centred on the heart and lungs. The creatures therefore had to have some means of showing their operation and so large glowing eyelike sensors were added to the front of their heads and a measured bleeping sound was included on the soundtrack when they became active.

The Cybermen's voices were also changed for this story. The two Cybermen featured for the bulk of the story spoke with a humming, emotionless drawl, quite unlike the electronic buzzing created by Hawkins for the previous stories. Hawkins' buzzing voice was, however, used for the Cyber-Planner, heard communicating with the Cybermen during the course of the adventure. The Cyber-Planner was described in the camera script for episode five as:

ANOTHER CYBERMAN, SEATED IN A STRANGE SEAT FROM WHICH METAL WIRES BEND OUT FROM THE BASE AND ATTACH THEMSELVES TO THE HEAD OF THE CYBERMAN.

The realisation of this creature was totally different and it was depicted simply as a glowing microphone-like device. The idea behind the Cyber-Planner was that this was a more sophisticated form of Cyberman, one which had been augmented to include the facilities for the complex planning of their numerous campaigns. The voices for the 'standard' Cybermen were created by Roy Skelton, whilst those for the Cyber-Planner were provided by Hawkins using the palate created for the previous stories.

The following Cyberman adventure, The Invasion, was once more based on an idea by Pedler, and was commissioned by producer Peter Bryant, from Pedler and Derrick Sherwin on 6 May 1968. Sherwin was at the time also acting as Doctor Who's script editor. Ultimately it was realised that Pedler's original synopsis was far too brief and Sherwin, who it was always intended would write the scripts from Pedler's synopsis, was left to craft and develop much of the plot himself.

The Cybermen were again redesigned for the story, and the Cyber Director made its one and only appearance, represented as a large and complex device constructed from perspex and metal, with a spinning central section

The Cybermen are strong and powerful. They can survive in space unprotected and need no oxygen to breathe. They have the strength of ten men and also have the ability to control the minds of others, either by a hypnotic ray or through a control device worn on the head, turning humans into their slaves. They stole a time machine from another race which allowed them to try to guarantee the success of previous missions – as when they attempted to ensure that Mondas was not destroyed during its fateful encounter with Earth in 1986. Their weaponry includes hand-held blasters which can stun or kill; certain Cybermen have had guns implanted in the lamp-like device at the top of their heads and others have had them included as a part of the chest unit. They can also fire a disabling bolt of energy from their fingers or from the lamp-like device. The energy bolt from their fingertips can also operate machinery.

and fitted with flashing lights. This was a very basic representation of the being as described in the script:

```
THIS IS BASICALLY A METALLIC BRAIN-CASE-SHAPE PULSATING WITH PERIODIC INNER PRESSURE
LIGHT COMING FROM INSIDE IT. TO IT GO LARGE COILS OF CORRUGATED TUBE FROM PERIPHERAL
MACHINERY COMPOSED MAINLY OF LARGE ELECTRICAL COILS (SPRING SHAPED) FLASHING WITH
LIGHT. THE SURFACE OF THE BRAIN CASE IS COVERED IN VEINS AND SMALL POINTS OF
LIGHT ARE TRACKING OVER IT.

THIS WHOLE COMPLEX IS HOUSED IN A TRANSPARENT UNIT WHICH HAS VARIOUS ELECTRONIC
LEADS RUNNING TO IT. THE WHOLE COMPLEX BEGINS TO PULSATE WITH LIGHT AND SOUND
WHEN IT IS REVEALED.

WHEN THE CYBER DIRECTOR SPEAKS IT IS WITH A SYNTHETIC VOICE BUT THE WORD FORMULATION
IS PERFECT, WELL MODULATED, CONTROLLED AND COMPLETELY WITHOUT EMOTION.
```

The Cybermen's costumes were once more based on a wetsuit but the arms and legs had a single rod fitted to them rather than the double rods of *The Wheel in Space*. The rods were attached to small hemispherical connectors positioned on the arms and legs as before.

The helmets retained the 'teardrop' hole on the eye, but the hole below the mouth was removed. Two 'pie case' attachments were present, one on either side of the head, from which the tubes leading to the top of the skull emerged. The chest unit was very much simplified, although retaining the gun fitting at the top of the central section.

One of the actors playing a Cyberman in *The Invasion* was Richard King, who, unknown to the BBC, suffered from claustrophobia. 'I hadn't been forewarned as to what the outfit would be, and in our business you tend not to reveal to the BBC your little afflictions. When I turned up, they gave me this rubberised suit, which was fine, but when the dressers came to put the helmet on and screw the helmet down – which is what they had to do – I started to get very irritable. I just couldn't stand it, but I had to in order to get through the job. The dressers were very understanding and would come between takes and remove the helmet so that I could calm myself down, ready for the next shot.

'The suits were very difficult to walk in and the way that the Cybermen walked, in a very staccato manner, was about the only way you could walk in the suit.'

One of the most memorable scenes from *The Invasion* is when the Cybermen emerge from hiding and are seen marching over London. In particular there is a scene of them on a long flight of steps, with St Paul's Cathedral towering in the background.

King remembered filming these scenes. 'At St Paul's, because of the limited field of vision that we had within the Cyberman costumes, which was further obscured by some gauze fitted over the eye holes, and also because the director wouldn't let us move our heads down to see where the steps were, we literally had to walk down the steps feeling the way with our feet.

The Cybermen are filmed emerging from a sewer in Central London. *The Invasion*.

'All in all, playing a Cyberman was very uncomfortable. The suits were difficult to wear, but the job was enjoyable in some ways. In this business, you have to put up with these things.'

The costume designer for the story, Bobi Bartlett, also remembered the filming at St Paul's Cathedral, but for very different reasons.

'There was a scene when the Cybermen came out of the sewers,' she recalled. 'And I was actually underground, in the sewers with them. The Cybermen's helmets had to be screwed together, with a single screw at the back attaching them to the main part of the costume for quick release.

The Cybermen advance, armed with flame-throwing weapons. *The Invasion*.

They were made of fibreglass, as they had to be lightweight, but the actors couldn't stay in them for more than about twenty minutes at a time before they became too hot and started to have problems with condensation as the eye visors steamed up. They could also get to feel claustrophobic. Consequently I had to be on hand throughout the filming, to take their heads off between shots and then screw them back on again when they were needed.

'Unfortunately, the director, who was usually extremely efficient, took an incredibly long time to film these particular shots of the Cybermen coming out of the sewers, so I was down there for ages, constantly taking

Cybermen's heads off and putting them back on again. What didn't help matters was that there were also lots of rats in evidence! I had to say to the director, "I'm sorry, but I'm not going down there unless you let me have some men with big torches to scare the rats off, because if I see a rat it won't be a Cyberman you'll get coming out of the sewers, it'll be me!" I got quite firm about it, because I knew that if I came out while they were filming, and ruined their shot, they would get extremely annoyed with me. In the end it worked really well and to great effect, as they conceded and gave me more warning before the Cybermen were needed each time.'

In a significant change from the previous Cyberman stories, *The Invasion* did not use Peter Hawkins or Roy Skelton to provide the voices. Instead an actor called Peter Halliday, who was also guest-starring as one of the human characters in the story, did the voices of the Cyber-Director and of the regular Cybermen. As a

result they were completely different from those that had gone before. For the Cyber-Director, Halliday adopted a kind of nasal emotionless drawl, not entirely dissimilar to the voice of the regular Cybermen in *The Wheel in Space*, while for *The Invasion*'s regular Cybermen (which spoke in only two scenes in the entire eight-part story), the voice was distorted and overlaid with electronic twangs.

Following the conclusion of *The Invasion*, the Cybermen didn't make a further major contribution to the series for the next five years, and missed any significant appearance with Jon Pertwee's Doctor during his time in the role.

The Cybermen outside St Paul's Cathedral. *The Invasion.*

This was unusual for a creature that had been such a success in the mid-to-late-sixties. Perhaps a contributing factor to this was that, shortly after submitting the initial storyline for *The Invasion*, Kit Pedler, together with Gerry Davis, was instrumental in the devising and setting up of a new BBC drama show called *Doomwatch*.

During the era of the third Doctor, the Cybermen did make two very brief appearances: as one of the images experienced by the Doctor while he is being attacked by the alien mind parasite housed inside the Keller Machine at Stangmoor Prison (*The Mind of Evil*), and as one of the trapped specimens in Vorg's Miniscope (*Carnival of Monsters*).

The Cybermen's next 'proper' appearance was in 1975, when Gerry Davis contributed a new story to the programme. This started life as a storyline and four-part story called *Return of the Cybermen* and was retitled *Revenge of the Cybermen* for production.

Because of the long gap between *The Invasion* and *Revenge of the Cybermen*, all the existing Cyberman costumes had been either lost or damaged and so the Visual Effects Department had little choice but to start again from scratch. To create the costumes, an external contractor was assigned, Allister Bowtell.

'The Cybermen were based on the same kind of thing that had gone before and were based around a wetsuit,' commented Bowtell. 'I think we were given a drawing to work from as well.

'We had to re-sculpt the head and the helmet was made from fibreglass. We had about ten people working on that costume, all doing different parts. I remember making the basic shell of the chest unit, for example, and then someone else filled it with bits and pieces from broken television sets.

'The designs evolved. The BBC designer would come down to the workshop while we were making the costumes and make comments and suggestions.'

Revenge of the Cybermen featured another new form of Cyberman, the Cyberleader. The costume for this higher-ranking Cyberman was effectively the same as all the others, but with a predominantly black helmet as opposed to the silver of the others.

The Cyberleader was played by Christopher Robbie, and, for the first time, the Cybermen's voices were provided by the actors inside the costumes.

'One had to try to find a vaguely mechanical voice,' Robbie explained in 1985. 'I think that I was led to believe when we were rehearsing it that the voice was going to be distorted through a synthesiser to a far greater degree than eventually it was. And that's why I was speaking in that staccato way with deliberate pausing, so that any distortion would still allow the words to come through.'

  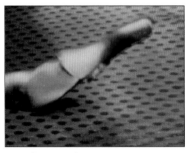

Left to right: Tom Baker (The Doctor) is menaced by a Cyberman in a publicity photograph for *Revenge of the Cybermen*. The Cyber Leader (Christopher Robbie). A Cybermat attacks. *Revenge of the Cybermen*.

Following *Revenge of the Cybermen*, the silver giants were not to make another appearance in *Doctor Who* for a further five years. These absences were down to a lack of suitable opportunity rather than from a conscious policy by successive production teams not to feature them. When they eventually did return, it was with yet another radically different look.

In 1981, producer John Nathan-Turner and script editor Eric Saward turned their attention to the Cybermen. Saward remembered the creatures from *Doctor Who*'s past and wanted to bring them back to the show, bigger and better than before. With Tom Baker leaving after seven years in the role to be replaced by Peter Davison, Nathan-Turner wanted something in Davison's opening season to make an impact.

With the working title of *Sentinel*, Saward's Cyberman story was commissioned on 24 July 1981 and eventually retitled *Earthshock* for production. As with *Revenge of the Cybermen*, the story featured a Cyberleader, and added a Cyberlieutenant to the ranks as well as numerous warrior Cybermen.

No consideration was given to reusing any costumes that might remain in the BBC's stores as Nathan-Turner wanted a radical new look for the creatures. The construction of these new costumes was given to a freelance company called Imagineering.

Imagineering were approached by the costume designer allocated to *Earthshock*, Dinah Collin. 'The Cybermen comeback was really quite difficult,' she explained in 1985. 'You are stuck with an image and because *Doctor Who* has such an enormous tradition, you can't devise a completely new thing. I was asked to actually rethink the costume. We had to have elements of the original shape – the head was the main thing. They ended up with those handles on the sides, which I've always thought was a mistake, but the handles were somehow part of how people remembered them. As for the rest of it, I think we found a flying suit which was ex-army surplus and covered with all these amazing tubes which we built up, and then put even more tubes on and that's how it evolved. The other Cybermen wore terrible wellingtons. I didn't get over that problem terribly well: I used moonboots, which were sort of better.'

'We did a lot of sketches ourselves,' said Richard Gregory, one of Imagineering's founders, 'to show Dinah how we thought the Cybermen should look and how they could be made and we were very lucky in that she agreed so many of them and we had a good amount of time in which to make them.'

The *Earthshock* Cybermen did bear a lot of superficial similarities to those of the sixties. The helmets retained the tubes on the sides of the head, but the creatures were given a more sculptured and 'hi-tech' facial appearance than before. One innovation, suggested by Nathan-Turner, was to give the helmets a clear perspex mouthpiece through which the actor's real mouth and chin could be seen moving. This was to reinforce the original concept that the Cybermen were not robots and that there was some remnant of a humanoid creature inside, and also to make clear which of them was speaking at any given time – something Nathan-Turner was particularly keen to achieve.

The basis of the costume was, as Collin stated, an RAF G-suit. These suits were covered on the outside with a capillary system of tubes, all leading to a series of larger and larger tubes through which water was pumped in order to cool pilots when on high-altitude missions. The G-suit was taken apart and reconstructed on a cotton boiler suit in order to ensure that they would fit the actors. The capillary tubes echoed the tubes featured on the arms and legs of the Cybermen in previous stories, and, as before, they were all connected up to the chest unit.

The chest unit was considerably smaller, and was split into two sections, upper and lower. Behind a perspex panel mounted on the front of the upper unit could be seen the bas-relief impression of a heart and veins,

Cybermen have also been disabled in the past by radiation and a gravity weapon. Also highly effective was the Cerebration Mentor, developed by Professor Watkins for Tobias Vaughn. This projected a ray of selected emotion at the creature, and caused madness or death. Another weapon deadly to Cybermen is the glitter gun. This fired gold dust mined from the planet Voga, and was an important factor in the defeat of the Cybermen in the Cyberwars that saw its development.

The Cybermen are ruthless and their lack of emotion means that it is impossible to reason with them. The only reason they will heed is that of pure logic, and even then the reasoning must result in a win for the Cyber race. Despite their great power, the Doctor has managed to defeat them on each occasion he has encountered them, and following the Cyber Wars, the great race is all but defeated. There is little left other than isolated groups of Cybermen, struggling to find a way to survive.

Top: The Cyberleader (David Banks) discusses tactics with his lieutenant (Mark Hardy). *Earthshock*. Below: The Cybermen emerge from hiding on board a freighter bound for Earth. *Earthshock*.

The Cybermen are systematically wiped out by the Raston Robot. *The Five Doctors*.

A Cyberman patrols Cyber-Control. *Attack of the Cybermen*.

while the lower part of the unit was connected to the upper part via a flexible ribbed section.

The costume was completed with moonboots for the feet and heavy motorbike gauntlets for the hands, both of which were sprayed silver to match the rest of the costume.

To play the Cyberleader, actor David Banks was hired. Like Christopher Robbie before him, he also had to provide the voice for the creature he was playing. 'There is a difficulty when wearing the costume, as to where you put the radio mike. In *Earthshock* it was put up in the top of the helmet and held there with tape, but in the studio, it got hot, the tape came undone, and it slowly slid down my face. We had visible jaws in those costumes and we had a bit of a continuity problem as the microphone appeared in the jawline.

'It's probably nicer to feel in control of what you are doing and saying when you are saying the lines yourself rather than having someone speak them for you.'

After their return in *Earthshock*, the Cybermen again started to appear on a semi-regular basis, and the first of these appearances was in the 20th anniversary story *The Five Doctors*. The costumes used in *The Five Doctors* were identical to those in *Earthshock* – although they were reportedly a new batch built from scratch – with the exception that the perspex mouthpieces were sprayed over with silver. This was, apparently, not a deliberate design change, but one which came about gradually as the suits were touched up by the dressers between takes on location. David Banks recalls that even as early as *Earthshock*, the mouthpiece was being sprayed silver to try to hide the radio mike as it slipped down his head.

Banks again returned to reprise his role as the Cyberleader and remembered one scene where the Cybermen were literally torn apart by a powerful and lethal robot. 'I had the idea of holding some milk in my mouth and then spitting it out when I was attacked. I was fitted up with explosive charges and I sucked up the milk through a straw. If anything had gone wrong, I could really have choked.

'Stuart Fell, the stuntman, had green smoking slime stuck to his helmet, and he was suffocating, couldn't get his helmet off, couldn't shout. We thought him falling on the floor was just good stunt work ...'

Although the Cybermen were the major monster to appear in *The Five Doctors* – the story also featured cameo appearances from a Dalek and a Yeti – it wasn't long before they were back in another story of their own. *Attack of the Cybermen* started life as a storyline called *The Cold War* commissioned on 10 January 1983 and written by a friend of Saward's under the name Paula Moore. More so than any other Cyberman story, *Attack of the Cybermen* was heavily reliant on *Doctor Who*'s past history and told of an attempt by the Cybermen to divert Halley's Comet into the Earth and thus change history by preventing Mondas (which had been Earth's 'twin') from being destroyed when it returned to our solar system in 1986. In *The Tenth Planet* we had seen that it was Earth's continued presence in the solar system that sealed Mondas' fate. In addition, the Cybermen had made their base in London's sewer system (*The Invasion*) and also had a base on the planet Telos (*The Tomb of the Cybermen*). The Cybercontroller from *The Tomb of the Cybermen* also returned, albeit in a redesigned form, played, as before, by Michael Kilgarriff – and, in a nicely original touch, the Cybermen patrolling the sewers were painted black rather than silver so that they would be camouflaged in the darkness.

Once again the costumes were reused from *Earthshock* with little modification, aside from those colour schemes. The costume for the Cybercontroller, however, was new. The basis for this costume was again one of the flight suits, but in keeping with the original design as seen in *The Tomb of the Cybermen*, it had no chest unit, and the helmet was highly domed and did not feature the distinctive 'handle' on each side. In another nod to the original Cybercontroller, the dome of the helmet was originally painted silver with a red tint to give the impression of a brain beneath. This idea was dropped, however, and the dome was resprayed plain silver, although, as this was done partway through recording, the red tint can still be seen in certain shots in the transmitted story.

The Cybercontroller (Michael Kilgarriff). *Attack of the Cybermen.*

The Cybermen's final appearance in *Doctor Who* was in a story made to mark the programme's 25th anniversary in 1988 – a silver anniversary in matrimonial terms – and what better monsters to return for such an anniversary? The story was commissioned from writer Kevin Clarke on 20 January 1988 under the title *The Harbinger* but was later retitled *Silver Nemesis* to reflect the nature of the anniversary.

The Cybermen underwent yet another redesign for this story, this time courtesy of costume designer Richard Croft. One of Croft's innovations was to make use of a chroming process on the helmets and chest units so that they seemed to be made from a highly polished and reflective silver metal. In an unfortunate side effect, over time, the silver chrome oxidised and changed to a gold colour – and gold is fatal to the Cybermen.

The costumes were again based on the flight-suit principle but, by this time, the RAF were no longer making the suits that had been used as the basis for the previous costumes and so Croft had to create something similar. Instead of the capillary tubing on the arms and legs, he used clear plastic tubing connected together with electrician's junction boxes, which encircled the lower legs and lower arms of the Cybermen. The gloves were American baseball catcher's mittens and the actors wore lace-up boots on their feet, a concession to comfort that had actually been granted from *The Five Doctors* onwards.

Top: The Cybermen advance. *Silver Nemesis.* Bottom: Even the Cybermen are no match for a gold-tipped arrow. *Silver Nemesis.*

'These costumes were designed for comfort,' said David Banks, who once more returned to play the Cyberleader. 'They're lighter, the head is larger, and you can unclip the back panel and get it off yourself. It's still very uncomfortable, though, in the hot sun.'

One final idea for *Silver Nemesis* that was not to make it into the final scripts was the reintroduction of the Cybermats. A design for the creatures had been devised by visual effects assistant Mike Tucker for the story but was not included. A further redesigned version of this Cybermat later appeared in a documentary made by the BBC to mark thirty years of *Doctor Who* in 1993.

With the conclusion of *Silver Nemesis*, the Cybermen were not to appear in *Doctor Who* again before its cancellation as a BBC production in 1989. After numerous appearances, spanning some twenty years, they have certainly made their mark. Perhaps they will return to torment the Doctor once again.

CHAPTER 4

THE ICE WARRIORS

I was chosen for my size. We had these cumbersome costumes to wear. Very uncomfortable but very pleasing because you frightened everyone you met!

SONNY CALDINEZ ON PLAYING AN ICE WARRIOR

Created by writer Brian Hayles, the Ice Warriors were a race of gigantic, intelligent, lizard-like humanoids from the planet Mars who could indulge in conversation and could also scheme and plot. Speaking in 1978, Hayles explained how the Martian giants had originated. 'They were evolved because we wanted to have an adventure which introduced a new kind of monster, and not necessarily rivalling the Daleks or the Cybermen. At the same time we wanted something from outer space, and I happened to be interested in Mars and concocted, from the evidence that we knew at that time of conditions on Mars, a kind of reptilian biped that might conceivably just have existed. Having got the monster and where they came from, we wanted to do a setting and I think I'd read somewhere about a mammoth, I think, discovered in Russia, buried in the ice, and the thought came to me that perhaps we could find the Ice Warriors buried in the ice, and then develop it from there.'

In Hayles' camera script for the first episode, when one of the creatures was first found buried in the ice of a glacier, the following description was given:

THE ICE WARRIORS

The Ice Warriors (1967) 6 episodes
W. Brian Hayles d. Derek Martinus

Varga, an alien from Mars, is found in a glacier by human scientists on Earth. He revives and sets about preparing his ship and his crew to conquer the Earth.

The Seeds of Death (1969) 6 episodes
w. Brian Hayles (and Terrance Dicks)
d. Michael Ferguson

The Martians plan an attack on Earth by using a matter transmission system on the Moon to send deadly oxygen-absorbing Martian spores to destroy Earth's atmosphere. ➡

INSIDE THE ICE, DISTORTED BUT RECOGNISABLE, IS WHAT APPEARS TO BE A HELMETED WARRIOR. THE HELMET IS HOOD-LIKE AND OMINOUS, IN THE STYLE OF THAT USED UNDER THE OPENING TITLES OF 'HEREWARD THE WAKE'. THIS IS VARGA.

Later, as the Doctor examined the frozen body, the Warrior was described as having an electronic earpiece:

ALMOST A SCULPTURAL DESIGN AS IN MODERN SPACE HELMETS

And finally, at the end of the first episode, the following description appeared:

WHERE ICE HAS FALLEN AWAY FROM ITS HELMET, THE ELECTRODE IS NOW TOUCHING BARE METAL.

ON THE NEARBY HELMET, WE CAN SEE WHAT LOOKS LIKE A STRIP OF GLASS, PHOTO-ELECTRONIC CELL FACETS. THEY BEGIN TO PULSE WITH LIGHT.

The War Games (1969) 10 episodes
w. Malcolm Hulke & Terrance Dicks
d. David Maloney

During the Doctor's trial at the end of the story, an Ice Warrior is seen on a monitor screen as one of a number of examples of the evils the Doctor has fought.

The Curse of Peladon (1972) 4 episodes
w. Brian Hayles d. Lennie Mayne

The Doctor inadvertently attends a Galactic Committee of Assessment which is under threat by saboteurs. The Martian delegate helps the Doctor uncover the true miscreants.

The Monster of Peladon (1974) 6 episodes
w. Brian Hayles d. Lennie Mayne

A breakaway group of Martians are plotting with Federation enemies to start a war. The Doctor uncovers the plot and helps to foil the Martians' plans.

Bernard Bresslaw has the finishing touches made to his Warrior make-up. *The Ice Warriors.*

The costumes were again designed by Martin Baugh. 'If you say "Warrior", that's armour, and if you say "Ice", that's cold and hard,' he explained. 'It was those ideas together that gave me the concept for the creatures. They were a bit like a crocodile, really, and the design was of a crocodile with a shell. You think of these people fighting their way through ice, so they've got to be uncrushable, and this leads you to think of crustaceans like lobsters or turtles. The armour wasn't meant to be something they put on in the morning: it was intended as an integral part of them, like a turtle's shell. The helmet was based on a Viking helmet, again carrying through the idea of the warrior.

'They were built by Jack Lovell, and he and I used to have lengthy discussions about using fibreglass and what we could achieve for the costumes.

'I remember that the crew bolted me into one of the costumes just before a dinner break – it was the first time that we'd ever issued the dressers with spanners, because the costumes were held together with nuts and bolts. The costumes stank as well. The rush was always so great that I think the costumes arrived from Jack on Friday and we used them on Saturday, and the fibreglass was pretty pungent.

'Wearing the costume was terrible and, unlike the actors who had to wear them, I wasn't being paid to wear it – and it was five minutes before lunch!'

The director, Derek Martinus, remembers that they had many problems with the costumes.

'They were made of fibreglass and were very smelly inside. Fibreglass cures as it sets and gives off gases, and, especially at the start of recording, the actors tended to get a bit cured as well.

'To cast the Warriors I first looked through *Spotlight* to see who was over six foot four and I came across Bernard Bresslaw, so I thought why not. I talked to his agent, who told me that he wouldn't dream of doing it, so I had lunch with him and he said he'd do it, but that there might be a problem as he wore glasses. It was very tough work for Bernard as he couldn't see properly and had to be navigated around the set.'

'I was at the Edinburgh festival when I was asked to play the Ice Warrior, and that was in 1967,' recalled Bresslaw when speaking about the role in 1980. After discussions with Martinus, Bresslaw, who had made his name in the TV series *The Army Game* – working alongside William Hartnell – and who had also appeared in a couple of Peter Rogers' *Carry On* films – agreed to play the part of Varga.

'Then the BBC ...wardrobe got in touch with me and said, "About your wardrobe ..." So I thought I'd go into Bermans or wherever you normally go to get your costumes ... but no. It was something like the London metalwork company! Something very strange, a firm that normally made yachts. So I went down there and was measured up very carefully – normally when you go for a costume fitting it's a tape measure to the chest and waist and that's it, but here they used callipers and took very detailed head measurements ... I just didn't know what was in store for me!

'I wasn't prepared for the incredible lizard-like structure which was mostly fibreglass, rubber and plastic that

Bernard Bresslaw is fitted with the Warrior helmet during a make-up session for his role as Varga. *The Ice Warriors.*

was meant for me. Of course, it meant that you couldn't see me at all, which was a shattering blow initially to my morale and ego.'

The Ice Warriors stood about seven foot tall and were encased in a green, scaly carapace. Their heads were covered in a helmet which featured perspex panels covering the eyes and a lower opening through which the mouth could be seen. Their arms ended in clamp-like hands which also contained an inbuilt sonic weapon. Matted fur could be seen at the joints of the creatures' arms and legs.

'It was very uncomfortable in costume,' said Bresslaw. 'The problem was the joints – there was very little mobility or flexibility. Fibreglass is pretty rigid, so the joints had to be rubber. The visor was plastic, transparent plastic. It was difficult to move and it was enormously hot inside.

'They made up my eyes for some reason – I mean, you couldn't see my eyes through the visor. My mouth was painted green, with latex, which hardens to a rubbery consistency to give the reptile like skin effect. It took ages to get into costume.

'I had enormous fun doing it, but the thing about playing in something like *Doctor Who* and being asked to play the first Ice Warrior is that it really gives an actor a very free reign to create not merely a part but an alien being. That's a marvellous challenge. It takes a lot of thought and brings the best out of you, really. You can't rely on your face and you can't rely on your body, in effect, because you're encased in this costume – and that in itself makes a statement. Once seen, an Ice Warrior makes an impression on the viewer, and so you've got to find something to go with that, and that really is a challenge.

'There was a problem in how to play, vocally, the Ice Warrior. There, the costume was a help. I saw it in reptilian terms, obviously, and so thought of lizards and the hissing sounds that snakes make, and that gave it to me. I worked very hard, taping the voice and playing it back to myself to get the right effect, and the director was very pleased. It was essentially my own interpretation. That was why it was such an exciting thing to do: it was entirely me – no electronic gadgetry in the reproduction of our voices.'

In fact, because of the problems with speaking in the costumes and make-up, all the Warrior voices were pre-recorded by Bresslaw and one of the other actors to play a Warrior, Roger Jones, and then played back during the recording to allow the actors to open their mouths and move their lips accordingly.

Following the filming at Ealing for *The Ice Warriors*, several changes to the Warrior costumes – and some others – were requested by Martinus. In a memo dated 3 October 1967, he said:

On the whole the costumes are highly original and most successful. Many thanks. However there are a few things that must be done before we go into the studio.

1. Please see that full movement is possible in all 'human' costumes.

2. The Warriors. Costumes must be tailored to allow much more freedom of movement.

3. The head must be capable of moving fully from left through

ICE WARRIORS

CHARACTER

Mars was a cold and dying planet and so its intelligent inhabitants decided to send a scout party to Earth in order to assess that planet's ability to sustain life. Unfortunately the scout ship crashed and was buried, and all aboard were feared dead. In fact they had been buried in ice, which preserved their bodies until they were revived during Earth's third Ice Age around the year 3000.

The expedition leader, Varga, intended to carry out his mission and to conquer the Earth for the Martian race. However, his ship's power was very low after so long in the ice and, ultimately, he, his crew and his ship were destroyed by the humans' use of a ioniser – a heat-ray being used to hold back the glaciers from engulfing the Earth. It was on Earth that the Martians were given their nickname 'Ice Warriors'. This was first coined by Walters, one of the scientists who discovered Varga's body, and later by the Doctor's companion Jamie. In fact, the creatures are simply Martians and refer to themselves as 'Warriors'.

It was evident, however, that Mars had once been home to a thriving race of Martians. They had augmented the bodies of their warriors with electronic eyes and 'ears' and each was equipped with a fearsome sonic weapon built into its hand. Their science was based on the mineral trisilicate, which, until its discovery on the planet Peladon, was known to exist only on Mars, and their knowledge of sonic technology was second to none. ➡

Alan Bennion (Slaar) prepares for recording in the lunar control room of T-Mat. *The Seeds of Death.*

37

180° to the right. The actor must also be able to look down to his feet. The helmet appeared to be very top heavy. Anything that can be done to make it far lighter and better balanced would be worthwhile.

4. Bodily movement must be improved to allow the actor to crouch and to give free movement of the arms. The actors complained of great discomfort under the crotch. Can anything be done about this?

We have to remember that Varga is a long part, involving much more than is usual with a 'Who' monster. He has only his voice and movement to make his impact. If only a limited amount of alteration is possible, Varga must come first. He must have freedom and comfort.

Left: A costumed Warrior waits with a member of the production team by the entrance to the Weather Control Station on Earth. Right: A Warrior strides through the Martian foam. *The Seeds of Death*.

At the same time as sending this memo, Martinus also contacted Bernard Wilkie of the BBC's Visual Effects Department. In this note he requested that, 'Ice Warrior sound sensor to be built into hand of Warrior.' And, 'Check to get "eyes" and "ears" of Warriors in working condition.'

Although there was an initial plan for the Warriors' eye panels to glow, this idea was ultimately dropped as the costumes were very hot to wear, and the addition of a light behind each eye would have increased the temperature and discomfort of the actors significantly.

To enable the Warriors to be able to look at their feet – possibly initiated by their need to look at and operate the controls in their space craft – Baugh designed a flexible neck piece made from rubber and latex. The end result of all these changes between the material filmed at Ealing and the studio recording was that Varga's costume is visibly different on screen depending on where the footage originated.

The 'sound sensor' built into the hand of the Warriors by Visual Effects was intended to be a devastating sonic weapon. The effect of its being fired was achieved by reflecting the intended victim in a large sheet of mirrored plastic called mirrorlon, which was mounted on a wooden frame. When the centre of the reflection was pressed from behind at the moment of attack, the image distorted. This impressive yet simple visual effect was retained throughout all the stories in which the Ice Warriors appeared.

Hayles believed that the Ice Warriors were successful because they were unusual. 'I think it was because, out of all the monsters, they were slightly more emotional. They could have emotion, they could latch on to people, although they were essentially Martian. They could, in fact, relate to people, and therefore, when you have a creature like that, whether it's good or bad, in terms of good and evil, you can find some point of identification with them.'

Following their initial appearance, Hayles was asked to engineer their return in a further story. He was asked on 22 July 1968 to submit an idea and came up with an outline called *The Lords of the Red Planet* in which the Martians invade the Earth using the moon as a base. This outline was progressed to a full scene breakdown, dated 5 August 1968, but, after completing rewrites to the scripts for the first two episodes, agreement was reached with Hayles that assistant script editor Terrance Dicks would carry out major revisions and rewrites on the final four episodes of the story.

The Warrior costumes used in this story, which was retitled *The Seeds of Death* for production, were the same as those for *The Ice Warriors*. In fact, the original costumes would be used in all the stories in which they appeared. There were, however, some additional pieces of information about Martian culture revealed. Leading the attack on the moon was a creature named Slaar (in the original outline there had also been a second creature called Visek). Slaar looked significantly different from the Warriors in that he was of a slighter build and wore no scaly body armour. His helmet was also sleeker. The 'traditional' Warriors in *The Seeds of Death* were reduced, for the best part, to being silent guards, speaking only when they had to. Their voices were again pre-recorded, this time by Steve Peters, and played in during recording of the episodes.

In *The Seeds of Death*, Slaar was played by Alan Bennion, who went on to play this variant of the Warriors – which was eventually termed an Ice Lord – in a further two stories.

'They started off with a latex suit,' he explained when asked about the costume in 1993. 'Then there was

They had developed spacecraft and travelled in fleets to try to occupy the Earth in the 21st century after Slaar the warlord had prepared the way by invading the moon and sending Martian seed pods to Earth so that they might absorb the oxygen from the atmosphere and convert Earth into a planet more like Mars for the Martians to inhabit. This attempt failed and the Martian fleet was lured into the Sun, where it perished.

At some point in their history, the Martians made their peace with the rest of the galaxy and became members of the Galactic Federation. Their ambassadors to the Federation sought to improve the lot of all life forms, and the Martians' noble and dignified bearing and upbringing made them ideal and honourable members. Nowhere was this honour more evident than when the delegate Izlyr, present on Peladon with his lieutenant Ssorg, helped the Doctor for no other reason than the fact that the Doctor had saved his life. This put Lord Izlyr in debt to the Doctor, a debt he intended to repay.

Although the Warriors had been accepted into the Federation, there were still factions within the race who were at odds with the Federation's aims. A small group of Martians led by Lord Azaxyr determined to supply the Federation's enemies in Galaxy 5 with trisilicate mined on Peladon. The Doctor managed to prevent this plot from reaching fruition and, as a result, Galaxy 5 surrendered–as they realised they could not win without the mineral supplies.

As well as the lumbering, carapace-protected Warriors, who are intelligent and cunning and have been placed in charge of missions to other planets (like Varga), there are also Lords who seem to be in a higher ruling caste within Martian civilisation. These creatures are less well protected than the Warriors and, although they enjoy augmented sight and hearing, they do not all have sonic weapons built into their hands. Above the Lords seems to be the Grand Marshal, although only one of this level has been seen, in overall command of the fleet intending to invade Earth in the 21st century.

Frank Gatliff (Ortron), Sonny Caldinez (Skel) and Stuart Fell (Alpha Centauri) during studio rehearsals for *The Monster of Peladon*.

the helmet, which came down to end-of-nose-level. The bottom half of my face was still visible but they then started sticking little pebbles of stuff around my mouth. I remember I was most upset, because I'd just had my teeth capped, very expensively, and I was there in make-up looking in the mirror thinking "Oh, the teeth look good don't they?" and then Michael Ferguson [the director] came in and said, "I think we'll have the teeth blacked out as well!" So I disappeared completely.

'They put transparent orange gel in the eye holes and then, for some reason, they put in a very fine mesh, a sort of wire netting, as well. Then they discovered that the gel was glaring into the cameras, so they came round with some anti-glare spray, which meant I could hardly see a thing!

'Because hearing was so difficult I couldn't hear a cue. If I had the first line in a scene, the floor manager would normally give me a hand signal to start. However, I couldn't see anything, so he had to give me a karate chop on the back of the legs.'

Top: The Martian Lord Azaxyr (Alan Bennion). Bottom: Studio rehearsals for *The Monster of Peladon*. Donald Gee (Eckersley), Stuart Fell (Alpha Centauri), Alan Bennion (Azaxyr), Sonny Caldinez and Frank Gatliff (Ortron). Note that Sonny Caldinez is not wearing his full Warrior costume for Sskel.

As well as Slaar, *The Seeds of Death* featured another Warrior variant called the Grand Marshal, although only his head was seen. He was similar in appearance to Slaar but with added glittery embellishments on his helmet. The Grand Marshal, played by Graham Leaman, spoke normally, without hissing – the rationale for this being that the air on the Marshal's ship was suitable for the Martians, whereas the air in the lunar base was not. This is a good example of the production team taking care over small details, all of which combine to give a greater sense of realism to the characters.

Following *The Seeds of Death*, Hayles continued to submit ideas and storylines to the production office and eventually Dicks picked up on several elements contained within two ultimately unused storylines, *The Brain-Dead* and *Shape of Terror*, and suggested that Hayles work on an outline which would enable the production team to make a totally studio-bound story in order to try to offset a number of stories with extensive and costly location shoots. The story that Hayles came up with was rumoured to have been initially called *The Curse*, but the scripts were eventually commissioned on 14 May 1971 with the title *The Curse of Peladon*. These were based on an undated and un-named storyline apparently written by the production team which set out the basic premise of the story and summarised the plot.

The Curse of Peladon featured a novel twist on the idea of the Doctor's enemies always being foes, and presented the Ice Warriors as allies for the Doctor rather than the bad guys. 'Having done them twice as the dirty villains,' explained Hayles, 'I wanted to play a trick, perhaps turn the whole thing upside down. Very often when you find monsters like them or the Daleks or the Cybermen, you know they're going to be villainous. So we started off the series, and as soon as they appeared everybody would say: "Ah ha. They're into something dirty." And, of course, we turned them round and they actually became, in a sense, the co-heroes of the plot with a certain nobility of purpose. But if you followed their psychology, they were still basically the same people. It simply happened that, for once, their motivation was similar to the Doctor's.'

For *The Curse of Peladon*, Izlyr's costume was the same as Slaar's, but with a helmet of a slightly different shape and the addition of a belt and a cape. 'I asked for that cape,' said Bennion, 'because I felt that my original costume didn't make my figure look its best. It gave me more bulk and a bit of "top". Without the cape, I felt I looked a little bit like a kind of pregnant lizard.'

Playing the Warrior Ssorg was Sonny Caldinez, who had played Warriors in both *The Ice Warriors* and *The Seeds of Death*. 'They wanted some very big people to play Ice Warriors because they had to dominate all the scenes in which they appeared,' he explained. 'I was chosen for my size. We had these cumbersome costumes to wear. Very uncomfortable but very pleasing because you frightened everyone you met!

'It's very difficult working inside a costume. The Ice Warrior's costume was very uncomfortable to wear. You

Original outline for a four-part story prepared by Terrance Dicks and Barry Letts. This outline was given to writer Brian Hayles and was developed into the story The Curse of Peladon.

FOUR-PART DOCTOR WHO SERIAL

<u>Setting</u>. An alien planet on the remote fringes of the Galaxy. Inhabited by a race of fierce warrior-like humanoids, ruled by a king and a Priest caste. Their civilisation is at approximately the mediaeval stage of development – codes of honour, trial by combat etc. They worship some kind of sacred Beast, a giant ghostly version of which appears at times of crisis. The story will take place entirely in the Citadel, a mountaintop castle/temple. This is a taboo area to which only nobility are admitted, on pain of death. (There will be no location filming).

<u>Background</u>. The King, a newly acceded modern and enlightened figure wants his planet to join the Galactic Federation, a kind of U.N. of all intelligent races. The High Priest secretly fears that this will mean decadence and decay for his people.

A group of delegates from the Galactic Federation are to attend the formal coronation of the King. They will make use of the occasion to decide upon the King's application for Federation membership.

<u>The Delegates</u>
One Ice Warrior – Mars has ostensibly given up its aggressive colonisation policy, solved it's climate problems and joined the federation. <u>Two other non-humans</u> from other member planets. <u>The Earth Delegate</u> – not yet arrived when the story opens.

<u>Story Development</u>. A teaser in which someone – delegate or temple guard is killed – or maybe only terrified by an apparition of the sacred Beast, which then vanishes.
The Tardis materialises in the middle of the subsequent confusion. Jo and the Doctor emerge, hide and are eventually caught. Their skins are saved by the fact that the Doctor is taken for the Earth Delegate, a masquerade which he is forced to continue. (Perhaps he justifies Jo as an Earth Princess, and has to treat her with reverence in public.)

Once established in this role the Doctor finds that someone is making determined attempts to kill him. Attempts are also made to kill other delegates, and generally to stir up trouble between the delegates (internally) and between the natives of the planet. There are various apparitions of the sacred Beast, scaring the wits out of everyone, and killing the odd extra (but not too many deaths). ➡

were bolted in. You couldn't go to the toilet, you couldn't sit down, you couldn't lie down and you stood in one place for a long while and just sweated.

'In one story my character was killed and I had to fall over. I had about four foot of fibreglass in front of my stomach and I was a bit dubious about falling on the floor. When I did it, I nearly decapitated myself down below because that's where the bolts holding the costume together were. It wasn't funny at the time, but that was one of the hazards of the job.'

The Ice Lord Azaxyr (Alan Bennion). *The Monster of Peladon.*

Alan Bennion remembers that Caldinez's costume started to get tight as, over the years, the actor put on weight between appearances. Men were always running up with spanners to loosen it. I remember he had to fall over an awful lot and he couldn't get up again, so the same little men had to come and put him on his feet again.'

Despite the discomfort, Caldinez remains proud of his association with *Doctor Who*. 'I'll never get fed up of being a monster, because, deep down inside, I want to frighten people all the time! I like to see shock on people's faces.'

The fourth, and final, appearance of the Ice Warriors came at the end of the Jon Pertwee era, in a 1974 story that was devised as a sequel to *The Curse of Peladon.*

In *The Monster of Peladon* an Ice Lord called Azaxyr, again played by Alan Bennion, was in charge of an invasion force of Warriors, and Caldinez was on hand as the leading Warrior, Sskel.

'We were quite a team by then,' said Bennion. 'I think it was probably the fact that they knew we more or less fitted the costumes. I think it got to the point where we'd done the job before and they liked our work, so we were automatically contacted.'

Once more, the original costumes for the Warriors were reused and Azaxyr's outfit was the same as used for Izlyr in *The Curse of Peladon.*

The costume designer for *The Monster of Peladon* was Barbara Kidd. 'The Ice Warrior costumes were just lethal,' she said, 'They were fibreglass shells that were bolted together so that once the guys were inside them they couldn't get out, there was no release mechanism. They also couldn't sit down easily and unfortunately the actors had to wait around for hours before they got to their scenes. When they did sit down, their heads would disappear into their bodies like a turtle.'

After *The Monster of Peladon*, the Warriors did not appear in *Doctor Who* again. A part of one of the original Warrior costumes was glimpsed in the 1975 story *Genesis of the Daleks* as a mutant creature, and there were plans to include the Warriors in a story intended for the 23rd season, written by Philip Martin with the working title *Mission to Magnus*, before the original stories in that season were scrapped during a hiatus in the production of Doctor Who during 1985. They were due also to have appeared in a story in season 27, but this too came to nothing as production of the series was discontinued at the end of season 26.

Despite the fact that the creatures appeared in only four stories, their impact was such that they are still fondly remembered by all who saw them in action. The combination of their impressive build and hissing voices made them all the more appealing to the viewers who liked their monsters to be truly monstrous. The fact that they were also eloquent and could construct and operate complex machinery added to their charm.

Wendy Padbury (Zoe) and Sonny Caldinez in an uncharacteristic pose during the recording of *The Seeds of Death.*

Bernard Bresslaw outside television centre during a press call for *The Ice Warriors.*

CHAPTER 5

THE SEVENTIES

I was encased in green latex. It wasn't so bad out on location, but in the studio, you did sweat. I used to take the headpiece off at the end of the day and literally pour out a pint of sweat.

PETER BIRREL ON PLAYING A DRACONIAN

By the end of 1969, *Doctor Who* was in many ways not the programme it had been at the end of 1964. The stories with historical settings had been phased out and, with the change from William Hartnell playing the Doctor to Patrick Troughton, the show had seen a slight shift in emphasis from its educational roots to a far more entertainment-based programme. Science fiction was the preferred story type, which meant that the Doctor had to visit a new alien planet every few weeks, or discover some threat lurking on Earth. These threats had to be seen, of course, and this meant more and more monsters, aliens and other villains.

This reliance on alien planets and space/time travel was to change, however, because at the close of the sixth season in mid-1969, in plot terms the Doctor was captured by his own people, the Time Lords, and sentenced to exile on Earth in the 20th century. The secrets of the TARDIS were also taken from him so that he could no longer roam the galaxy.

The reasons for this decision on the part of the production team were mainly down to the budget. Monsters cost money and the show was becoming increasingly expensive to make. The decision to bring the Doctor down to Earth was intended to allow more to be made of the budget. Therefore, when *Doctor Who* returned

THE NESTENES AND THE AUTONS

Spearhead From Space (1970) 4 episodes
w. Robert Holmes d. Derek Martinus

The Doctor arrives on Earth at the same time as a shower of plastic meteorites containing the Nestene Consciousness. Before long, a plastics factory is producing deadly shop mannequins.

Terror of the Autons (1971) 4 episodes
w. Robert Holmes d. Barry Letts

The Master arrives on Earth and summons the Nestene Consciousness. Commandeering a plastics factory, the Master plans to take over the world.

after a six-month break, not only would the show feature another new actor as the Doctor – as Patrick Troughton had decided to leave the part, handing over to Jon Pertwee – but it would also be structured to minimise the overall expense. This meant fewer monsters, fewer stories (to keep the cost of new sets to a minimum) and, with the Doctor exiled to Earth, more filming on location (which would not need the additional effort of being made to look like alien planets).

A deadly Auton disguised as a shop dummy. *Spearhead from Space.*

The threats faced by the Doctor were also to change. With the errant Time Lord stranded on Earth, any menace he faced either had to have originated from Earth, or to have arrived there from somewhere else. There would still be monsters, but their origins and motivations would change.

Despite these apparent limitations, there was no shortage of monsters and creatures during the first years of the seventies. Writers thrive on a challenge, and writing for *Doctor Who* posed challenges that could not be found elsewhere.

One of the things that *Doctor Who* is always remembered for is its effect on young children. People still recall with fondness watching the show from 'behind the sofa' or, when it became too frightening, from the safety of a parent's lap. Nowhere was this 'sofa' effect more evident than in *Spearhead from Space*, the first story of the seventh season, which introduced viewers not only to a new incarnation of the Doctor, but also to an alien foe which, as it had no body of its own, had to use something else. The Nestene Consciousness, as it was called, could actually inhabit and animate anything made of plastic. The scene that everyone remembers from this story came when the tranquillity of a shopping street was shattered as plastic window dummies came alive and, smashing their way out of the shops, proceeded to kill anyone in their path.

'Terrance Dicks asked me to write the opener for that season introducing Jon Pertwee,' explained the story's writer, Robert Holmes, in 1981. 'It had therefore to be an Earth story. That almost certainly meant an alien invasion story. I wanted aliens that could pass as humans (they act better) and so came up with the idea of a species that could animate plastic.'

The plastic figures inhabited by the Nestene Consciousness were called Autons and the figure of an Auton was described in the script for episode one as follows:

A SMOOTH, SOMEHOW FACELESS FIGURE RAISING AN ARM UP TO STRIKE

Because the plastic facsimiles – *Facsimile* had, in fact, been a working title for the story – were essentially humanoid in appearance, costume designer Christine Rawlins didn't have many concerns about their appearance. Although the action was set on Earth, a time period had not been specified and so Rawlins tried to make all the costumes of indeterminate date. 'With the Autons,' she said, 'they wore boiler suits. The thing about boiler suits is that they are simple, straightforward – dateless – and come in sizes to fit everyone.'

To complete the look of the Autons, blank plastic masks were created by the Visual Effects Department, and scarves were added by Rawlins to hide the join between the mask and the boiler suit.

There was one further innovation in the design of the Autons and this was a gun concealed within their hands. Holmes described this in the scripts as follows:

WITH A QUICK TWIST, IT UNHOOKS ITS LEFT HAND. THE WRIST
SOCKET IS AN OPEN ENDED TUBE WHICH IT RAISES AND POINTS

THE NESTENES AND THE AUTONS
CHARACTER

The Nestene Consciousness is an entity from a distant planet. Its natural form is akin to an octopus and it has an affinity for plastic, which allows it to inhabit and animate anything made from that material.

In order to colonise other worlds, fragments of the Consciousness are hurled into space contained within many spherical plastic containers. These containers, or energy units as they are called, fall as meteorites on to the world marked for colonisation. When they arrive, they influence the native life form into creating host bodies for them out of plastic. Once their agents have form, then equipment is created with which to create a body for the collective being of the Consciousness. ➡

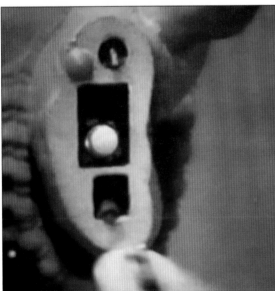

Top: An Auton steals an energy unit from the UNIT troops that were carrying it. *Spearhead from Space.*
Bottom: An Auton gun. *Spearhead from Space.*

This concept was refined and the Autons were eventually equipped with fake plastic hands, the fingers of which were hinged at the bottom allowing them to drop down, revealing a small gun barrel which then emerged from what remained of the hand. With the addition of a small explosive charge to represent the firing of the gun, and suitable sound effects, the illusion of the Autons being equipped with deadly weaponry was achieved.

The Nestenes and Autons appeared in two stories in the seventies, *Spearhead from Space* and a sequel, *Terror of the Autons.*

Originally titled *The Spray of Death*, *Terror of the Autons* saw the Nestenes and the Autons teamed with a character who was to become one of the staple ingredients of *Doctor Who* during the Jon Pertwee era, the Master. Holmes wanted to make more use of the concept of the Nestenes' affinity to plastic and devised a story in which they would invade the planet by arranging for the distribution of many hundreds of plastic daffodils and death-dealing troll dolls which would be activated when it rained.

Ultimately, Holmes' original storyline was changed so that it was only plastic daffodils that were distributed, and they were to have been activated by radio signal rather than by the unpredictable British weather.

New Auton threats were introduced such as a telephone cord which rises and tries to strangle the Doctor and a single Troll Doll programmed to activate when exposed to heat and to strangle whichever human happened to be nearest. The Troll Doll was played by a diminuitive actor called Tommy Reynolds who experienced acute discomfort at being encased in the rubber costume.

Any item made from plastic can become an Auton – a carrier of a fragment of the Consciousness – but if the Consciousness is withdrawn or blocked, then the plastic becomes inert once more. The Consciousness is a single creature and all its component parts are linked together. Therefore if the linkage is disrupted, for example by waves from an ECT machine, then the creature cannot function and the Consciousness is withdrawn.

Earth has seen two attacks so far from the Consciousness. The first was repelled by the Doctor, but on the second occasion, the Nestenes had an ally in the shape of the Master, a renegade Time Lord and the Doctor's arch enemy. With the Master's help, plastic daffodils, each containing a Nestene imprint to kill, were created and distributed across Britain. The Master also created a killer plastic Troll Doll and a black plastic armchair which suffocated its victim.

Despite the assistance of the Master's imaginative and devious intelligence, the Doctor was able once more to prevent the Nestenes from gaining a foothold on Earth by convincing the Master that they would never allow him to rule alongside them. With the Master convinced, the two Time Lords sent the Consciousness back into space.

'We had terrible problems with that,' explained visual effects designer Michealjohn Harris. 'I put it out to be made by an outside contractor, and it was made out of foam plastic stuck edge to edge. You cut it rather like a dress pattern and stick it together edge to edge and then surface it with a sort of latex surface to give it texture and quality. The contractor who made it was really unreliable, terribly drunk, and she didn't turn up with it. We were all ready in the studio about six o'clock in the evening and it was supposed to be there the night before. We had awful problems: the seams kept coming apart and the stink of the adhesive and the rubber was asphixiating the poor lad inside …'

'Tommy had to wear a rubber suit,' remembered Jon Pertwee, 'and sit on a large model radiator. However, inside the suit he got hotter and hotter and in the end he collapsed in the studio as the heat from the studio lights was unbearable.'

The Autons were also included by writer Terrance Dicks in the original draft scripts for *The Five Doctors* in 1983.

The scenes in question came during a sequence in which the Doctor's companion, Sarah Jane Smith, finds herself lost in a deserted town street after having been plucked from Earth by a Time Scoop.

The scene in the draft script for *The Five Doctors* read as follows:

Channing (Hugh Burden). *Spearhead from Space.*

The Auton Troll Doll (Tommy Reynolds). *Terror of the Autons.*

TELECINE 9:

Ext. Ruined High Street.
Day

Frightened and confused, SARAH is stumbling along a street – a strange surrealist street of half-wrecked buildings. She sees that one of them is a ruined shop.

Mannequins are scattered about, looking eerily like corpses.

SARAH stumbles against one, and for a moment thinks it is a dead body. She kneels to examine it and smiles in relief.

Suddenly it sits bolt upright, reaching for her throat . . .

SARAH screams and jumps back. She turns and runs – straight into another MANNEQUIN, reaching out for her.

She dodges round it – but now the other MANNEQUINS – all Autons – have come to life and are encircling her. They stalk menacingly towards her.

Suddenly the PERTWEE DOCTOR zooms along the street in Bessie, and stops.

PERTWEE DOCTOR: Quick, Sarah Jane. Get in!

SARAH jumps in and the PERTWEE DOCTOR roars off.

The AUTONS stretch out their arms. Their hands drop back on hinges to reveal guns.

They open fire, but by now the car is zig-zagging down the street, energy-bolts exploding all around it.

The car reaches the far end of the ruined street and finds its way barred by a road block.

The PERTWEE DOCTOR and Sarah leap out and start moving the broken planks and rubble which make up the barrier.

AUTONS move in and attack them.

SARAH and the PERTWEE DOCTOR fight them off using bits of barricade as weapons.

They return to clearing the road block.

PERTWEE DOCTOR: Quickly, Sarah.

More AUTONS lurch closer reaching out . . .

Working desperately they manage to clear the barricade and are getting back in the car when:

An AUTON trains its wrist-gun at the PERTWEE DOCTOR'S HEAD at point-blank range . . .

Suddenly the AUTON reels and falls. ONE by ONE the other AUTONS stiffen and fall.

The PERTWEE DOCTOR gets out of the car and examines them.

PERTWEE DOCTOR: Extraordinary.

SARAH: They're just dummies.

PERTWEE DOCTOR: They are now. Before they were Autons, plastic replicas of humanity, animated by the Nestene Consciousness. It seems to have been – withdrawn . . .

SARAH: Let's get away from here.

PERTWEE DOCTOR: Agreed.

A Silurian. *Doctor Who and the Silurians.*

This sequence was dropped simply because there was not the time to do it. In the transmitted episode, Sarah simply stumbled over a cliff. 'A lot simpler,' explained Dicks.

The Nestenes were simply the first of many alien races that found Earth a good place to visit during the period of the Doctor's exile here. As previously mentioned, the challenge facing the writers was to come up with numerous original and plausible reasons as to why this should be so.

'Basically in science fiction, there are only two stories: we go to them, or they come to us,' explained writer Malcolm Hulke in 1979. 'Everything else is a variation on those two themes. I decided to write a "they come to us" story, and then thought of a way to give it a twist. The twist was that they were already here – and had always been here, even before humankind existed. So, going back into history that far, I thought of reptile people, since reptiles were the main class of animal around at that time.'

Two of the three members of the Silurian Triad. *Warriors of the Deep*.

The story that Hulke devised was initially called *The Monsters* but was retitled *Doctor Who and the Silurians* for production (this is, incidentally, the only time that the words '*Doctor Who and the*' actually form a part of the on-screen story title).

The reptile creatures were called Silurians after their supposed period of origin and in Hulke's scripts were very sketchily described as follows:

THIS IS AN INTELLIGENT MAN-LIKE CREATURE . . .

ALL WE SEE OF THE CREATURE IS A DISTANT FIGURE WHICH MIGHT WELL BE HUMAN.

Later on, the creature's hand was described as:

A SCALY ALMOST HUMAN HAND

The costume designer given the job of realising the creatures was Christine Rawlins. 'I remember the Silurians quite well,' she said. 'The costumes were very uncomfortable to wear, and got very sweaty inside.

'Jim Ward of Visual Effects designed the heads and put the lights in, and I was responsible for the bodies. They were actually sent outside the BBC to be made. We were looking at dinosaurs and prehistoric animals, and so the scaly suit evolved.'

The reason for the Silurian heads needing lights inside was that the creatures had a third eye, positioned on their foreheads, which they used to operate machinery and to defend themselves. When in use, this third eye glowed red. The eye was powered from a small battery, which was operated by a switch that the actor worked with his foot.

'The costumes were made from sheets of moulded rubber,' continued Rawlins. 'Ghastly to wear, and, as far as I remember, they weren't tailored to the individual actors. We just made some standard sizes and they had to fit: that was the only thing we could do so far in advance.

'I remember Jon Pertwee being very anxious about the join between the head and the body, which he thought was too obvious. It wasn't absolutely ideal, but we had to be able to lift the actors out very quickly if anything went wrong, because they could hardly breathe in there. I think it looked better when we got them into the more controlled situation of the studio, after the location work, because it could be covered up more easily there.'

The Silurians were considered to be a reasonable success and Hulke was asked by producer Barry Letts if he wanted to bring them back. Rather than just cash in on the creatures, however, Letts told Hulke that they had to come from under the sea. The reason for this, according to Hulke, was that the Navy had told the BBC that they would be happy to assist with a *Doctor Who* show

THE SILURIANS AND SEA DEVILS

Doctor Who and the Silurians (1970)
7 episodes
w. Malcolm Hulke d. Timothy Combe

A group of Silurians are roused from hibernation in caves under a moor in Derbyshire. They decide to reclaim the Earth for themselves.

The Sea Devils (1972) 6 episodes
w. Malcolm Hulke d. Michael Briant

The Master makes contact with a nest of underwater reptiles and plans to use them to aid in his plans of conquest.

Warriors of the Deep (1984) 4 episodes
w. Johnny Byrne d. Pennant Roberts

The members of a Silurian triad revive a squad of Sea Devil Warriors and together they attack and invade an underwater Sea Base in an attempt to trigger a global war between the humans.

and that Hulke was chosen to write it because in the distant past, he had been in the Navy.

Hulke's story outline was called *The Sea Silurians* and was retitled *The Sea Devils* when the scripts were commissioned on 29 March 1971.

By the time *The Sea Devils* came to be recorded, the name of the creatures had changed from Silurians because the production team had realised that the Silurian era could not have been their point of origin. To try to get around this, a line was included in *The Sea Devils*, in which the Doctor explained that their true name should be Eocenes, as the Eocene era was a far more likely period for them to have originated from.

The costumes for the creatures were markedly different from those of the Silurians. The main difference was in the head. The Sea Devil's head was actually perched on top of the actor's own head, and he looked out of the creature's neck. The heads were created by visual effects assistant John Friedlander, and in 1981 he was asked about their construction. 'They were worn as hats,' he recalled. 'They wanted the characters to be much taller and so the actual Sea Devil head was worn as a hat on top of the actor's

A Sea Devil, underwater cousin to the Silurians. *The Sea Devils.*

head and they looked out through the necks. I modelled the heads up normally in clay, built up the fin part and I joined them using a kind of netted fabric I'd found for the webbing.'

The body of the costume was constructed from latex and rubber and, whereas the Silurians had been nude – they wore no clothing – the Sea Devils covered their modesty with simple smock-like outfits made from blue netting. The creatures' heads were based on that of a turtle and large gills were added to the sides of the head to reflect the fact that they were amphibious.

At one point in the story, the Sea Devils had to emerge from the sea. Jon Pertwee recalled what happened. 'The director had briefed them all beforehand: "Now, I want you to wade into the surf, about twenty yards back, and on my signal, duck down under the water. After three seconds, start coming back up out of the sea and walk towards us."

'Well all went fine until the men in the costumes tried to duck down under the water. I should perhaps explain that the actual Sea Devil's heads that sat on top of the actor's head were naturally full of air and try as they might, the actors could not get under the water without the monster heads popping up off their own heads to the surface. In the end, they submerged the heads first to try and get some water into them, and this worked to an extent, except that when the actors finally came to emerge from the water and stumble back to the beach, water was pouring from the heads all but drowning the actors beneath. Had the director wanted to use the original soundtrack, rather than overdubbing it with music, eight million people would have heard a stream of foul and abusive epithets that would've shamed a three badge stoker.'

With the involvement of the Navy giving *The Sea Devils* a very documentary feel, the show was considered to have been a great success. This could have been the end of the story, but in the eighties, when producer John Nathan-Turner was looking for past monsters to make a comeback to the show following the successful reintroduction of the Cybermen, he decided that it was time that the Silurians and Sea Devils returned.

Writer Johnny Byrne was commissioned to write the scripts for the story, called *Warriors of the Deep*, on 10 September 1982. As

Top: The Sea Devils emerge from the sea. *The Sea Devils.*
Bottom: The Sea Devil Warrior Leader Sauvix (Christopher Farries). *Warriors of the Deep.*

over ten years had passed between this and the original stories, none of the original costumes were available. In addition, Nathan-Turner was keen on updating the look of the Doctor's returning foes. Therefore both the Silurians' and the Sea Devils' costumes were changed.

Top: Alpha Centauri [Stuart Fell; voice: Ysanne Churchman]. *The Curse of Peladon*.
Bottom: The Ice Lord Izlyr [Alan Bennion] confers with Alpha Centauri. *The Curse of Peladon*.

In the final camera scripts for *Warriors of the Deep* neither the Silurians nor the Sea Devils were described and the look was down to costume designer Judy Pepperdine and visual effects designer Mat Irvine. The new Silurians were still reptilian, but now had a hard shell-like carapace covering their torsos. The third eye was still present, but now simply flashed in synchronisation with the creature's speech. Their faces and voices were also completely different from the original Silurians.

The Sea Devils, however, underwent an even more drastic change. Rather than the blue string vests, the Sea Devil Warriors seen in *Warriors of the Deep* wore samurai-style armour. They also for the most part wore helmets which covered the bulk of their heads so that only the front of the face and neck was visible. Despite these changes, the heads and voices of the creatures were very similar to their seventies counterparts.

Playing the Sea Devil Warrior Leader, Sauvix, was Christopher Farries: 'The costume was made from rubber and the head I wore above my own head was mechanical. As I was playing the Leader, I was the only one to have a mechanical head. The eyes opened and closed operated by remote control. I looked out of some small holes in the neck of the monster. It was very hard work acting in that costume.

'*Warriors of the Deep* was made over the summer of 1983, which was a very hot summer. I remember particularly the scene where the Sea Devils woke up from hibernation. We were kneeling in a tank as dry ice swirled around our lower halves. We were freezing from the waist downwards and up above it was so hot that it was unbelievable because we had the studio arc lamps shining down on us. I remember the sweat falling down my back. I lost exactly one stone during the making of that *Doctor Who*.'

Although the Doctor faced a great many alien menaces during the seventies, only a few were considered successful enough to warrant a return appearance. Some of these have been discussed above. Another creature – alien not menace – which made two appearances was once described by the Doctor as 'a hermaphrodite hexapod' and was named Alpha Centauri.

This bizarre-looking being first appeared in a story by Brian Hayles called *The Curse of Peladon*. The story outline prepared by the production office for Brian Hayles to work from did not specify, aside from the Ice Warriors, the alien races that would be seen. Hayles therefore created two new alien characters to fulfil the roles described in the outline as 'non-human' delegates: the machine-like Arcturus and the effete Alpha Centauri. Hayles' camera scripts did not contain any description of Centauri and so the designers had a free reign to create whatever they wanted.

The costume created by designer Barbara Lane for Centauri consisted of a large tube-shaped body to which were attached three pairs of flexible arms, each terminating in a handlike 'beak'. On the top of the body rested the head, which consisted of a large egg-shaped dome in the front of which was mounted a single massive eye. The head could swivel from side to side and the eye was equipped with an eyelid which could be made to blink by the operator.

It has been recounted by those involved in the production how the costume did not originally have a cloak covering its back and when the creature was unveiled in the rehearsal rooms for the first time, it looked too much like a giant-sized item of the male anatomy for comfort. The addition of a cloak helped to break up the lines of the shape and this unfortunate similarity was, for the most part, removed.

Inside the costume was stuntman Stuart Fell. 'They cast me as a stunt performer to play inside this costume, not because I had to do a lot of stunts, but because it was very uncomfortable and they wouldn't have expected an actor to put up with that sort of thing.

'This character was in every other scene for four episodes,' recalled Fell. 'He was one of the major characters and had a lot of lines, which meant that he was in a lot of scenes. This was in the days when the BBC didn't have the facilities for editing so in the studio they would have all the different sets laid out and when one scene finished, you'd have to move over to a different set for another scene very quickly. This meant that there was no opportunity to get the head off and to have a breather. So once they'd put me in the costume, I was stuck there for two and a half hours.

'In rehearsals, I remember that the head arrived and had only just been made. It was fibreglass and the fumes from it were very potent. Under the studio lights it became very stuffy inside the costume and, in fact, it was probably very unhealthy.

'There were a lot of complicated mechanisms and movements needed in order to make the creature appear convincing. He had six arms and they all had to move. In some scenes I'd use the arm at the top right and in another scene I'd use the one middle left. I also had to keep the character moving because otherwise it would have ended up looking like a salt cellar standing there. They'd built this one huge eye into the head and during the dialogue it was important that the eyelid flicked across from time to time. The head could also move from side to side and my job, really, was to convince people that it was this creature that was talking and not someone else doing a voiceover.'

The voice for Alpha Centauri was provided by actress Ysanne Churchman. 'I recall the amusement of the rest of the cast' she said 'as they watched Stuart and me huddled in a corner of the rehearsal room discussing exactly how Alpha would react to each situation in order to make his movements coincide with my vocal interpretations.'

Alpha Centauri went on to reappear in the second of Hayles' Peladon stories, *The Monster of Peladon*, in which the only change to the costume was a new cloak. Both Fell and Churchman returned to reprise their roles.

Doctor Who was always successful when it tried to present monsters which echoed elements of real life. Thus, the Cybermen played upon perfectly natural human concerns about limb and organ transplantation and also the loss of one's humanity. The Ice Warriors presented a convincing reptilian alien life form from Mars at around the time that humanity was striking out for the stars and preparing to send men to the moon for the first time.

A fear of snakes and lizards is another common human characteristic, and another of the memorable monster races to appear during the seventies was partly inspired by this phobia.

The Draconians were, like the Silurians and Sea Devils, the creation of Malcolm Hulke. In 1979 he explained the origin of the story that introduced them, *Frontier in Space*. 'The BBC said to me, "We've just bought a whole load of models of space ships from Lew Grade's show that he's had on ITV [Gerry Anderson's *UFO*]. We can paint 'em up different colours – can you write a story which will use these?"

'It was obvious that with that amount of hardware it'd be what's known in the trade as

Top: Sarah (Elisabeth Sladen), the Doctor (Jon Pertwee) and Alpha Centauri in the Queen's throne room. *The Monster of Peladon*. Bottom: Alpha Centauri in the corridors of the Citadel. *The Monster of Peladon*.

The Draconian Prince [Peter Birrel] together with another Draconian on Earth. *Frontier in Space.*

a "hardware show" with a lot of flying about. But there has to be conflict because without conflict you've got no drama and this leads your thinking fairly naturally to the idea of what *Frontier in Space* was about: a kind of *Star Wars* and you've got two sides so -– who are they? Why are they at war? The idea came of these two great empires with an imaginary frontier drawn between them, across which their spaceships weren't supposed to travel   but of course they did and that gave us the story.

'The two sides as far as I was concerned were the Soviet Union and America with somebody else trying to tickle 'em up and get them to go to war with each other when they were quite capable, although very different, of living in a kind of peace.'

In Hulke's script, the two empires were represented by Earth and the planet Draconia from where the Draconians, a race of intelligent and noble lizard people, originated. The camera script for episode one described them as follows.

THE DRACONIANS ARE BASICALLY HUMANOID IN THEIR BODY SHAPE, BUT THEIR FACES AND HANDS ARE DRAGON-LIKE. THEIR HANDS ARE CLAWED. THEY CARRY GUNS OF A DIFFERENT DESIGN OF THOSE OF THE EARTH MEN. THEY WEAR MILITARY UNIFORM AND INSIGNIA.

Later, when the Draconian Prince – the main Draconian character in the story – first appeared, the following description as given:

THE DRACONIAN AMBASSADOR, WHO IS A PRINCE, SON OF THE EMPEROR, WEARS THE ORNATE UNIFORM OF A DRACONIAN COURT OFFICIAL ... HE IS HUMANOID, BUT WITH DRAGON-LIKE CHARACTERISTICS ABOUT THE HEAD AND FACE, AND WITH CLAWED HANDS. HE IS A YOUNG WARRIOR, PROUD AND A LITTLE ARROGANT, LIKE ALL DRACONIANS.

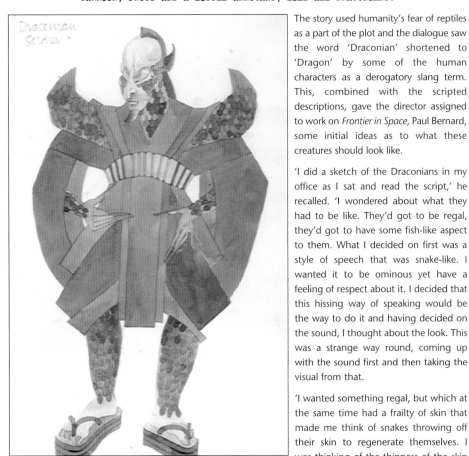

Barbara Hidd's original costume design for the Draconian. Note the ultimately unused flip-flop design for the shoes.

The story used humanity's fear of reptiles as a part of the plot and the dialogue saw the word 'Draconian' shortened to 'Dragon' by some of the human characters as a derogatory slang term. This, combined with the scripted descriptions, gave the director assigned to work on *Frontier in Space*, Paul Bernard, some initial ideas as to what these creatures should look like.

'I did a sketch of the Draconians in my office as I sat and read the script,' he recalled. 'I wondered about what they had to be like. They'd got to be regal, they'd got to have some fish-like aspect to them. What I decided on first was a style of speech that was snake-like. I wanted it to be ominous yet have a feeling of respect about it. I decided that this hissing way of speaking would be the way to do it and having decided on the sound, I thought about the look. This was a strange way round, coming up with the sound first and then taking the visual from that.

'I wanted something regal, but which at the same time had a frailty of skin that made me think of snakes throwing off their skin to regenerate themselves. I was thinking of the thinness of the skin and I wanted to feel that we could see

into their face, although I knew that we wouldn't be able to do that. So I started to think about possibly framing the face with something flimsy, a material that was scale-like.

DRACONIANS

Frontier in Space (1973) 6 episodes w. Malcolm Hulke d. Paul Bernard

Earth and Draconia have established an uneasy frontier between the two empires which is being threatened by the activities of a third party. The Doctor and Jo become involved and must find the real culprits.

CHARACTER

The people of Draconia are very like humans in their morals and outlook. There are good and bad sides to most races and the Draconians are no exception. Their development followed a more dynastic nature than that of humanity and the Draconians are, as a result, a race divided between the nobles and the 'ordinary' Draconian people. All are ruled by the Emperor and follow and obey the rules of state regarding who may come into the presence of their ruler. The Emperor's power stems from the great families and court business is carried out in consultation with the nobles. One area in which Draconian society seems a little out of step is that females are not treated with the same accord as males – indeed, females are forbidden to speak in the presence of the Emperor.

The Draconian Emperor is serious about maintaining good relations with Earth to the extent that he sends his son as the Draconian ambassador during discussions to try to avert a recurrence of war between the races, which seems ever more likely.

The Draconians are also loyal, but can be devious in their dealings with others. This has resulted in the war of words and recriminations in which neither the humans nor the Draconians are prepared to believe the others' assertions that they are innocent of any crimes.

This distrust goes back a long way and is fuelled by the humans' instinctive fear of the Draconians and vice versa. In summary, humans and Draconians are very similar people with similar aspirations, fears and concerns.

Director Paul Bernard's original sketch of the Draconian head showing the arching collar added by Barbara Hidd during discussion.

A Draconian. *Frontier in Space.*

'Aloofness was another thing, and the sketch came out of all these thoughts. They didn't exactly end up looking like my sketch but they were pretty close. They dropped the skin-like framing, but kept the scales and the serpent/lizard feel to it.'

'They weren't sure about the kind of bumps on the face at first until I did it and they liked it,' said Friedlander, who created the final masks. 'It was these lumps that stuck out, I think, that made the masks so comfortable to wear on the faces. There was an air pocket under each so they didn't adhere too rigidly to the face.'

'I also wanted to get a sense of size to the creatures, and dignity,' explained Bernard. 'I was emphatic that I didn't want them to be seen as baddies. I wanted grace and stature.' He discussed his thoughts with costume designer Barbara Kidd and together they worked out the look of the creatures. 'She added to my original sketch the outline of a samurai-like collar, which was the way that we were thinking,' said Bernard. 'I wanted the costumes to reflect sea-greens and purples to bring over the creatures' nobility. I wanted them to be simple and Barbara managed to bring a superb elegance to her work with me on the show.'

'I did see a pencil sketch of a head, based on a sort of dragon, and the body was from me,' confirmed Kidd. 'I did a drawing from the head which was then worked to. The basis for the costume was a samurai warrior.'

Several actors were cast to play the noble Draconians, among them Peter Birrel, who played the key part of the Draconian Prince.

'I was encased in green latex. It wasn't so bad out on location, but in the studio, you did sweat. I used to take the headpiece off at the end of the day and literally pour out a pint of sweat.

'On my feet, I had to wear something like a pair of plastic flip-flops like you would wear on the beach, but in order to make me taller, they put four or five additional soles on them. So I was teetering around like a girl in her first high heels. Out on location, in the inevitable quarry that every *Doctor Who* seemed to use, it was unbelievable, I was running over rocks. The fact that I didn't break my ankle was astonishing.'

Kidd remembered that there was a problem with the shoes. 'The Draconians' shoes were originally made from flip-flops with lots of soles glued on, but on location they all broke so we ended up using something else in the end – I can't remember what, unfortunately.'

Birrel also recalled the distinctive Draconian mask. 'The only part of my face that actually showed through the latex mask was my bottom lip and around my eyes, which were made up to match the mask. The problem was that I sweated so much that the make-up sank in and at the end of each day I used to lie back in the make-up chair with hot towels over my face – which was very nice. But apparently this treatment didn't really work as my wife used to say, when I came home from the studio, that I looked like a corpse with deep green rings around my eyes. It took weeks for the colour to come out completely.

'What was quite strange about the Draconian masks was that although they were a full head mask and although they all came out of the same mould, they seemed to take on the characteristics of our faces. My wife said that when she saw a shot of several Draconians on screen together, that she knew exactly which one was me. After about ten minutes of wearing it, the mask sort of moulded itself to the contours of your face.

'I remember we were out at a fuller's-earth quarry, with dust flying everywhere. The part of the quarry that we were filming in was half way up a hill with a pathway leading to it, and the make-up truck was at the bottom of the hill. We used to get dressed and made-up and then walk up the path to the location. Although we seemed to be in the middle of nowhere, there was always a small crowd of people who would stand and watch us film. Among them was a group of schoolchildren.

'As Jon Pertwee walked up the hill, these children all pointed and went, "Look! That's Doctor Who, that's Doctor Who!" Then Katy Manning walked up and they all went, "That's Jo, that's Jo!" And when I emerged

Top: The Doctor (Jon Pertwee) is captured by the Draconians. *Frontier in Space.* Bottom: The Draconian Prince (Peter Birrel). *Frontier in Space.*

from make-up and started up the hill, one little boy screamed and ran away. "Well, that worked!" I thought. I enjoyed that. With television, you never really know what the audience's reaction is. Sometimes you get unexpected feedback and this helps greatly because you realise that you therefore don't have to worry about how you look and can concentrate on the performance.

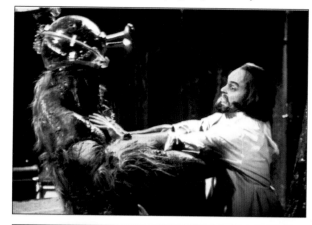

'In effect, I played a human being in a reptile skin. I was very lucky in that my character was the first to appear on screen, so I set the pattern for how the Draconians would be. Early in rehearsals the idea came up of speaking with a sibilant voice and also, when I sat down, I would sit with my hands bending inwards like a lizard's would. These traits were taken up by the other actors playing the Draconians, but basically they were well-written characters and we played them as though we were human.'

Not all of the Doctor's adversaries in the seventies were humanoid, however, and one of the more memorable of the creations he faced was a stitched-together headless monstrosity, built by a Frankenstein-like scientist with the aim of providing a new body for his master, who existed only as a disembodied brain.

Top: The monstrous body (Stuart Fell) containing Morbius' brain wrestles with its creator, Doctor Solon (Philip Madoc). *The Brain of Morbius*. Bottom: Doctor Solon. *The Brain of Morbius*.

This gruesome creation appeared in a story called *The Brain of Morbius*, which had been commissioned from writer Terrance Dicks by script editor Robert Holmes. Dicks' original idea had come out of a discussion about myths. 'One of them was the Frankenstein myth of a man making a monster,' he explained. 'I came up with the idea of a galactic super-criminal who has a super robot assistant – a sort of devoted robot Jeeves. The criminal, Morbius, is fleeing from his enemies, and his spaceship crashes.

'Morbius is smashed up to the extent that the robot can save only the head. And having been saved like this, he demands a new body. The robot is well intentioned, but limited as robots are. Now for some reason, spaceships do crash on this planet. So the robot goes out, scoops up the remaining bits of alien life forms and whacks them together into a roughly functioning body, on to which he puts Morbius' head. But as Morbius has always been something of a handsome Greek god, he is far from pleased.

'That was the story – it was gruesome, macabre and funny. But it was also logical: the robot would do that. Bob and I worked out the story, and I wrote a set of scripts which he seemed happy with.'

Unfortunately, during the subsequent development of the story, the producer, Philip Hinchcliffe, decided that the robot would be too expensive and difficult to realise and so Holmes was instructed to remove it from the story. Dicks was at this time out of the country and so Holmes had to carry out the rewrite himself. When Dicks returned, he was less than happy that his script had been changed without his consent, but agreed that it could go ahead as long as his name was removed from it. When Holmes asked Dicks what name he would like to use, Dicks suggested, vaguely, that it be 'something bland'. Thus the transmission of *The Brain of Morbius* saw the story credited to 'Robin Bland'.

In the script, the patched together monster was described as follows:

... A MONSTROUS BODY, THE PRODUCT OF SOLON'S LABOURS WITH VARIOUS DISPARATE LIFE-FORMS THAT HAVE CRASHED ON THE PLANET. A HYBRID OF FUR, FEATHERS AND SCALES, AND IT HAS NO HEAD.

A blinded Sarah (Elisabeth Sladen) approaches the disembodied brain of Morbius. *The Brain of Morbius*.

The director assigned to *The Brain of Morbius* was Christopher Barry. 'The design of the monster came from the script. I think it described it as a pot pourri, a hotch potch. We came up with the idea that it would be built from bits and pieces of other creatures but that became rather difficult to realise. Rowland Warne [the costume designer] thought we could have panels of flesh without being specific as to their origin.'

'We cut up lumps of foam and stuck them onto a cotton jumpsuit which had been layered with textured latex and foam rubber,' explained Warne. 'We then covered the foam with Terylene wadding dipped in latex. We built muscles down the spine – which in fact were to conceal the zip – and I used real surgical clips on the body, and also coffee beans to give the skin the right texture.'

'What we specifically didn't want to use were any metallic or non-organic panels,' added Barry, 'because the only thing we wanted to look false and inorganic was the head that gets fitted later.'

One of Sutekh's servicer robots (Nick Burnell) prowls the woods around the Old Priory. *Pyramids of Mars.*

MUMMIES

Pyramids of Mars (1976) 4 episodes
w. Stephen Harris (Robert Holmes, from an idea by Lewis Griefer)
d. Paddy Russell

The ancient Osiran god Sutekh is preparing to escape from his captivity. But can the Doctor stop him?

CHARACTER

The mummies were in reality Servicer Robots created by Sutekh to carry out his will while he himself was trapped immobile in a pyramid in Egypt. An unwary archaeologist, Marcus Scarman, became a human host to Sutekh when he uncovered his tomb. Scarman travelled back to England and started preparations to build and fire a pyramid-shaped rocket at a pyramid on Mars which was holding Sutekh prisoner.

The mummies were impervious to attack and simply obeyed commands. The Doctor was able to disable one of the creatures and used its framework to plant dynamite on the rocket, preventing it from being fired.

The mummies are controlled by an amulet which emits impulses picked up by a small pyramid shaped crystal embedded in their back.

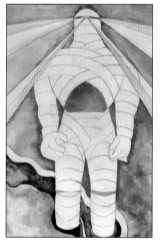

Top: Barbara Kidd's retrospective painting of how the Mummies could have looked. Bottom: A Mummy stands in the pyramid on Mars. *Pyramids of Mars.*

Originally, the creature did not have a head, and later in the story, a large goldfish-bowl-like helmet was fitted, into which the disembodied brain was placed. Because of this requirement that the creature be 'headless', a short actor had to be cast to play it. This role eventually went to stuntman Stuart Fell as, not only did the creature have to act and react to the other characters, it also had to perform a tricky fall at the story's climax. 'My head was at shoulder height within the costume,' Fell revealed, 'and the bowl and brain were on top of my head and were very heavy. At the end the creature had to run up a cliff and fall off. I twisted my neck quite badly falling off the cliff because of the weight of the head.'

'The fall was quite a remarkable achievement,' remembered Barry. 'Stuart actually fell about eight feet on to mattresses. You see him take one look round to see where he's got to go and then over he goes! He actually hits the camera on the way down which is why the picture bumps as he goes out of shot.'

As usual for the actors who played the monsters, the main problem for Fell was the heat. 'The facilities we had in those days meant that, as with Alpha Centauri, I had to stay in the costume all day,' he said. 'The monster was made of fur so it was even hotter than usual and I had to breathe through the fur and this was very difficult to do because of the heat. Between scenes, I would put a straw in my mouth and push it out through the costume in order to help me breath. I regretted that a few days later because I developed an infection in the back of my throat.'

In the same year as the headless Morbius monster, the Doctor faced a number of bandage-wrapped mummies. These creatures, although loosely based on the Egyptian mummy, were, according to the *Doctor Who* universe, robots.

They appeared in a story called *Pyramids of Mars,* which had started life as a story outline by writer Lewis Griefer, commissioned by Robert Holmes in July 1974. Griefer had built a story around the myths of ancient Egypt, with the Egyptian god Shebek planning to destroy the Earth by sending contaminated grain to the moon. The moon would be eroded when the grain germinated and the Earth's life cycle would be destroyed.

Holmes worked with Griefer on the outline throughout the summer of 1974, but unfortunately Griefer fell ill and was unable to deliver the scripts by the agreed date in October. When they finally arrived in December, producer Philip Hinchcliffe felt that they needed a significant rewrite but by this time Griefer was teaching in Tel Aviv and could not carry out the work. Holmes therefore undertook to rewrite the scripts himself and the story underwent a significant restructuring as a result.

The mummies were designed by Barbara Kidd and, as there was no significant description of them within Holmes' scripts, she had an almost free hand. The basis of the costume was a fibreglass support created by John Friedlander, which was then covered with a bandage-like material. 'This story was hell because the fibreglass supports for the mummies were really difficult to get in and out of,' recalled Kidd. 'It was really painful for the guys to put them on. Then Tom Baker had to put one of them on and that was just horrible: the skin on his arms was all scratched.'

One of the actors playing the mummies was Melvyn Bedford. 'The only provision was that we were about six feet in height,' he said in 1980. 'The costumes were pretty uncomfortable and very hot. When we were filming on location this wasn't too bad as the weather wasn't very warm, but when we were in the studios it was very much hotter.'

'The costumes comprised a fibreglass body which was joined to the head,' explained Kidd, 'and this was covered with an elasticated fabric to form the actual binding. It had to be elasticated, because to create the shape we wanted it had to stretch around the edges. Otherwise you have to do bandaging as seen during the First World War to build up the shapes. This is lovely as it builds up all sorts of intricate patterns but was unfortunately too complicated for us to use here.

'The costumes were made in sections, pre-wrapped, so to speak, although there may have been parts that were wrapped each time to link the sections together. They didn't survive very well, unfortunately. They took quite a bashing.'

Kidd was ultimately disappointed with the way the mummies were seen in the story. 'I think there was quite a lot of contention about the mummies because they didn't work as well as we'd hoped. I felt quite strongly about it and I didn't think they worked as well as they might have done. As a result I did my own painting after the production had finished showing how perhaps they might have been.'

The seventies, as with the sixties, saw a large number of monsters appearing in *Doctor Who* for just one story, never to be seen again. Some were particularly memorable, like the Zygons, the Axons, giant spiders, the Krynoid and the Fendahl. Others were less successful, and creatures like the Gell Guards, the Minotaur, the Nucleus of the Swarm and the giant squid Kroll failed to make a significant impact, despite every effort having been made to ensure their success.

Another race of monsters who were not the overwhelming success it might have been were the Mandrels. These had been devised by writer Bob Baker for his story *Nightmare of Eden* – which was commissioned under the title *The Nightmare of Evil* – as a mud monster. In the rehearsal scripts, when a Mandrel was seen for the first time, it was described as follows:

```
THEY ARE CONFRONTED BY A BLUE MIST, OUT OF WHICH LURCHES A
MANDREL, A SLIMY MUD CREATURE FROM THE SWAMPS OF EDEN, ITS
                  GREAT ARMS GRASPING ...
```

Later, in the second episode, the following description appeared:

```
K-9 IS BEING PROBED BY MANDRELS. A TENDRIL MOVES TOWARDS HIM,
                      THEN ANOTHER,
                      AND ANOTHER.
```

A final description appeared at the start of episode three:

```
FROM THE SWAMP RISES A MANDREL DRIPPING WITH SLIMY MUD
```

It is clear from these extracts that Baker had intended the Mandrels to be dripping, tendrilled, slimy creatures, perhaps even composed of mud. Unfortunately, *Nightmare of Eden* was affected by a severe lack of money due to the high cost of a story in the same season partly filmed in Paris, France (*City of Death*), and also because of an ambitious six-part story with which the season was scheduled to end (*Shada*, which was ultimately cancelled partway through production due to industrial action at the BBC).

MANDRELS

Nightmare of Eden (1979) 4 episodes w. Bob Baker d. Alan Bromly (and Graham Williams)
Arriving on a luxury cruise liner the *Empress*, the Doctor uncovers a plot to smuggle the dangerously addictive drug vraxoin.

CHARACTER

The Mandrels originate from the muddy swamps on the planet Eden. There they would have stayed if it hadn't been for the fact that, if killed, the Mandrels decompose into a pure form of the addictive drug vraxoin. This fact brought them to the attention of drug smugglers who hatched an ingenious scheme to smuggle the drug by capturing the Mandrel, on holographic dimensional crystals and killing them only when the Mandrels were safely past all the security checks.

The Mandrels' only desire is to roar and fight, both of which they do pretty well. Their elongated arms are tipped with vicious claws and their mouths are wide and cavernous.

This shortage of money resulted in cutbacks and the dripping mud monsters could not be achieved. Costume designer Rupert Jarvis made a game attempt to convey the creatures as described in the script. The final costumes were tall and impressive and featured glowing green eyes and a wide fringed mouth as well as elongated arms

The Doctor [Tom Baker] wrestles with a Mandrel. *Nightmare of Eden*.

operated by the simple mechanism of the actor inside the costume holding wooden lengtheners in his hands, with pressure grips to make the clawed fingers on the end of the arms flex.

The head of the costume was given shape by a wicker framework which was covered with padding and fur, while the trunk, legs and arms were made from latex rubber, patterned with scales and painted a dark, muddy brown-black. It was not possible to create the creeping tendrils as described in the script and so these were dropped.

David Korff and Rob Goodman were both hired to play Mandrels in the story.

'I'd done costume work before and I realised when I saw the costumes that this was going to be a hot job,' said Goodman. 'It was like having your own private sauna. I lost a few pounds during the making of that *Doctor Who*. We had a few days' rehearsal for it and I hope it all worked out OK. I'm only five foot nine, but I must have been well over six foot in the costume.

'Being encased inside a costume skin and trying to act through that can be quite restrictive, but it can be likened to Greek theatre, where the actors work through masks. If you get the mental attitude right then it seems to project through the mask or costume. It's getting the frame of mind right to start with. In terms of movement inside the costumes, something intended as a subtle movement has to be made much bigger so that it becomes subtle when viewed from outside.

'The Mandrels had tunnel vision. You weren't looking through the eyes of the costume, which were somewhere above your head: you were looking through the nostrils.'

'We each had an assistant to help us in the costumes,' recalled Korff, 'because they were hard to work in and we couldn't really see where we were or what we were doing.

'I remember one scene when there were about five Mandrels trying to get through a small hatch on a spaceship at the same time. I was the short one at the back and the crew were pushing us to try and get us through.

'One of the costume's arms got ripped off when we were attacking the passengers on this ship, and there was a bare human arm seen emerging from the body of a Mandrel! The scene was stopped and the costume went off for repairs.'

For the first time in a great many years, the press took an interest in these new *Doctor Who* monsters. The *Sun* reported that the Mandrels were unduly terrifying and that because of this no photographs had been taken of them in the studio (which was not true). In fact, when the story was transmitted, a reviewer for the *Doctor Who* Appreciation Society described the Mandrels as 'cute rejects from the Muppet show', not quite the terrifying horror described by the *Sun*.

Nightmare of Eden was transmitted as part of *Doctor Who*'s final season of the decade. Every story in the season featured a monster and yet none of them seemed to have the necessary impact. The Daleks made a return appearance in *Destiny of the Daleks*, but the story was primarily about Davros; Skaroth was a disappointing spaghetti-faced alien played by Julian Glover in *City of Death*; the Tythonian ambassador Erato was a giant ambulatory green blob in the descriptively titled *The Creature from the Pit*; and, in what was, with the loss of *Shada*, to be the final story transmitted in the season, the bull-headed Nimon showed promise in *The Horns of Nimon*, but ended up looking like masked men wearing platform shoes and tights.

There was, however, one creation which was originated and made a significant impact in the seventies and which returned several times to battle the Doctor – the Sontarans.

The Mandrels on the rampage in the corridors of the space liner Empress. *Nightmare of Eden*.

CHAPTER 6

SONTARANS

APPEARANCES

The Time Warrior (1973/4) 4 episodes
w. Robert Holmes d. Alan Bromly

A Sontaran officer called Linx crash-
lands on Earth in the 13th century and
is forced to kidnap scientists from the
20th century to repair his ship. The
kidnappings also alert the Doctor, who
sets out to investigate.

The Sontaran Experiment (1975)
2 episodes
w. Bob Baker & Dave Martin
d. Rodney Bennett

Sontaran Field-Major Styre is
experimenting on a captured group of
GalSec astronauts to determine Earth's
resistance to Sontaran invasion. ➡

*We just had this very silly idea that he should have this helmet,
and when he took the helmet off the head would be almost exactly
the same size and shape.*

COSTUME DESIGNER JAMES ACHESON SPEAKING IN 1987

The Sontarans were the latest in a line of *Doctor Who* monsters to follow an emerging pattern. The creators of those monsters which had gone on to make numerous appearances in the show had not necessarily started with that intention. The creatures were devised for a single story and, when that appearance was deemed particularly successful, they were brought back. Occasionally a writer might hope that their creation would be a success, and, in the sixties, both the Zarbi and the Mechanoids were promoted as 'the next Daleks'. What made those creatures which did return successful was some elusive spark of originality of concept, and a believability which set them apart from the rest. Like the Daleks, Cybermen and Ice Warriors, the Sontarans fitted this pattern nicely, fulfilling all the requirements: an interesting and eloquent alien, a distinctive look and a believable history.

Robert Holmes had been one of a number of regular contributors to the show throughout the seventies and had contributed many popular science fiction scripts to the series. Eventually, script editor Terrance Dicks suggested to Holmes that a story set in the past might be nice. 'Basically, the choice of the kind of story is the job of the script editor and producer,' explained Dicks. 'When we did *The Time Warrior*, Bob hated writing historical shows. "Well," I said, "I want a show set in the Middle Ages." I eventually dragged him kicking and screaming into the Middle Ages.'

'The genesis of the Sontarans came about, I think, because at the time of writing *The Time Warrior* I had been reading, or trying to read, *Clausewitz on War*,' said Holmes in 1980. 'Terrance Dicks asked me to write an historical

Linx [Kevin Lindsay] catches the Doctor [Jon Pertwee] in the doorway to his ship during a publicity session for *The Time Warrior*.

adventure for the Doctor. Now this is an area I have always shied away from, remembering some of those early stories about Nero's Rome and the travels of Marco Polo. (I have a feeling that *Doctor Who* was originally developed by Auntie as a format for making history interesting for children; fortunately the fantasy side soon took over.) Anyway, after some argument, Terrance and I compromised on a story that would be a mix of science fiction and historical fiction.'

The Invasion of Time (1978)
6 episodes
w. David Agnew (Graham Williams & Anthony Read) d. Gerald Blake

The Sontarans use a race called the Vardans as an advance guard to invade Gallifrey. The Doctor, who has been aiding the Vardans in order to trap them, must stop the Sontarans from gaining the secret of time travel.

The Two Doctors (1985) 3 episodes
w. Robert Holmes d. Peter Moffatt

The Sontarans are in league with the scientist Dastari in an attempt to discover the secret of time travel.

The story started life as an outline written by Holmes as a citation from a Sontaran named Hol Mes to another named Terran Cedicks. Story outlines, explained Holmes, 'are boring things which plot the main course of action, and just to make life more interesting, I wrote mine in the form of a citation.'

A storyline called *The Time Fugitive* was commissioned on 26 February 1973 and the scripts, now titled *The Time Survivor*, were commissioned on 5 March 1973 before the story was finally retitled *The Time Warrior* for production and transmission.

In the script for episode one of *The Time Warrior*, Holmes described the Sontaran, who was named Linx, as follows:

```
LINX WEARS SONTARAN SPACE ARMOUR, NOT UNLIKE A GLEAMING, SOPHISTICATED VERSION OF
                    THE KNIGHT'S ARMOUR OF THE PERIOD.
```

When Linx finally removed his helmet at the end of the first episode, the following description appeared:

```
 AS LINX TURNS WE ZOOM INTO A CLOSE--UP OF HIS HIDEOUS TOAD-LIKE ALIEN FACE.
```

In charge of make-up for the story was Sandra Exelby. She recalled that, although the Visual Effects Department had worked out the rough costume and make-up designs for the Sontaran, pressure of work meant that they were unable to carry them through. The work therefore passed to the make-up and costume designers. 'They had designed the costume and the facial features of Linx up to a point. At our first planning meeting, the director was trying to explain the kind of thing he wanted. I can't remember if it was I or the costume designer who suggested that he should look half man, half frog and to lose the neck as we thought that would make him look more froglike. The actual construction of the head was the responsibility of Visual Effects because at that time the Make-up Department didn't have any facilities for making prosthetics – you can class it as an early prosthetic because it did use a certain amount of foam.'

'I can remember that the head had been modelled by John Friedlander, I think before I got on the story,' recalled the story's costume designer, James Acheson, in 1987. 'We just had this very silly idea that he should have this helmet, and when he took the helmet off the head would be almost exactly the same size and shape.

'I often worked very closely with John. He was very, very clever. He was making people speak through rubber masks long before he had the right materials available. Nowadays there are very sophisticated foaming techniques for making extremely flexible rubber that people can actually stick to their face. The whole area of prosthetic make-up has really made vast strides in the last ten years, but John was out there doing, I think, very sophisticated and clever things long before anyone else.'

The actual mask for the Sontaran was made from fibreglass matting, without the hardening resin. First, a cast of actor Kevin Lindsay's face was taken by Exelby. The matting was built up around the cast into the shape of the Sontaran's head and then covered with a thin layer of latex. This was then painted and hairs were punched in at selected points.

'The top lip actually went inside Kevin Lindsay's own lip as a flap,' explained Exelby. 'I stuck the bottom lip to his chin so that he had some movement there. I then used make-up to paint his lip in the same sort of browny green colour as the rest of the mask. I also had to stick the mask down around the eyes.'

Kevin Lindsay as Linx, both in and out of his mask.
The Time Warrior.

The costume created for Linx was a silver-black military-looking suit with a belt on which could be attached his communicator and gun. The creature had only three fingers on each hand. Around the neck was a large collar on to which the domed helmet could be fitted. At the back of the neck was a projecting aperture, described in the script as a probic vent. The costume was very hot and constricting, and, unknown to anyone working on the production, Lindsay suffered from a heart condition.

'He didn't mention anything of that to me,' stated Exelby. 'On the location filming there wasn't really any bother because, being outside, you don't have to contend with the heat of the lights in the studio or the lack of air. In addition, most of the time if we were doing shots of him in the helmet we didn't put the actual Sontaran head on at all.

'Parts of the studio recordings were all right because he had the helmet on. When he didn't have the helmet on, we put the head on, but then there were some scenes where he had to put the helmet on and off over the head. There was one scene where you saw him put the helmet on and he had to keep it

on for the rest of the scene, and at the end he came over to me and said, "Oh, I feel dreadful." So I asked him if he wanted to sit down for a minute and he said, "No, I think I'm going to fall down," at which he fell down! I took the helmet and the head off him and they got the nurse down from the medical centre to look at him.

'He told me that his ticker was a bit dodgy and he had to watch it sometimes. It was the heat of the studio and the claustrophobic aspect of having both the mask and the helmet on at the same time. The costume was made from a quilted lurex material and was deliberately thick and padded to make him look squat. He didn't have a good time, poor Kevin. But he was very good about it.'

At the conclusion of *The Time Warrior*, Linx was killed, but viewers did not have long to wait before the Sontarans returned.

During the planning stages of the 12th season of *Doctor Who* in 1974, outgoing producer Barry Letts, incoming producer Philip Hinchcliffe and script editor Robert Holmes, realised that they were going to have to make some budgetary cuts. This was achieved partly by using the same sets for two stories (*The Ark in Space* and *Revenge*

Top: Styre (Kevin Lindsay) forces Krans (Glyn Jones) and Erak (Peter Walshe) to torture Vural (Donald Douglas) in his attempts to measure human strength. *The Sontaran Experiment.*
Bottom: Styre reports back to the Marshal of the Sontaran fleet. *The Sontaran Experiment.*

of the Cybermen) but also by including a two-part story made entirely on location to complement *The Ark in Space*, which was made entirely in the studio.

Holmes decided to reintroduce the Sontarans and, on the recommendation of Terrance Dicks, turned to experienced *Doctor Who* writers Bob Baker and Dave Martin to come up with a story which fulfilled all the requirements the reduced budget had imposed upon it.

The Destructors, as the story was initially called before being retitled *The Sontaran Experiment*, took place on a devastated Earth. Baker and Martin had areas of Dartmoor in mind when they planned out the story and originally suggested using an abandoned priory as the Sontarans' base. Having obtained some initial costings from Raymond Cusick, who was acting as the chief assistant to the Head of Television Design, Hinchcliffe started to question the requirement to use a priory as this necessitated a number of sets to be erected on location. By 22 August 1974, a decision had been taken to move the setting from medieval to prehistoric and Dartmoor was also confirmed as the location to be used. Strangely, although the documentation clearly uses the word 'prehistoric', the story was actually set in the far future, at a time when Earth had been ravaged by solar flares and was believed uninhabited.

As Linx had been killed at the conclusion of *The Time Warrior*, a new Sontaran was introduced called Styre, and Kevin Lindsay returned to play him. By way of concession to Lindsay's heart condition, the Sontaran costume and mask were redesigned to make them lighter and less constricting. The original mask had disappeared following completion of *The Time Warrior*, which meant that a new one had to be made anyway. In addition, Lindsay was required to wear the Sontaran's outer helmet only for a single scene at

Styre (Kevin Lindsay). *The Sontaran Experiment.*

Top: Roth (Peter Rutherford) and Sarah (Elisabeth Sladen) are captured by the Sontaran Styre (Kevin Lindsay). *The Sontaran Experiment*.
Middle and Bottom: Two photographs taken during location filming for *The Sontaran Experiment* at Dartmoor.

the end of the first episode. Styre was also given five fingers on each hand but aside from this the general physical appearance of the Sontaran remained unchanged.

Barbara Kidd, the story's costume designer, remembered that during the lunch break Lindsay used to stay up on the Dartmoor tor that was being used for the location as he didn't want to have to come all the way down and then go back up again. 'At lunchtime he used to sit up there on his own and someone would bring his lunch up to him.'

The Sontaran Experiment actually featured two Sontarans. As well as Styre, a Sontaran Marshal was also featured, although this character appeared only on a monitor screen. Lindsay played both parts and the same mask was used, although the Marshal was distinguished by the addition of two circular 'insignia' to the front of his spacesuit collar.

Following *The Sontaran Experiment*, the Sontarans stepped into the background, although their sworn enemy, the Rutans, made an appearance in Terrance Dicks' *Horror of Fang Rock* at the start of the 15th season. This creature was as unlike the Sontarans as could be imagined: a glowing green formless blob, not unlike a jellyfish, but with the power to change its shape into that of any other creature.

The Sontarans' surprise appearance at the conclusion of the story *The Invasion of Time* at the end of the 15th season in 1978, may never have happened if production on the story originally intended to fill that slot had gone smoothly and as planned.

The Invasion of Time was a last-minute replacement for writer David Weir's original scripts (called *The Killer Cats of Gen Singh* (spelling uncertain)). These had been considered unusable when they were eventually delivered one week before the director was due to join the production. All that producer Graham Williams and script editor Anthony Read could do was to create another story themselves, utilising some of the initial design work that had already been undertaken.

Williams and Read turned to Robert Holmes for advice, and he suggested a similar approach to that used for *The Ark in Space* and *The Sontaran Experiment*, namely to combine a four-part story and a two-part story into one. He also gave his permission for the Sontarans to return in the final two episodes of the replacement story.

The Sontaran costumes seen in *The Invasion of Time* were all newly created and were of the same design as seen in the previous stories, being made from a padded, quilted silver-black material. The helmet, however, underwent some changes. An additional ridge ran from the forehead down to the back of the helmet and above the enlarged eyeholes was engraved a geometric decal. The commanding Sontaran was named

Sontarans are technologically advanced, having developed cloning to the extent that they can create millions of Sontarans at one time. They have mastered space travel and use distinctive one-Sontaran spherical geodesic ships. They also have the technology to create a universal translator device and also a pencil-like weapon which can, at a distance, strike a weapon from an opponent's hand, kill, stun or mesmerise, depending on the circumstances.

In order to assess the strength of humanity to a Sontaran invasion, the Sontaran Grand Strategic Council sent Field-Major Styre of the Sontaran G3 military assessment survey to carry out the task. As well as his own equipment and spacecraft, Styre used a complex robot to hunt and capture human subjects for his experiments. He had also concealed a miniature camera and microphone on the spacesuit of one of the captured GalSec humans which transmitted intelligence back to his ship.

Their spaceships use an osmic projector, which gives them limited time travel capabilities. However, the Sontarans have made attempts to gain a greater control of time, both through an abortive invasion of the Doctor's home planet of Gallifrey, and by joining forces with the scientist Dastari when he attempted to create a time capsule using the biological imprint of a Time Lord – the Doctor – to prime the device.

Both attempts failed and the Sontarans, for the moment at least, remain a space-travelling only race of quite remarkable warlike prowess.

The Sontarans invade Gallifrey. *The Invasion of Time.*

Stor, and on his helmet this decal was outlined in black and was painted silver, whereas for the regular Sontarans, although the decal was present, it was painted the same gunmetal colour as the rest of the helmet. Also on Stor's helmet was a raised band around the lower part, above the collar. The probic vent on the back of the collar was also slightly altered, with the addition of a horizontal slot across the centre of a raised oval-shaped protuberance.

The Sontaran troopers wore black, three-fingered gloves, whereas Stor's hands were made from flesh-toned latex and also sported three fingers.

The Sontaran mask was also redesigned, but more drastically, so that the actor's eyes appeared to be sunken into the head and the actor's real mouth was seen, rather than his lips being attached to the latex lips of the mask. It was painted a uniform orange colour, with black rings around the eyes and mouth. This gave the effect of the Sontaran having a much smaller mouth than previously.

Kevin Lindsay had died since completion of *The Sontaran Experiment* and so Derek Deadman was hired to play Stor. Interviewed in 1993, Deadman had one main memory of playing Stor: the heat. 'The costume was extremely hot and the mask was latex,' he said. 'When I was asked if I could move more quickly down some steps I remember it was quite impossible – not only because of the heat; I couldn't see either!'

The Invasion of Time marked the final appearance of the Sontarans for many years, until producer John Nathan-Turner turned to them in his continuing desire to see monsters from the Doctor's past return to the series. Writer Andrew Smith, who had scripted the Tom Baker story *Full Circle* for the series in 1980, was commissioned to write a storyline on 10 January 1984 with the title *The First Sontarans*. Further details of this outline are not known, but the seed of bringing back the Sontarans had been sown and the following month Holmes was persuaded by script editor Eric Saward to resurrect his creations for a rematch against the Doctor, in a story which featured not just one but two Doctors.

'We were moving to the forty-five-minute time slot and this was going to be the season "biggie",' said Holmes, 'and Eric Saward wanted someone with experience of writing what is virtually an old six-parter and asked if I'd mind writing it. Then they said, "Can we have Sontarans?" I don't really like bringing back old monsters but I didn't think the Sontarans had been well used in their last appearances so I was glad to redress the balance.'

Holmes was commissioned to write the script for the first episode of the story, which had the title *The Kraalon Inheritance*, on 13 February 1984 and those for the remaining two episodes on 9 March. Nathan-Turner had for several years wanted to set a story in New Orleans in America following the promise of co-production funding from the American distributors of *Doctor Who*, Lionheart, via BBC Enterprises (now BBC Worldwide), the commercial arm of the Corporation. The American writer Lesley Elizabeth Thomas, who had been in discussion

Top: Commander Stor (Derek Deadman). Bottom: The invading Sontarans are affected by a blast of sound. *The Invasion of Time.*

with the production office since 1981, was formally contracted on 23 April 1984 to provide a scene breakdown with the title *Way Down Yonder*. According to Nathan-Turner, this didn't have 'that elusive *Who*-ish quality about it' and so Holmes' story, which had been given a similar brief regarding the location, was the one chosen for production. Ultimately the co-production deal fell through and so the location was changed to Seville in Spain as location filming there could be achieved within the standard allocated budget whereas a trip to New Orleans could not.

The story's title was changed from *The Kraalon Inheritance* to *The Androgum Inheritance* and finally to *The Two Doctors* for production. Other working titles that have been associated with this story are *Parallax*, *The Seventh Augmentment* and *Creation*, although these do not appear in any known BBC documentation.

Because seven years had passed since *The Invasion of Time*, there were no existing costumes available for reuse and so new costumes were created for the two Sontarans featured in *The Two Doctors*.

Group Marshal Stike (Clinton Greyn). *The Two Doctors.*

Once more the basic costume was made from a black, quilted fabric, but for this appearance the collar, elbow pads, boots and belt were silver. The collar, however, was not attached to the costume and the probic vent was of a slightly different design from those previously seen.

Group Marshal Stike (Clinton Greyn). *The Two Doctors.*

The main area of difference was in the masks. Here, the two Sontarans were designed to look different from each other, and the masks were far more sculptured than before. The actors' lips were not incorporated into the mask, but instead could be seen within the stationary sculpted lips of the Sontaran head. The heads also had prominent beards but the hands once more had three fingers on each. Clinton Greyn, who played Group Marshal Stike, was significantly taller than Tim Raynham, playing Major Varl, and adopted a far more militaristic posture and approach to the character than seen before in the series.

'I found playing behind a mask very challenging,' commented Greyn in 1991. 'It cuts off most expression so angles of the head, gestures and reactions have to be made interesting – Sontarans aren't mechanical, like Daleks.'

The Sontarans returned once more to television screens in a 'special' edition of *Doctor Who* recorded for the children's programme *Jim'll Fix It*. In this, Jimmy Savile OBE 'fixed it' for people to fulfil their dreams, and a young Gareth Jenkins had written in saying that he had his own *Doctor Who* costume and asking whether he could meet Colin Baker and go inside the TARDIS. A roughly eight-minute programme was recorded with Baker playing the Doctor, Janet Fielding playing his companion, Tegan, and two Sontarans, played, as in *The Two Doctors*, by Greyn and Raynham.

This skit was recorded on 20 February 1985 and transmitted on the same day as the second episode of *The Two Doctors* (23 February 1985), marking the final time in studio for the Sontarans, although the third and final episode of *The Two Doctors* was to be their final appearance on *Doctor Who*.

CHAPTER 7

THE EIGHTIES

THE MARSHMEN

Full Circle (1980) 4 episodes
w. Andrew Smith d. Peter Grimwade

The TARDIS becomes drawn into E-Space and arrives on the planet Alzarius where a colony of Terradonians have been working to ready their ship for take off for many years. Their legends speak of Mistfall when strange creatures emerge from the swamps, and, as the Doctor soon realises, the time of the next Mistfall is imminent.

> *When I first played Sil I wanted to make him as scary as possible, and when people were writing into* **Points of View** *complaining about this disgusting monster, I thought I had succeeded because that was exactly what I had wanted to do.*

NABIL SHABAN ON PLAYING SIL

Towards the end of the seventies, *Doctor Who* had become increasingly whimsical. There was a lighter tone to the stories than had been present earlier in the decade and it seemed that the strident complaints of Mary Whitehouse and her National Viewers' and Listeners' Association concerning the suitability of *Doctor Who* for its target audience had resulted in a gradual toning down of the horrific content. *Doctor Who* was simply not as frightening as it had been, and producer Graham Williams was opting instead for more science-fictional concepts and stories including a strong humorous element. The appointment of Douglas Adams as script editor, later to find fame through his *The Hitch-Hiker's Guide to the Galaxy* concept, also added to the light-hearted material contained within the final season of the seventies.

As previously mentioned, this season was perhaps disappointing for viewers brought up on a diet of terrifying adversaries. As it happened, the end of the seventies saw Williams moving on from the post of producer and John Nathan-Turner taking over control of the show. Nathan-Turner was to produce *Doctor Who* from 1980

The Marshmen emerge from the Alzarian swamp during Mistfall. *Full Circle.*

until its ultimate cancellation as a BBC production in 1989.

Nathan-Turner's appointment resulted in another change in focus for the programme. Science writer Christopher H. Bidmead was brought in as script editor to inject more realism into the stories and to ensure that any featured scientific concepts were in some respects rooted in reality. This resulted in stories which were perhaps more intelligently written and conceived, and the previous emphasis on monsters shifted to more human-based threats.

Doctor Who turned away from the simplicity of some of the recent stories towards a more complex and 'glossy' production, more geared towards television in the eighties. Unfortunately, some of the scripts suffered as a result and action tended to take over from plotting. In addition there was an increasing awareness within the series itself of *Doctor Who*'s own continuity and history and this was often adhered to, arguably to the show's detriment. Occasionally, however, the programme did present original and groundbreaking material, and there are several examples of monsters which live on in the memory of those who saw them.

An early example of innovative storytelling came with a storyline called *The Planet that Slept*, commissioned from author Andrew Smith and retitled *Full Circle* for production, which introduced a hyper-evolutionary race of creatures from the planet Alzarius, perhaps better known as the Marshmen.

In an article written in 1981, Smith explained the background to his tale. 'A good *Who* story is, I think, one which is acceptable on a number of levels. This I tried to achieve with *Full Circle*. To those who wish, it is a straightforward monster story with Our Heroes threatened by a group of hostile, bloodthirsty killer beasts. It is also, again to those that wish, I hope something a little juicier than that, an intriguing tale not only of xenophobia but of self-deceit, loyalties, and many other aspects.'

One of the most intriguing aspects of Smith's story is that it describes the ongoing process of evolution, but over a very contracted period. Thus, the process starts with a strange mist, then gourd-like river fruit are found to have eggs inside them. The eggs hatch and the river fruit burst open to reveal huge spiders. Then reptilian marsh creatures emerge from the waters of the planet – there is an implication that the spiders change into the marsh creatures, but this is never explicitly stated. The creatures adapt to breathe air and then attack the humanoid occupants of a crashed spaceship – the Starliner. With the humanoids dead, the marsh creatures literally develop into the humanoids they killed, ready for the next cycle of evolution to begin.

'The Marshmen are hyper-evolutionary creatures. Their metabolisms change to suit their surroundings,' wrote Smith. 'The Marshmen's change into humanoid form came about through their presence in the Starliner more than as a link in a predetermined natural sequence,' he continued, quoting the Doctor's line from the story – 'The environment evolved the creatures most suited to survive in it' – by way of example. Smith described the Marshmen in his script for episode two of *Full Circle* as follows:

```
ONE BY ONE, THE MARSHMEN BREAK THE SURFACE OF THE MARSH, HORRIBLE HALF MEN/HALF
        BEASTS AND SLITHERING DOWN THEIR FACES, MOUTHS GAPING AWFULLY.

THEY ARE VERY TALL, WITH A SLIGHT CROUCH, AND WITH LARGE, HEAVY EYEBROWS WHICH CAST
                    SHADOWS OVER THEIR EYES.
```

The costumes created by designer Amy Roberts were based on a diver's wetsuit. Each suit was turned inside out in order to present a rough surface on which panels of thin latex rubber imprinted with the design of a small seashell could be stuck to give the effect of scales. The suits were also given latex breasts and nipples and a flap of latex covered the zip. A pattern of purple veins was added extending down the torso from the neck, and from the hands up the arms. The masks were also modelled on top of inside-out wetsuit headpieces, with purple veins again in evidence on the head in a pattern echoing the shape of a spider, and extending down the neck. The outfits were completed with shell-patterned latex-covered gloves and feet.

Because the suits had to be immersed in the water for the scene in which the creatures emerge, a wetsuit

A Marshman. *Full Circle.*

was deemed the ideal solution, as the actors inside would remain dry and warm for the duration.

'It has to be said,' commented Roberts in 1981, 'that they were not the most comfortable costumes to wear, especially the headpieces, and inevitably the actors were a little hot! The only problem for them

The Marshmen attempt to leave the Starliner. *Full Circle*.

appearing from underneath the swamp was to hold their breath long enough! I did only one "design" for the Marshmen costumes after preliminary rough sketches and working drawings for myself, and that was approved by the director and producer. The final costumes were a reasonable approximation of that design but I wasn't entirely happy with them.'

Two of the actors hired to play Marshmen were Barney Lawrence and Keith Guest. 'We were filming at a place called Black Park,' recalled Lawrence, 'and that conjured up to me images of black water with fetid bubbles coming up.'

'It was like that, too,' said Guest. 'One end of the park had this marshy area which was very unpleasant and had "things" floating in it. There was one chap who was right at the front. There wasn't much water there and he had a very difficult task getting under the water. However, once we were under, our wetsuits all filled with water so that when we came up and took a great gulp of air, we found ourselves breathing in this brackish water.'

'We had to go under the water in our costumes,' said Lawrence, 'and then stay under until the water went calm. We had to count to seven. So we all tried to get under the water but we couldn't because the costume was so buoyant that we all floated. To get around this they got some heavy stage weights, attached a rope to them and then sunk them to the bottom of the lake. We could then haul ourselves down into the water using the rope and hold ourselves under until it was time to emerge, when we would let go of the rope and pop up like a cork out of a bottle.'

Although the wetsuits were made to keep the actors warm in the water, they were incredibly hot in the studio. 'I remember leaving wet footmarks wherever I went as the sweat poured off me and out the legs,' commented Lawrence.

'One of the days in Black Park,' recalled Guest, 'was a blazing hot day, and at one point we'd been lined up to do something and we all put the helmets on – which was the last thing we did before a shot – and they were very heavy. Then the director decided he was going to shoot something with K-9 instead and I remember Tom Baker going absolutely spare and saying that the director couldn't get people dressed up in all this gear and then leave them waiting in the heat. Under the studio lights it was actually worse, and I remember somebody actually passed out from the heat at one point.

'The hands were made from surgical gloves with latex "skin" stuck to the outside of the gloves. Someone found a small hole in one of their gloves and I remember seeing a stream of sweat pouring steadily from the end of the glove. Just squirting out of the hole. Incredible.'

Despite all the discomfort that seems to be part and parcel of playing a *Doctor Who* monster, Lawrence commented that he found the working atmosphere to be very good indeed.

On location in Black Park, the actors are helped into their Marshman costumes. *Full Circle*.

A Marshman is prepared for filming. *Full Circle*.

'I felt so much a part of *Doctor Who*,' he explained, 'that I wrote in to John Nathan-Turner after it was finished, rather cheekily suggesting that one of the Marshmen be found in the TARDIS and be regenerated as the next companion. They never took up my suggestion, though.'

Although the Marshmen were a one-off, there were two original eighties *Doctor Who* monsters which went on to make return appearances, featuring in stories in their own right. The first of these was the Mara, a creature from within a dream.

Although the Mara appeared in both *Kinda* and *Snakedance*, the creature itself was never seen. It took the form of humans possessed by the creature or it manifested in the form of a snake. A large snake costume was created by designer Barbara Kidd for the conclusion of *Kinda* and in *Snakedance* the creature appeared as a series of ever-bigger rubber snakes, operated by the visual effects team.

Kinda and *Snakedance* were both particularly effective stories and their strength, rather than in costume, make-up or visual effects to create an impressive monstrous foe, was in psychological horror, driven by the script and by the acting. The author of both stories was Christopher Bailey, who drew on Buddhist imagery and meaning to drive his storylines. *Doctor Who* has not often dealt with true psychological drama and yet the dream imagery of these two stories resulted in several memorable and harrowing scenes of the Doctor's companion Tegan being tempted by the Mara into giving up her bodily form for it to inhabit.

The Mara manifests as a snake. *Snakedance*.

The other creature to make a return appearance was a charismatic maggot-like creature called Sil.

SIL

Vengeance on Varos (1985) 2 episodes
w. Philip Martin d. Ron Jones

The Doctor arrives on the planet Varos in search of zeiton 7 ore for the TARDIS. Sil, representative of the Galatron Mining Corporation, is also there for apparently the same reasons. The Doctor and Peri find themselves in the middle of a real life 'video nasty' as they try to escape the Punishment Dome with their lives.

The Trial of a Time Lord (1986)
14 episodes parts 5-8
w. Philip Martin d. Ron Jones

On Thoros-Beta, Lord Kiv, ruler of the Mentors, is in search of a new body in which to house his expanding brain. Sil is also present, seeking to perhaps profit from the situation, and the Doctor is apparently acting very strangely indeed.

Sil was created by writer Philip Martin for a story called *Vengeance on Varos*. This had begun life over two years previously as a scene breakdown called *Domain* commissioned on 13 April 1982, which was developed into scripts in the latter part of 1982 and early 1983. During this process it was retitled to *Planet of Fear* until it finally became *Vengeance on Varos* for production.

'Sil came about in three stages, really,' explained Martin in 1987. 'When I was thinking about having an alien, I read something of Asimov's which said that you never seemed to see water-based creatures. This is partly because they don't like water in TV studios. You drop it on the floor and the paint, for some reason, immediately blisters. Designers hate it. If he's in water, he's probably an amphibian, he's probably a mutant. The designer came up with that.

'Then we had a real stroke of fortune, in that we had Nabil Shaban, who made the character his own, not only in terms of acting, but in intensity and motivation. He turned it into something wonderful. It's been a delight in the studio watching him work and adding so much to it.'

In Martin's script for episode one of *Vengeance on Varos*, Sil is described as follows:

```
SIL IS SMALL, REPTILIAN, A NATIVE OF THE WATERY WORLD OF
                      THOROS-BETA.

HE IS SUPPORTED IN A WATER TANK BY TWO HUSKY HELMETED
                      BODY SERVANTS.

SIL LIFTS HIS VOICE BOX AND SPEAKS INTO IT WITH A HIGH
SHRILL WHINE THAT IS TRANSLATED (NOT ALWAYS ACCURATELY)
                      INTO ENGLISH
```

For the casting of Sil, director Ron Jones heard about Nabil Shaban through three different sources.

'One was Martin Jarvis' wife,' explained Shaban in 1987. Martin Jarvis had been cast by Jones to play another part in *Vengeance on Varos*. 'She had seen me in a documentary and she knew they hadn't cast Sil yet and she had read the script and told them she knew someone who could play it. Martin had met me in the street once and told me how impressed his wife was with the work I was doing. So he went back to Ron Jones and said:

"My wife thinks Nabil Shaban should play Sil." Then one of the production assistants on *Varos*, who had worked with me on the same documentary, also recommended me to Ron, and one of the assistant floor managers who, although he wasn't working on *Varos* but had worked on other *Doctor Who*s, also recommended me. So finally about three sets of people had told Ron that I should play the part, so he decided that he should see who this Nabil bloke was.'

'Nabil Shaban was exactly right as Sil,' commented Jones. 'I wanted him to appear as slimy as possible, and Nabil gave a lovely performance of the right kind of eye-rolling evil. The voice was designed to be quite sinister as well. Of course, it's very hot in all our monster costumes and after takes Nabil had to be kept cool with face fans.'

The original idea was that Sil would be seen floating in a tank of water, but when this was attempted in the studio, it was realised that it was impracticable. Sil was therefore placed on a supported shelf above the water tank, giving the impression that he carried his water about with him wherever he went.

'One of the problems with the goldfish-bowl idea,' explained Shaban, 'was the reflection of the studio lights. To give the impression of me actually being in the water they could have done double glazing and had water in between the two pieces of glass. It would have looked quite amazing but it was a question of budgets and time, and *Doctor Who* always compromises quite heavily on the original idea.'

During the studio recording for *Vengeance on Varos*, Nabil Shaban had to be kept cool by helpers holding miniature fans to his face.

Because Shaban suffered from an illness called osteogenesis imperfecta, which had resulted in his legs being underdeveloped, the costume created for Sil by visual effects designer Charles Jeanes was able effectively to reflect the amphibious nature of the character. Instead of legs he was given a stubby maggot-like tail into which his real legs would fit, the rest of Shaban's body being concealed within a sculpted latex trunk. The costume was completed with a head mask which revealed Shaban's real face, made up to match the rest of his body. A set of false pointed teeth completed the transformation.

The placing of Sil above the tank of water made it apparent to the audience that the creature really did have no legs (otherwise an able-bodied actor could conceivably have played the character with his legs strapped up or otherwise hidden) and the effect was totally convincing. Despite this unexpected benefit, Shaban was disappointed with the decision not to be inside the tank. 'I was supposed to sit inside this tank and I tried to persuade them to put snakes inside the tank with me, but in the end they didn't use the idea at all as it was supposed to be in the script.'

Sil was an instant hit with the production team and plans were made to feature the character in another story, again written by Martin, in the 23rd season the following year. This was the Ice Warrior story initially called *Planet of Storms* and later *Mission to Magnus*. This story was ultimately abandoned when the BBC put production of *Doctor Who* on hold for a year.

Martin was then commissioned, by way of consolation, to write a segment of the new 23rd season which was being devised as a single 14-part story called *The Trial of a Time Lord*. This segment initially had the working titles *The Planet of Sil* and then *Mindwarp*.

Nabil Shaban returned to play Sil, this time on his home planet of Thoros-Beta, and others from his race were also seen. Sil's costume was updated, being made more comfortable for the actor, and rather than the tank of water, the character was carried around in a futuristic-looking sedan chair. The mask was also changed for something more comfortable, a move that Shaban applauded. 'My headpiece was much more comfortable in *Mindwarp*. The whole process of putting it on took about two hours. The make-up takes about an hour. The first hour was spent trying to glue the head on to myself and then glue the extra frill on to the mask.'

Sil's character also changed somewhat between *Vengeance on Varos* and *The Trial of a Time Lord*. 'Mindwarp is much more tongue-in-cheek because they were very conscious of the need to cut down on the violence,'

Top: The Doctor (Colin Baker) with Sil (Nabil Shaban). *The Trial of a Time Lord*. Bottom: Sil with his two slaves. *The Trial of a Time Lord*.

Top: A specially created skeleton for the Kandy Man, used in his final scene after he has been all but destroyed by boiling candy. *The Happiness Patrol.*
Bottom: A back view of the Kandy Man (David John Pope) showing some of the electronic components installed by Artem. *The Happiness Patrol.*

explained Shaban. 'When I saw the script, the emphasis had shifted to more comedy, but I don't know whether that was a direction, as a viewer of *Doctor Who*, I would necessarily have liked. I preferred – not just as a kid – *Doctor Who* when it was intellectually stimulating but also scary. When I first played Sil I wanted to make him as scary as possible, and when people were writing into *Points of View* complaining about this disgusting monster Sil, I thought I had succeeded because that was exactly what I had wanted to do.'

Sil was one of the success stories of the eighties. *Doctor Who* was always creative in the conception and realisation of the numerous monsters that it has presented over the years. Some, like Sil, are obviously organic and whether the viewer can be persuaded to believe that such a thing could truly exist rests with the combined skills of the writer, designers, director and actor.

All these elements also came together in a story called *The Happiness Patrol*, written by Graeme Curry. The story was commissioned as *The Happiness Patrol* and underwent a title change to *The Crooked Smile* midway through development before the title reverted to the original for production. The story was set on a planet where it was an capital offence to be unhappy. The creature placed in charge of arranging and carrying out the executions was called the Kandy Man and was described in the script as follows:

```
THE KANDY MAN IS HUMANOID BUT NOT HUMAN. HE
  IS ACTUALLY COMPOSED OF SWEET SUBSTANCES
(WITH A ROBOTIC SKELETON, COMPLETELY UNSEEN,
DEEP INSIDE HIS SYNTHETIC BODY). HE IS CHUBBY
  AND JOLLY LOOKING, BUT AT THE SAME TIME
ELEGANT AND SINISTER. THE COLOUR OF HIS SKIN,
  LIPS ETC. SHOULD SUGGEST SWEETS AND SUGAR
 CONFECTIONS RATHER THAN HUMAN FLESH. HE IS
              TALL AND POWERFUL.

HE WEARS A WHITE LAB COAT, A BOW-TIE AND RED
 FRAMED MOVIE STAR GLASSES - THESE AND OTHER
   ARTICLES OF HIS APPAREL (THE PENS IN HIS
       POCKET ETC) ARE ALSO MADE OF CANDY.
```

Because the description suggested an essentially man-like creature with a 'sugary' complexion, it was the story's make-up designer, Dorka Nieradzik, who was given the task of devising the Kandy Man's appearance.

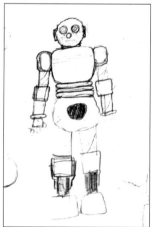

Two design sketches for the Kandy Man. Top: an early sketch by make-up designer Dorka Nieradzik. Bottom: a sketch created by the costume's builder Robert Allsopp while the actual construction of the creature was being planned. *The Happiness Patrol.*

Nieradzik claimed that there was never any question of creating the effect using make-up alone, however. Nathan-Turner and the story's director Chris Clough had always thought in terms of a costume being constructed, as they wanted the character's robotic nature to be readily apparent to viewers.

Nieradzik therefore came up with the idea of the Kandy Man being, quite literally, a 'sweet' robot. In her initial thoughts, she gave him rotating eyes and panels of flashing lights to try to emphasize his mechanical origins, and also metallic teeth. She also decided that there should be a pipe running from his chest to his chin, with red liquid constantly pumping through it as though constantly lubricating the robot's joints. The idea of dressing him in a lab coat was dropped as Nieradzik felt this would obscure too much of the body.

The costume was constructed by Robert Allsopp, a freelance costumier, and an outside effects company called Artem made and installed all the electrical parts. Haynes and Kulp, a dental firm, made a set of metal teeth for the actor to wear.

After preliminary discussions with Nieradzik, Allsopp first put together a prototype version of the costume to establish the shapes and sizes of all the various body sections. This had to take into account space to include Artem's eye mechanics and chest panel lights. There also had to be enough room for a small pump which was used to circulate liquid through the tubing.

Once the prototype had been approved, Allsopp started work on the final costume. This comprised a number of separate elements which clipped together like a suit of armour. The main requirement in the design and construction of all the different pieces was that they should look convincingly like sweets.

The robot's head was covered with hundreds of individual pith balls, arranged in a pattern of concentric circles and sprayed differing shades of blue. The balls were not all the same size but gradually reduced in size towards the centre of the face, which was cast in latex and polyurethane foam to allow the mouth to move freely. There was an early suggestion to include candyfloss hair on top of the head, but this was abandoned.

Left: David John Pope is helped into the Kandy Man costume. Right: The prototype costume created for the Kandy Man by Robert Allsopp. *The Happiness Patrol.*

The main chest section was moulded in fibreglass and given a pattern of red stripes so that it resembled a humbug or boiled sweet. It was then covered in clear plastic sheeting to suggest that the sweet was wrapped.

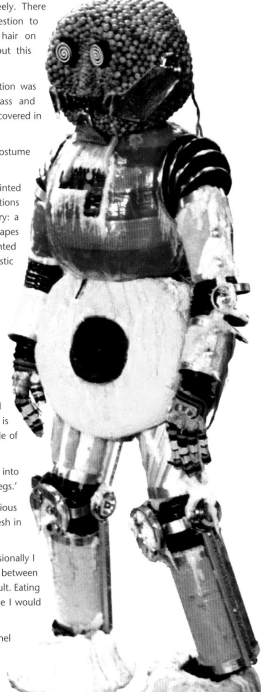

The hip and waist section was made from suitably textured foam rubber, so as to give the costume a little flexibility at this joint, allowing the actor to bend slightly for comfort.

The Kandy Man's arms and legs were made from fibreglass and polypropylene pipes, jointed with flexible aluminium ducting and aluminium strip callipers. The different arm and leg sections were all constructed and treated to suggest different types and colours of confectionery: a striped stick of rock was created by fixing a combination of coloured and clear plastic tapes under a translucent fabric; a barley sugar was made from smooth, polished fibreglass, tinted orange; and a green, sugar-coated jelly was created by covering a base shape with plastic granules which had been run through a coffee grinder to give them a more irregular and crystalline look and then mixed with an iridescent sequin dust to add sparkle.

The marshmallow feet were carefully designed so that, as each one in turn bore the weight of the robot, it squashed up slightly, just as real marshmallow would. This realistic impression was enhanced by the addition of a special 'sugary' coating designed to crack slightly as the foot was compressed.

'A whole part of being a *Doctor Who* monster is wanting to do it,' explained David John Pope, who was cast as the Kandy Man after a chance meeting with Gary Downie, one of *Doctor Who*'s regular Production Assistants. 'I had watched the programme as a child and remember sitting behind the sofa as the Daleks came on. There's another side to it, which is wondering what your friends are going to say when they see you dressed as a man made of sweets. In the end, it was a job but was also great fun.

'The costume was very uncomfortable. The fibreglass tubes on my arms and legs would cut into me and at the end of each day I had bruises on my upper arms, across my chest and on my legs.'

It took 45 minutes to get Pope into the costume before each recording session as the various body sections had to be linked up around him. He saw out through areas of fine wire mesh in the head, just below the rotating eyes.

'I was locked into the costume every day. Once I was in it, I could not get out, but occasionally I took the head off. After two or three days I started insisting that they take the arms off between takes because it was becoming too painful. Going to the toilet was very difficult. Very difficult. Eating was also impossible. I certainly couldn't go to the BBC canteen and have a meal because I would have emptied the place, so food was brought to me.

'At the end of the story the Kandy Man dies by being covered in fondant cream in a tunnel while he is trying to escape and he ends up coming down a chute. Chris Clough, the director, had rigged up a slide for me. I had to climb up a ladder and slide down. Of course when I reached the bottom the costume stopped but I didn't and everything cut into me. After a trial run, I realised that this would happen and I refused to do it. Sylvester McCoy also said that they couldn't ask me to do that.' In the end, the costume was sent down the chute, but without Pope inside.

'It was fun at the time,' Pope said. 'Appearing as a monster was a bit like people being invited on to *The Morecambe and Wise Show*. Everyone always said they didn't want to do it but you got a real buzz if you were asked. It's nice to have done it, and I probably would do it again!'

Earl Sigma (Richard D Sharp), the Doctor (Sylvester McCoy), and Gilbert M (Harold Innocent) with the Kandy Man (David John Pope). *The Happiness Patrol.*

One aspect of the costume that subsequently underwent modification was the hands. Allsopp had supplied specially made, one-piece hands to match the rest of the body, but Nieradzik thought they looked too much like rubber gloves. She therefore decided to use only certain pieces of them, attached directly to the actor's own hands. This allowed for natural movement and bending of the fingers, and although it was more time-consuming – the hands had to be built up from scratch each day and needed constant repair work – the end result was judged to have been worthwhile.

A further modification came when the costume first appeared in the studio. Pope's own mouth was felt to be too prominent and humanoid on the robot's head and so a metallic mouth shield was hastily constructed and fitted to the head to cover it up and direct attention away from it. Certain scenes remain in the transmitted episodes in which this metal shield is not present.

When the story was transmitted, John Nathan-Turner received a letter of complaint from H.B. Stokes, the Chairman and Chief Executive of Bassett Foods PLC. He was concerned that the character of the Kandy Man bore a distinct resemblance to their registered-trademark character Bertie Bassett. Furthermore, he commented that as the Kandy Man had 'a most unsavoury nature', it could lead to a negative effect on the sale of their products. Stokes concluded by asking that a disclaimer related to the similarity of the Kandy Man to their character be made, or that the character be changed to have a promotional effect on confectionery rather than a negative one.

The BBC carried out an internal investigation and were convinced that no attempt had been made to deliberately copy the Bertie Bassett character, and that the only similarity was that they were both made from sweets. The BBC's head of copyright replied to Stokes to this effect and went on to say that the character appeared in only three episodes, had been 'killed' at the conclusion of the story and that there were no plans for it to return.

The Kandy Man had been one of the more ambitious monsters to have appeared in *Doctor Who* and as the eighties drew to a close, so the quality of the creatures featured seemed to improve. There had been a great many advances in technology over the previous decade, and new materials were also available for the designers and sculptors to work with. Using much of this new technology, one of the most impressive beings featured on the show was a demonic creature summoned by the witch Morgaine to devour the Earth during the story *Battlefield*.

Written by Ben Aaronovitch, *Battlefield* began life as a story outline entitled *Storm Over Avallion* which itself was a reworked version of a previously rejected outline called *Nightfall*. In the outline for *Storm Over Avallion*, dated 12 September 1988, the demon is described as 'a tall menacing humanoid figure in black knobbly armour like skin, horns protrude from its body'.

In a later story treatment, dated 20 September 1988, the demon is referred to as a 'Death Elemental' and the description has been simplified to 'a massive humanoid in black spiky armour, (or is that skin).'

The final concept of the Destroyer was of a humanoid character who transformed into a demon towards the end of the story. The descriptions of the creature therefore came at various points in the final scripts. The pertinent pieces which described the creature were as follows:

```
SHADOWS FADE TO REVEAL THE DESTROYER, APPARENTLY AN ORDINARY, RATHER
        ARISTOCRATIC HUMAN MAN, IMPECCABLY DRESSED.

    THE DESTROYER SMILES AND HOLDS UP ITS FREE HANDS.
    THE SKIN ON THEM PEELS BACK TO REVEAL TALONS.

        HORNS ARE GROWING OUT OF THE DESTROYER'S HEAD.
```

Top and Middle: The Doctor (Sylvester McCoy) with the Kandy Man (David John Pope). Bottom: The Kandy Man discovers that his feet have been stuck to the floor with lemonade. *The Happiness Patrol.*

THE DESTROYER

Battlefield (1989) 4 episodes
w. Ben Aaronovitch d. Michael
Kerrigan

When the witch Morgaine sets her
sights on the Earth, it seems that no
one can stop her. No one, that is,
except her old enemy Merlin ...
or the Doctor, as he now seems
to be known.

THE DESTROYER'S CLOTHES BEGIN TO RIP.

ITS CHEST IS EXPANDING.

SCALES CAN BE SEEN IN RENTS IN THE CLOTH.

IT HAS BECOME GIGANTIC, A HUGE CREATURE WITH GLOWING GREEN EYES AND
HIDE LIKE ARMOUR.

ITS FEET AND HANDS ARE TALONED CLAWS

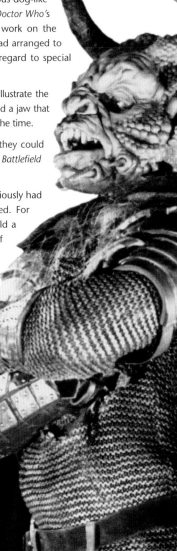

The Destroyer was brought to life by freelance effects designers Susan Moore and Stephen Mansfield.
Normally, the creation of such a creature would be under the jurisdiction of an assigned BBC designer – for
example, costume or visual effects – but, for the Destroyer, Moore and Mansfield were contracted
direct by *Battlefield*'s director, Michael Kerrigan. However, the concept actually originated some
time before that.

Moore and Mansfield had been responsible for some of the more successful and technically
complex effects creations over the previous couple of years. Between them they had created the
alien Chimeron baby that hatched from an egg (in *Delta and the Bannermen*), a vicious dog-like
creature (*The Happiness Patrol*) and the impressive facial meltdown of Kane, one of *Doctor Who's*
evil villains, at the climax to the story *Dragonfire*. They had been contracted to work on the
Haemovores in *The Curse of Fenric* (see chapter 8) for the forthcoming season and had arranged to
talk to the *Doctor Who* production team about several ideas that they'd had with regard to special
make-up and creatures.

'We took with us a number of maquettes [small models], masks and photographs to illustrate the
concepts that we had in mind,' explained Mansfield. 'For example, one of the masks had a jaw that
was built out from the face, showing that you don't have to use the actor's own jaw all the time.

'One of the maquettes was of a demon-like creature and suggested the scope that they could
have with such a character should they require it. It was a happy coincidence that *Battlefield*
featured a demonic entity.

'We sat and talked with John Nathan-Turner for about an hour and a half, and he obviously had
a great deal of interest in the way things were done and what could be achieved. For
example, one of the things we discussed was the problem of not being able to hold a
long close-up shot of a monster, simply because it wouldn't stand up to that kind of
close scrutiny. This is of course quite true. He was also very keen on getting a lot more
movement into the faces of the monsters.'

Moore and Mansfield left some of the maquettes and Polaroid photographs
with Nathan-Turner, and started working on the Haemovores.

'It was when we were completing the Haemovores that we next heard
anything about the Destroyer,' said Moore. 'The director's secretary
phoned us up! This was quite unusual – usually it was one of the
designers. She explained that Michael Kerrigan wanted to talk to us
about doing the Destroyer, so we went up to see him and, together
with the designers from Visual Effects, Costume and Make-up, who
would also be involved, we discussed how the Destroyer might be
realised.'

It was at this point, as with most complex effects work, that the script
was adapted to fit in with what time, money and facilities would allow.
'In the original script,' explained Mansfield, 'the Destroyer started out as an
ordinary guy who transformed into a demon. They had already cast Marek
Anton in the part because he had the ability to sort of scrunch himself up and
then expand himself again as he transformed – that was the original idea.

'About halfway though the meeting they decided to lose the idea of the
transformation and make him appear as a demon from the outset. The only
remaining nod to the original transformation concept is that he pulls a section
of his chest armour off at one point.'

Having arrived at an agreed position of what the Destroyer would do and

Creating the Destroyer: Top Down: the fibreglass under-skull; the unpainted latex mask; the painted latex mask; Stephen Mansfield puts the finishing touches to the head.

how he should appear, it was down to Mansfield and Moore to take the original maquette and turn it into a realistic and believable demon.

'What they essentially wanted was a mask, and they were very keen on keeping the image of the maquette – the traditional idea of a demon,' Mansfield explained. 'We had to change the mouth because the Destroyer has dialogue and wouldn't have been able to talk if the teeth appeared as they were on the maquette. What we tried to do was to give it a bit more character than most run-of-the-mill monsters. The Destroyer is supposed to be a very distinguished, proud-looking creature, which is one of the things they asked for.

'The head was modelled in clay, to get the proportions correct, then split up into sections – the horns, the ears and so on – for moulding. The mould was made by a chap called Mick Hockney. Then foam latex was pumped into it to make the mask.

'Because the mask was quite a way from the actor's head, we had to work out a method to get the eyes and the jaw, which are probably the most important areas, properly aligned. We used a fibreglass under-skull for the mask and then another under-skull which would fit on the actor's head. These were put one on top of the other, aligned and then stuck together with a fibreglass paste. This made it comfortable to wear as well as providing a strong base for the two main horns.'

Because of the pressure of time to complete the Destroyer, Mansfield called upon the services of Robert Allsopp to construct the two large, curling horns that crown the Destroyer's head. 'As the horns had to be very light,' explained Allsopp, 'I decided against using fibreglass on them. I eventually decided to use a kind of orthopaedic bandage which comes from Belgium. It's very lightweight, durable and doesn't need a negative mould.

'The horns were worked directly over the clay, just by wrapping the bandages around it. The bandages are hard to start with, but you soften them by applying heat, for example from a hairdryer. Once you've finished modelling, they cool down and harden again in the desired shape.

'Once they had been modelled and hardened, I split the horns to remove the clay and then resealed them before painting them black.'

To give the Destroyer more character and to provide the facial movements, Mansfield installed a cable control system for the face. 'The cable system operated his snarling top and bottom lips and a raising brow,' he said, 'which we tended to work backwards – in other words, we kept it raised and then lowered it when he frowned. We made sure that every time he talked we kept a rippling motion going on the mouth to give the impression of speech.

'All the cabling was hidden behind the cloak, which is why the Destroyer wears one!'

The Destroyer appears for only a brief time before he is himself destroyed, exploding in a climactic battle with

The Destroyer [Marek Anton]. Battlefield.

the Brigadier. This was another reason why the horns needed to be as light and yet as strong as possible: if they had been brittle, they would have shattered upon impact with the ground, something real horns would never do. In the event, the bandage horns just bounced around harmlessly.

The Destroyer's exploding head was made from wax, and several replicas were produced to allow for possible retakes. In fact, the destruction was recorded twice – once in the studio and then again at the Visual Effects Department's workshops. 'We had to take a latex cast from the mould that produced the actual head,' explained Moore. 'Then, from that latex version, we took a silicone multi-piece mould. That was next used to lay up four wax duplicates (a process painstakingly carried out by Tony Clark). The completed heads were assembled and then reinforced with fibreglass around the neck and in some other places so that the head would hold together. Finally, they were painted to match the real Destroyer's head.'

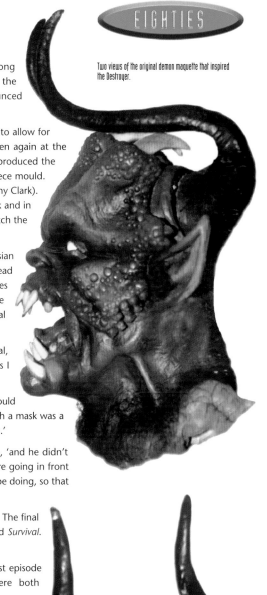

Two views of the original demon maquette that inspired the Destroyer.

Marek Anton was already appearing in *The Curse of Fenric* that same year, playing a Russian soldier. In a 1990 interview, he recalled playing the Destroyer. 'They made a cast from my head and they moulded it to my face,' he explained. 'I could do quite a bit if I stretched my muscles and things. They were my own eyes and by extending my jaw I would feel the side of the mask and move it around to move the mouth. I exaggerated my mouth and vocal movements. It was very tight though, not so much the mask but the scalp piece.

'I couldn't really see much either. I was carrying around fifteen-inch horns, masses of metal, medieval shoes and chains – I could hardly walk! I couldn't look down because as soon as I did, wires fell out of my head.'

Anton told another journalist in 1989: 'I enjoyed the Destroyer because it was the first time I could be something bigger than myself and show strength in an awesome character. Working with a mask was a very new experience for me which I did enjoy although it was excruciatingly painful at times.'

'Marek was in the costume for up to two and a half hours at a time,' commented Moore, 'and he didn't complain at all. He would stand in front of a mirror and really get into the character before going in front of the cameras. He also discussed with us, as we were operating the mask, what he would be doing, so that the facial expressions could be made to match. He was great.'

Battlefield was the first story in the 26th and final season of *Doctor Who* on BBC television. The final story to be transmitted (although it was actually made as the penultimate story) was called *Survival*. It was written by Rona Munro and featured a race of cat-like Cheetah People.

Survival had started life as an outline initially called *Blood-Hunt*, and then *Cat Flap*. The first episode was commissioned on 16 November 1988 and the remaining two episodes were both commissioned on 11 January 1989.

The Cheetah People were described in the scripts as follows:

```
THE CHEETAH PERSON IS HUMANOID IN SHAPE, ITS EXPOSED BODY IS
COVERED IN LIGHT GOLDEN FUR WITH IRREGULAR BLACK SPOTS, BOTH ITS
   HANDS AND ITS FEET WHICH ARE EXPOSED HAVE LONG JOINTS AND LONG
                              CLAWS.

THE CHEETAH PERSON IS WEARING CLOTHING IN THE FORM OF THE SKINS
  OF A VARIETY OF OTHER ANIMALS, BIRDS FEATHERS, TEETH AND BONES
    ARE HUNG AROUND IT AND THE HORSE LIKE TROPHIES. ITS HEAD IS
   AGAIN HALF HUMAN HALF CAT WITH CAT'S EARS AND WHISKERS. IT HAS A
                 DARK BLAZE OF FUR ON ITS FACE.
```

Their creation was the responsibility of the Make-up and Costume Departments, with Visual Effects providing special props as required.

In charge of Make-up was Joan Stribling. 'There were eight Cheetah People and we had to take face casts of each of the eight actors and actresses that were playing them,' she explained. 'The Cheetah faces were then sculpted and casts made of them. The main part of the prosthetic was made out of airbrushed cold-foam with hair attached. From the nose back, they are overhead masks, but for above the lip we used a hot-foam prosthetic piece to enable them to open their mouths and snarl.'

Hair was stuck on to the actors' cheekbones to give their faces a triangular cheetah shape; contact lenses and teeth then completed the transformation. Malcolm James, handling the visual effects for the story, created a prop cheetah paw with retractable

Top Down: A Cheetah Person; costume assistant Sara Wilkinson makes last-minute adjustments to one of the costumes; one of the Cheetah People on horseback at Warmwell Quarry; a mounted Cheetah arrives in Perivale. *Survival*.

claws operated by a cable-control mechanism. 'One of the shots was of a rope pulled across a pathway,' he said, 'and one of the Cheetahs comes along the path on horseback and sees it. It then stretches out its paw and cuts the rope with its claws. We wanted the claws to spring out and snip the rope. There was another shot with the Cheetah's claws raised up in front of its head and body in a fairly threatening, aggressive pose and we used the same prop for that sequence as well.'

The leading Cheetah Person, Karra, was played by Lisa Bowerman. 'I had a make-up test, and I knew I had to wear contact lenses and dentures, and the head-cast, they said, was just for other bits that were going to be stuck on. I wasn't quite fully aware of how much glue I was going to have on my face until the final make-up test, which took three-and-a-half hours. Eventually, they managed to get it down to a shorter time but there were a lot of problems – for example the glue they were using didn't stick because the weather was so hot.'

The heat was one of the main problems for the artistes playing the Cheetah People. Outside-broadcast recording took place in Warmwell Quarry in Dorset during a heatwave over the summer of 1989. Temperatures were well over 100 degrees and the Cheetah costumes had been made from fur and latex that covered the artiste's bodies completely.

'We were in a quarry and there was a lot of dust flying around,' recalled Bowerman. 'In addition, the make-up consisted in part of little bits of "fun fur" that were stuck to our faces. These used to work their way up into our eyes and once you've been put on standby and have put the lenses in, and then told that they don't need you yet and taken them out – after a few times, your eyes become quite painful and you also end up suffering from heat exhaustion. I found that the best thing was just to do nothing. To sit back and do absolutely nothing because if you got agitated about it then it became ridiculous and unbearable.

'On one particularly hot day, we were hanging around for hours and this girl, who was playing one of the Cheetah People, just decided she had had enough. She ripped the make-up off her face and walked off home. I couldn't blame her, really.'

Bowerman also recalls that the hands were made from gardening gloves. 'Originally our hands and arms were encased in fur – it was literally a complete catsuit – and they had spent ages working out how to make paws and they had these lovely pads made out of latex. But we had to ride horses and when we got up on them and picked up the reins, on a hot sunny day, the hands just shredded. The result was a very practical solution – gardening gloves.'

The Cheetahs in *Survival* were the last race of monsters encountered by the Doctor before *Doctor Who* was cancelled by the BBC. The final season had showcased several superb examples of the creativity and imagination which *Doctor Who* viewers had come to expect. From the blue-faced demonic horror of the Destroyer to the feline Cheetahs, the Doctor had fought and won out against them all.

There was one further 'classic' monster which appeared in this final season. Harking back to the vampire myths of old, *Doctor Who* presented a tale of death and power, of creatures from beneath the sea and of an enemy as old as time. The Haemovores marked a welcome return to the terrifying *Doctor Who* monsters of old.

CHEETAH PEOPLE

Survival (1989) 3 episodes
w. Rona Munro d. Alan Wareing

Returning to Earth, the Doctor discovers that all of Ace's old friends have mysteriously vanished. The cause is the Master, himself trapped on a distant planet, who is trying to lure the Doctor there so that he might escape.

CHARACTER

The Cheetah People are vicious, cunning and dangerous beings, loving to run, fight and feed. They track their human prey on horses, and play with them before moving in for the kill.

The worst thing that potential prey can do is to run, for the Cheetahs will attack in seconds. Standing still and calm is perhaps the only defence. Unfortunately, it's hard to stand still when a pack of snarling cat-people are inches away from your face.

The planet from which they come has strange powers. It can 'infect' others who visit with the spirit and nature of the Cheetahs, first turning their eyes into those of the big cat, and then their minds and bodies. In this way it entraps those who are unwary enough to venture there.

The planet is also in its last days of existence, with volcanoes and earthquakes ripping it apart. Unless the Cheetahs can find a way off-world, their race will die out.

Top: Ken Trew's original costume design for the Cheetah People. Bottom: Actress Lisa Bowerman (Karra) attempts to eat through her Cheetah make-up.

CHAPTER 8

THE HAEMOVORES

The effect I hope we achieved was that this creature had almost built itself a breathing apparatus which was incorporated into its own flesh, and the body had actually been stripped of skin.

COSTUME DESIGNER KEN TREW ON THE ANCIENT HAEMOVORE

The Haemovores were the creation of writer Ian Briggs and made their one and only appearance in the story *The Curse of Fenric*, transmitted as a part of the 26th season.

The Curse of Fenric was originally titled *Wolf Time* and the scripts were commissioned on 9 November 1988. The story underwent a title change to *The Wolves of Fenric* for production before *The Curse of Fenric* was settled upon as the final title.

Briggs' inspiration for the story had come out of vampire legends and from Viking mythology. The Haemovores were human beings who had been somehow converted into bloodsucking monsters and were, according to the scripts, the destiny of humanity. They appeared in numerous forms, and the oldest and most impressive of them was a creature called the Ancient One.

In the scripts for the story, this creature was described as follows:

```
THE ANCIENT HAEMOVORE IS MORE MONSTROUS THAN ANY OF THE OTHERS. IT WEARS A KIND OF
```

APPEARANCES

The Curse of Fenric (1989) 4 episodes
w. Ian Briggs d. Nicholas Mallett

The Doctor and Ace arrive at an army base towards the end of World War Two. The Doctor suspects that he has been manipulated by his old enemy Fenric, and when bloodsucking Haemovores emerge from the sea, his suspicions are confirmed.

CHAIN MAIL MADE FROM SMALL METAL OBJECTS OF THE LAST 1200 YEARS, WELDED
TOGETHER WITH CORAL.

Two views of the Ancient One's mask under construction

The task of designing the Ancient One fell to costume designer Ken Trew. Trew completed some design sketches of the Ancient Haemovore's head and then contacted freelance effects artist Susan Moore to talk about building that part of the creature.

At that time, it was assumed that make-up designer Dee Baron would handle the rest of the Haemovores and Trew realised that it would be sensible if the people involved in building the Ancient One were also involved with the 'standard' Haemovores in order to maintain consistency. Therefore Trew and Baron, together with Moore, her colleague Stephen Mansfield and Robert Allsopp (whom Trew had contracted to build the costume for the Ancient Haemovore), got together for the first of many meetings and discussions to work out how best to realise this race of creatures.

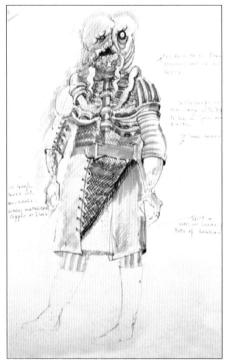

Costume Designer Ken Trew's design for the Ancient One.

'I had meetings with John [Nathan-Turner] and Nick [Mallett, the story's director] to work out what he, she or it should look like,' said Trew. 'Because there were a lot of Viking influences in the story, I initially tried doing something like the prow of a dragonship and then I started looking at Viking armour. Neither of these ideas seemed to work. Finally, I thought about vampires and blood. There was a line in the script about sucking blood and, without being obvious and using the Hammer vampire fangs, I wondered how you could get blood out of a person. I immediately thought of something along the lines of a leech. Then I considered that a leech only has one sucker so what about using something like an octopus arm? The concept carried on from there.

'I drew the head and misshaped it, working out how big it should be and what parts ought to be movable. I built in the gills and the suckers around the mouth and, because it was more developed than all the others, I put suckers all over the place. Then I considered how this mutated human figure would support its head and came up with the idea of the spine coming up out through the back of the head.

'The basic idea for the costume was of all the old rubbish that the Ancient One had collected from the bottom of the sea, all encrusted on him with barnacles. There were pieces that went over the shoulders and came out of the chest, like extensions of the lungs which actually went into a man-made bit at the back. There was a tube at the back and the ribcage was built out. The effect I hope we achieved was that this creature had almost built itself a breathing apparatus which was incorporated into its own flesh, and the body had actually been stripped of skin. By the time I'd finished it I thought "You've got a very nasty mind Ken Trew!"'

The design drawings were then passed to Moore, Mansfield and Allsopp to start working on the creation of the creature. Starting with the head, Moore takes up the story.

'I roughly assembled it in clay over a building-site helmet, because the mask was worn like a helmet (the actor looked out through the neck and the eyes were actually above his head). With the ordinary Haemovores, we were using actual face casts to work from and so the final masks had some character and expression; but with the Ancient Haemovore, although we had a face cast of the actor, we were faced with a shapeless lump of clay. Steve and I therefore worked it out between us to give it some character. It was a bit of a struggle but I think it worked.

'We also worked out, if this conversion from Human to Haemovore was some sort of infection, how it would spread. We decided it would go through the blood system, which is why all the veins on the head became swollen, started bursting out, became tentacles which then finally became the main ridgy bit down his back and also the tentacles which burst out the side and joined up round the back. All the Haemovores were worked to this idea, and the two closest to the Ancient Haemovore have embryonic bits of tentacle coming through their skin.'

The clay bust for the Ancient One.

Mansfield elaborates on the ideas by explaining that 'the skin is all sort of pushed away – it has become unimportant but it's still there. Similar to the Elephant Man, which was the sort of thing we were aiming for. We didn't want it to look like an alien creature: it had to look as human as possible. And Ken had a lot of that in his drawing, which was of great help.

'To operate the head, a simple air-controlled system was installed. One air line operated the eye-blink and the other worked the gill movement. The controls were worked by Ken's assistant, Andrew Duckett, who timed it from the script so that the eyes would blink normally in time with the dialogue. The mouth was attached separately via a harness to the actor's jaw so that it would move when the actor spoke the lines.'

Colour is always an important consideration and Moore explained how the colour schemes were worked out for the Haemovores. 'We chose blue around the mouth basically because we didn't want to use green. Everything that comes out of the sea is green these days, and blue is the nearest you can get to a deathlike pallor, tying in with the vampires idea. As in the past, we couldn't use oranges or reds because that suggests blood, which was taboo on *Doctor Who*, so it really only left blues, greys and whites. I would have liked greys and whites like a shark, but that wouldn't have been very effective on the screen and, taking into account that the masks had bone elements in them, it could have ended up looking like a polar bear walking up from the sea. Blue is an unusual colour and it registers well against flesh. It gave a drowned, *Evil Dead* sort of effect, which I quite liked.'

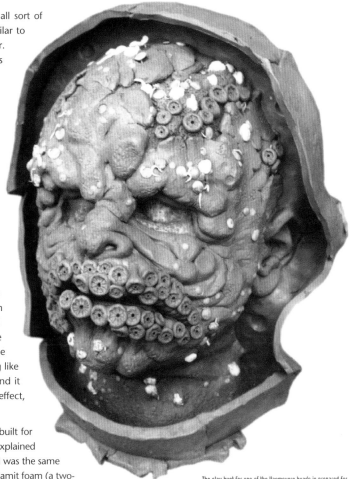

The clay bust for one of the Haemovore heads is prepared for moulding. Note the live seeds embedded in the clay.

As well as the head containing the air controls, a second head was built for the scene where the Ancient One emerges from the sea. Mansfield explained the difference from the construction point of view. 'The second head was the same as the first but without the mechanics and it was made out of solid foamit foam (a two-part chemical foam that expands when the chemicals are mixed together) rather than fibreglass, which would have resulted in a large air pocket inside. The mechanical one wouldn't actually sink but the water would soak into the foamit foam head and make it easier to keep underwater.'

Despite the construction of a second head, there were still problems in keeping it underwater, as Trew recalled. 'The only thing that operated on the second head was the jaw – that was the way it was built – but the jaw didn't have any drainage holes in so it sort of floated off. We had a bit of panic on the morning we used that, drilling holes under the jaw and through the top of the head so that the water would flow in and out easily. When he rose up out of the water on the screen, I thought it looked wonderful.'

The construction of the head was only one part of the process in creating the Ancient Haemovore. The costume had to be consistent with the concepts and designs worked out for the whole creature. 'Ken had done some superb drawings with a back view and everything, and then he and I had a look round the costume store to see what we could use on it,' explained Allsopp. 'This was both to save time, and also because the costume was meant to look as if it had been put together from other bits and pieces over the centuries.

'Using Sue and Steve's work on the other heads as a guide to texture and colour, I worked out the skin pieces that would show through the costume. I started by making a kind of vest in a stretch fabric for the body and then applied cast sections of latex to that, which had rib shapes and suckers moulded in. I moulded one set of ribs and a sheet of suckers about a foot square and then combined them to give the required effect. I interpreted the strange fleshy tubes that run over the shoulders and go into the mechanical bit at the back as being that he probably altered his body to enable him to be amphibian. I assumed that he constructed a kind of breathing apparatus which was part organic and part mechanical and that what used to be his lungs had grown into this external filter.

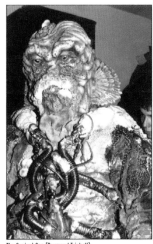

The Ancient One (Raymond Trickett).

'The vest piece stopped just below the waist and under that he wore very full baggy leather trousers that tucked into the top of boots that came to just below the knee. To give the idea of the creature growing and evolving over the centuries I made his toes burst through the ends of the boots and also fins growing from the back of the boots. He had an adjustable belt from which a variety of things hung. For these I tried to use as many different textures as possible: chain mail, scale armour and various bones, shells and bits of seaweed. There was also a kind of Viking belt buckle that was made from some small reproduction Celtic brooches that

I cut up and reworked into the buckle. I used metal plates and all sorts of bits and pieces hanging down off the belt. Part of an air-force breathing mask was used, various tubes were heated and then twisted, distorted and burnt and then had a plastic mesh tubing over the top to give them a layered look.

The Haemovores attack!

'Moving up to the shoulders, the left pauldron [shoulder plate] piece was a fibreglass cast of a horseshoe crab shell which then was combined with some bits of metal armour from the stores and also some real chain mail to again give the organic/metallic combination. The sleeves of the costume also had latex pieces where the body showed through and I made some wristbands to cover the joins at the end of the arms.

'I wanted the back part of the breathing apparatus to look like ship fittings so there's a little plaque on it saying "*HMS Hercules*" or something, as well as various bits of tubing and taps and things.

'Having got all the components together and worked out where all the fittings and clasps would be and how the actor would get into and out of it, I used the same paint techniques as used on the head for the body. Once it had been painted, I modelled up some barnacles in plastic filler and added lots of these all over the costume so it was all encrusted as though it had been in the sea for centuries. Finally the whole costume was worked with sprays and coloured lacquers to simulate the effect of rust and time on all the materials.

'It took about two weeks solid to get the thing together, with two fittings during that time to check that it would all fit together and match with the head and hands.'

Because the costume was fairly complex for the actor to wear, Allsopp was present on location for when it emerged from the sea, and as a last-minute addition, he and Andrew Duckett used seaweed collected off the beach to adorn the creature as it made its impressive entrance into our world.

As well as the Ancient One, *The Curse of Fenric* also featured his minions, the standard Haemovores. According to the script, these creatures appeared as follows:

AN ARMY RISING FROM THE SEA. THE HAEMOVORES' LEGS ARE ALL ADORNED WITH STRANGE METAL OBJECTS – SMALL PIECES OF METALWORK FROM DIFFERENT AGES IN THE LAST THOUSAND YEARS, SEEMINGLY WELDED TOGETHER WITH CORAL.

Later on, the following, longer description appeared:

THEY ARE IN VARYING STAGES OF DEGENERATION FROM HUMANS TO HAEMOVORES.

THE COMPLETE HAEMOVORES ARE LIKE HUMAN LEECHES, WITH A LARGE SUCKER REPLACING THEIR

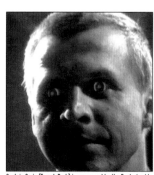

Captain Sorin (Tomek Bork) is possessed by the Doctor's old enemy, Fenric.

MOUTH, AND THEIR EYES CLOSED AND BULBOUS LIKE A FOETUS'S.

THE MORE RECENT HUMANS STILL WEAR TATTERED CLOTHES, FROM THE PREVIOUS HUNDRED YEARS OR SO. THE COMPLETE HAEMOVORES JUST HAVE SCRAPS OF RAGS HANGING OFF THEM. THEY ALL WEAR LIGHT STRINGS OF THE STRANGE METALLIC OBJECTS – METAL ARTEFACTS FROM THE LAST THOUSAND YEARS, WELDED TOGETHER LIKE CORAL.

The basic concepts for these creatures were worked out by all the main parties concerned. The BBC Visual Effects Department had initially come up with a concept based around a white leech-like creature which was to be operated as a puppet, but this was not used. One of the main problems facing the design team was that the costumes and make-up had to be used underwater.

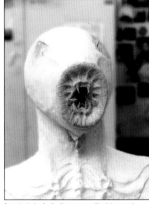
An early design for the Haemovores, ultimately unused.

Make-up designer Dee Baron explained that she knew from the start that this requirement would cause

difficulties. 'The Ancient One wasn't so much of a problem, as the actor's head was going to be completely encased and the mask was going to be quite heavy. But with the other Haemovores the problem was going to be keeping the prosthetics on in the water. What we decided to do was to make all the masks come around the back of the head. If you put on a section that only covered the face and not the back of the head then the likelihood of it coming off in the water was going to be very great.'

'It was the same thing with the costumes,' explained Trew. 'Most of the necks came up really high because the prosthetic pieces could then be anchored under them.'

'That's where we worked together very closely to make sure that we didn't cause any problems for each other,' confirmed Baron. 'We helped each other solve problems.

'On screen, the Haemovores don't appear that much, but we were using the masks over at least ten different days. To apply prosthetics properly you really need a new piece every time the make-up is redone but we didn't have the budget for that.

The Haemovores, mutated creatures from Earth's future.

As a result the pieces had to be strong and substantial so they would last for the duration of our filming.'

'What we worked out,' clarified Moore, 'was that we would use overhead masks, half-masks and quarter-masks. We decided to hold these masks on with elastic, which, when disguised, works fabulously, and Dee used latex-covered wigs to hide it.'

During the modelling of the masks, an interesting effect was achieved quite simply, as Mansfield remembered. 'We used little seeds, like lentils, in the clay to give texture and they started to sprout. This wasn't deliberate at all and the mask sort of modelled itself giving a rather good effect. We kept them all on because it looked good, like little tentacles.'

The half- and quarter-masks were made in latex and foamit foam while the final two were simply latex pull over head masks.

Each type of mask would give the actor a different 'look' or stage in their degeneration into a full Haemovore. These 'looks' were all devised in advance, as Trew explained. 'We worked the Haemovores out in periods. And by the time we got to Lulworth Cove for the location recording we had christened every one of them. They all had names. There were two Vikings (the Grace Brothers), a Victorian lady with a mop cap (Mrs Bridges), a twenties lady (Mary Quant) – I forget who the two Edwardian fishermen were – and a

Top: Designer Ken Trew is surrounded by his creations. Centre: Make-Up designer Dee Baron checks a Haemovore on location. Bottom: A Haemovore is prepared for bullet hits by two Visual Effects assistants.

Top: The Haemovores emerge from the sea. Bottom: Summoned by the Haemovores, the Ancient One is revealed.

First World War sailor (Popeye). All of the costumes were taken from BBC stock and then "dirtied down".'

'Once the actors and actresses were in these costumes there was no way of identifying them,' Baron added, 'so we used to talk to each other about Popeye and Mrs Bridges. It was terribly helpful when we filmed them emerging from the water. For instance they were using stones to weigh themselves down, so you would hear "Give Mrs Bridges another brick".'

After the colour schemes had been worked out, leather shoe sprays were used to colour the masks. 'I think it would have been better if we'd airbrushed them using acrylic paint,' said Moore. 'But as it had to be done quickly we used leather sprays with washes of acrylic on top of that. Another reason for using them was that it would be easier for Dee to retouch the colour on location if we used standard tints. Dee ordered a set of the same colours that we had, and I know she used them at one location as there were little Haemovore-shaped patches on the pavement! There were four colours that we used: an olive green, a dark blue, a light blue and a pink. The acrylic wash was dark blue and I rubbed that in all over to give the masks a pallid look.

'It was a very straightforward job in many ways because it used tried-and-tested techniques. There was nothing new involved, but there was an awful lot of it. For example, we had fifteen pairs of arms to prepare.'

Jean (Joann Kenny) and Phyllis (Joanne Bell) are transformed into vampire creatures.

'That again was a combined effort,' says Trew. 'We worked out these long gloves, and Dee arranged for the nails to be made to be added to the gloves.'

Baron commented that initially they were thinking of having metal nails, but Nathan-Turner thought that would be too like Freddy Krueger in the *Nightmare on Elm Street* films and so they were changed to ordinary nails.

The Haemovores worked well on screen and the story itself contained moments which echoed similar situations earlier in *Doctor Who*'s history, when both the Sea Devils and Marshmen emerged from the water to threaten the Doctor and his companions. Although the Haemovores did not speak aside from a few lines of dialogue given to the Ancient One, they dominated the story. Many scenes are reminiscent of the John Carpenter film *The Fog*, especially when the Haemovores attack a church wherein the Doctor, Ace and the local vicar are hiding.

The Curse of Fenric was the penultimate *Doctor Who* story to be transmitted. Despite the show's cancellation at the conclusion of the season, it seemed that *Doctor Who* had once again found its roots, and the presentation of new and original monsters was once more the way forward. Who knows what horrors the Doctor may have gone on to face had the show been allowed to continue?

Raymond Trickett in partial costume as the Ancient One.

CHAPTER 9

DALEKS & DAVROS

Being a real aficionado of science fiction, I hated stories which used bug-eyed monsters, otherwise known as BEMs. I wrote in my memo that there would be no *bug-eyed monsters in* **Doctor Who.**

CREATOR OF *DOCTOR WHO*, SYDNEY NEWMAN, SPEAKING IN 1988.

If the ban on bug-eyed monsters imposed by the BBC's Head of Drama had actually been observed back in 1963 then *Doctor Who* may not have lasted past its initial allocation of 52 episodes.

It was mid-1963 and comedy writer Terry Nation was on tour with Tony Hancock. Nation had been one of the main writers to salvage Hancock's ATV series in 1962, and Hancock liked to have him around while they were on tour even though by this time Hancock was not using any of Nation's material. Nation found himself effectively acting as a 'minder' for Hancock as they toured.

'We were working in a theatre in Nottingham that week,' he explained in 1989, 'and my agent called from London and said, "The BBC wants you to do a thing called *Doctor Who*. It's for the children's television slot, science fiction," and I said, "How dare they? I don't do things like that" But I'd been asked because of this *Out of this World* story.'

Nation had written one episode for this ABC series (*Botany Bay*) and had adapted two others (*Imposter* from a story by Philip K. Dick and *Immigrant* from a story by Clifford Simak) and this had brought him to the

APPEARANCES

The Mutants (1963-4) a.k.a. *The Daleks*
7 episodes
w. Terry Nation d. Christopher Barry
(1, 2, 4, 5), Richard Martin (3, 6, 7)

Arriving on the apparently dead planet of Skaro, the Doctor and his friends help the peaceful Thals to defeat the ruthless Daleks who intend to wipe out all life on the planet.

The Dalek Invasion of Earth (1964)
6 episodes
w. Terry Nation d. Richard Martin

The Doctor arrives on Earth in the future to find that the Daleks have invaded. He helps the human resistance fighters foil the Daleks' plan to mine the core of the planet.

The Space Museum (1965) 4 episodes
w. Glyn Jones d. Mervyn Pinfield

On the planet Xeros, in a museum of the Moroks' conquests, can be seen a lone Dalek casing. ➡

attention of Sidney Newman who was at that time – mid-1962 – the Head of Drama at ABC.

'Well, this particular night,' continued Nation, 'Tony and I had a big dispute. I wanted him to try some new material, and he wouldn't do it. We had a fight, and I'm not sure if I was fired or walked out, but the result was that I was on a train back to London thinking, "Hey, wait a minute! I'm out of work!"

'When I got back to London, I called my agent, and said, "If you haven't turned down that BBC thing, I'll go and talk to them."'

The result of this discussion with the BBC was that Nation was commissioned by *Doctor Who's* story editor David Whitaker to write a storyline called *The Survivors*.

This introduced the Daleks, a race of radiation-mutated creatures forced to live inside travel machines which were themselves limited to movement within a metal city, as they were powered by static electricity picked up through contact with the floor.

In his outline, Nation was vague about what these Dalek creatures looked like. There was a line which described one of the Doctor's travelling companions, Barbara, being grabbed 'by a pair of grotesque arms' and when the Doctor, together with his companions Ian and Susan, met the creatures for the first time, 'terrifying machine-like creatures' was all the description given. But later on the following description appeared: 'The "eye" of the suit is a television lens on a flexible shaft. The suit has no legs, the base being mechanised for movement.'

Nation has gone on record as saying that he always wanted to get away from the 'man in a suit' look that dogged film and television in the fifties whenever an alien creature was called for. 'My first requirement was to take the legs off,' he said. 'Further inspiration came from the Georgian State Ballet, the Russian dance troupe which was performing in London at the time. There was a dance that the women did where they wore floor-brushing skirts, and evidently took tiny steps, so they appeared to glide across the stage. There was no suggestion of what form of locomotion they were using. That's what I wanted for the Daleks.'

On the strength of the storyline Nation was initially commissioned by Whitaker on 31 July 1963 to write a six-part story. This allocation was increased to seven episodes about a week later when it became apparent that the story would work better in that format. As production work began, so a director was assigned. This was Richard Martin, fresh off the BBC's internal directors' course. To help him handle the complexities of working on the show, another, more experienced, director, Christopher Barry, was assigned to assist.

'Everyone asks me about the Daleks and who thought up their shape,' said Barry. 'Well, this is a tricky one to answer because, with hindsight, everything gels into what they actually turned out looking like. I do remember thinking, from what it said in the scripts, that it was an impossible thing to create. However, between Richard Martin, the designer Ray Cusick and myself, with the help of the backs of quite a few envelopes, we came up with some ideas. Of course it was Ray who made it all work and came up with the final design, but as with most television production, it was a cooperative effort. Ray must take the final credit for building the thing though.'

'I think the look of the Daleks was totally Ray Cusick,' asserted Richard Martin in 1995. 'Ray was very angry that he didn't get any recognition. That look was brilliant, and the casters were just about good enough in the studio. We all chipped in on the design. I asked, why two mechanical arms? I thought one should surely be a power tool and weapon when needed, and the other a multiple grabbing device.'

The Chase (1965) 6 episodes
w. Terry Nation d. Richard Martin

The Daleks track the TARDIS to the planet Aridius and from there chase the Doctor across time and space intending to kill him.

Dalek Cutaway (1965) 1 episode
w. Terry Nation d. Derek Martinus

On the planet Kembel, Space Security Service agent Marc Cory uncovers a Dalek plot to invade the solar system.

The Daleks' Master Plan (1965-6) 12 episodes
w. Terry Nation (1-5, 7),
Dennis Spooner (6, 8-12)
d. Douglas Camfield

The Doctor becomes involved in the Daleks' plot to invade the solar system and tries to prevent them from obtaining a vital component for their time destructor weapon, which is eventually turned on the Daleks themselves.

The Power of the Daleks (1966) 6 episodes
w. David Whitaker (and Dennis Spooner)
d. Christopher Barry

A newly regenerated Doctor arrives on the planet Vulcan and poses as an investigator to learn the truth about a buried capsule containing Daleks that has been discovered.

The Evil of the Daleks (1967) 7 episodes
w. David Whitaker d. Derek Martinus (1-7), Timothy Combe (7)

The Daleks kidnap the Doctor in order to help them discover the 'Dalek Factor' – the impulse to destroy – which they intend to spread across all time and space. ➡

Creator and creation. Terry Nation with a Dalek.

Raymond P. Cusick was one of a team of designers working at the BBC at that time, and he had been assigned to work on *Doctor Who* after the original designer selected for the story, a man by the name of

Ridley Scott, was unavailable for all the required dates. Scott went on to become a respected and influential film director with works such as *Alien* and *Thelma and Louise* to his credit.

Cusick recalls: 'When the idea of *Doctor Who* was put forward, Jack Kine, who was then in charge of the Visual Effects Department, wanted three new visual effects designers to take on the show but he was not allowed to recruit more staff. As a result of this he didn't want his department to have anything to do with it. He put the whole thing out to contract, to Shawcraft Models, who were based in Uxbridge and run by Bill Roberts. Kine's assistant, Bernard Wilkie, was more helpful. I used to go and ask his advice on bangs and explosions, how we could do that sort of thing.

'Although Barry Newbery and I were booked to design the sets, we also ended up designing the visual effects and all the props, so we had twice the amount of work. It was just too much, and a third designer called John Wood was eventually brought in to ease the load.'

The Daleks in their city on Skaro. The Mutants (a.k.a. The Daleks).

By the time production started on Nation's story, it had been assigned the overall title *The Mutants*. In his final script for the second episode of *The Mutants*, called *The Survivors*, Nation described the Daleks as follows:

```
FOUR HIDEOUS MACHINE-LIKE CREATURES. THEY ARE LEGLESS, MOVING ON A ROUND BASE.

THEY HAVE NO HUMAN FEATURES.

A LENS ON A FLEXIBLE SHAFT ACTS AS AN EYE.

ARMS WITH MECHANICAL GRIPS FOR HANDS.

THE CREATURES HOLD STRANGE WEAPONS IN THEIR HANDS.

ONE OF THEM GLIDES FORWARD. IT SPEAKS WITH AN ECHOING METALLIC VOICE.
```

From these descriptions, and in discussion with Christopher Barry, the basic idea of the Dalek was mapped out. Cusick provided numerous design sketches and drawings, which were then used as the basis for further discussion with Bill Roberts.

Mervyn Pinfield was *Doctor Who*'s Associate Producer and he had some ideas of his own about how the Daleks should look. 'When we were discussing the Daleks,' recalled Cusick, 'Mervyn was saying that he was worried about the cost. "What if we got some cardboard tubes and sprayed them silver?" he said, and of course the last thing I wanted was a man in a robot suit. One of my childhood memories is going to an exhibition at Earl's Court and seeing a robot in the entrance. It seemed very big, but I was small, and it was a huge man-like thing with bulbs in its eyes that flashed. The last thing I wanted was for the Dalek to look humanoid in any way. But that was how Mervyn was thinking of them. Although our budget was tiny, I thought that we could stretch it to make the Daleks work.

'My desire to make the Dalek look completely unlike a man in a suit was the reason that the operator ended up sitting down because I wanted to make them smaller than average human size. The original Daleks were about five feet high.'

Cusick actually started from the basis of a man sitting in a chair. One of his initial designs shows just this, with a shell drawn around the seated figure to completely enclose it. Once the designs had been agreed, the

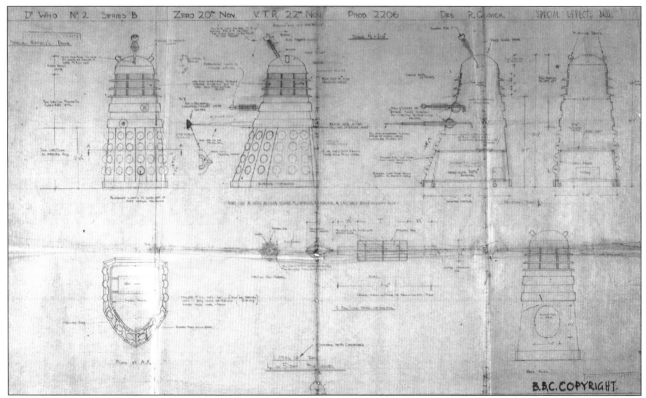

The original construction drawing for the Dalek drawn by A Webb from Raymond P Cusick's original specifications.

props were constructed by Shawcraft Models (Uxbridge) Ltd. The money to create the Dalek props had to come from the £2500 budget allocated for each episode. Of that amount, only £200 was set aside for the work being carried out by Shawcraft. This meant that Shawcraft had a total budget of £1400 to build the Daleks and any other special props and models for the story.

The eventual look of the Daleks owed much to Cusick's interpretation of Nation's descriptions. They stood around five feet three inches tall and were essentially pepper-pot shaped (although Cusick has denied any influence from this particular item of tableware). The prop could be broken down into several distinct parts. At the bottom, there was a platform with casters on which the Dalek could move about. Moving up the prop, there then was a segmented base section which was moulded in two fibreglass sections through which numerous lines of blue studs were inserted from behind. Then there was the shoulder section from which protruded the creature's gun and sucker arm. Next came the neck section through which the operator looked. And finally came the head – a domed section from which emerged a single eye on a stalk.

'We were pleased that we'd done it, Chris Barry and I,' said Cusick. 'Given the budget and the facilities, we'd actually done it and it looked quite promising. We had a viewing for their debut appearance, and we all went to this viewing room and Terry Nation was there. We were sitting watching it and I was watching Terry out of the corner of my eye, and there wasn't any reaction, no reaction at all. So I said, "What do you think of the Daleks, Terry?" He went, "Oh, they were all right". That was it!

'Later on, Terry and I were on a BBC2 show called *Late Night Line-Up*, talking about Daleks and *Doctor Who*. It went on until quite late and I'd missed my last train and Terry offered to give me a lift home. He told me on the way back that the only reason that he wrote *Doctor Who* was because he was short of cash. I think he thought that that was it: there wouldn't be any more. We all thought that. It was only later on that they realised that the Daleks had been somewhat successful. One day Verity Lambert, the producer, called me into the office and showed me the mail – there was one small sack of post for the artistes and about ten big sacks all about the Daleks.'

The actors who played the Daleks were all small men – they had to be to fit inside the cramped shells. Over the years a great many actors have suffered for their art and have crammed themselves into the Dalek casings to play the creatures. One of the first was Kevin Manser, who recalled in 1987 that they didn't actually see a Dalek machine until after rehearsals had started: 'We had just got the moves worked out and walked around and we *still* hadn't seen what we were going to operate!'

Robert Jewell, another of the original operators, also remembered in 1987 that 'up to the first rehearsal they were still talking about how they were going to operate it and how they were going to make it move, and

Two of Raymond P Cusick's initial sketches of the Dalek.

Top two images: The Daleks under construction at Shawcraft Models. Lower two images: The Daleks during studio recording for *The Dalek Invasion of Earth*.

finally they got down to doing it on the very basic idea of us pushing it around with our feet.

'One funny thing happened during rehearsals one day: the Daleks had this sucker arm with this plumber's thing on the end and of course it would have to be me involved but I was swinging the arm around to do something and it caught on one of Jacqueline Hill's bosoms! She squealed a bit and I said "Cup B. Cup B. Cup B ...", so we always used to go around shouting "Cup B, Cup B ...". It was a bit of a joke for quite a while.'

One of the most memorable aspects of the Daleks was their voices, originally provided by actors Peter Hawkins and David Graham. Hawkins was a well-known voice actor and had provided the vocalisations for Bill and Ben the Flowerpot Men in *Watch With Mother* and all the voices for *Captain Pugwash*. He later went on to narrate *The Family Ness* and also provided the voice of 'Money' in a series of animated television advertisements for the Access credit card. Graham had been working extensively for Gerry Anderson and had provided many voices for Anderson's puppet series, including *Stingray* and *Fireball XL5*.

'I used to sit behind the set with a hand microphone and a ring modulator and grind out the voices,' Hawkins explained. 'When I was doing the voices for two or three Daleks, I used to grade them into different pitches to distinguish between them.'

The voices for the Daleks were one of the things that Barry had to develop. He made contact with the Post Office's Joint Speech Unit and asked about 'synthetic speech'. In return, they provided two examples: one generated by a vocoder (a device which could blend human speech with the sound from a musical instrument) and the other by computer simulation. Barry was interested by the vocoder, but by this time had realised that some, if not all, of the Daleks' speech would have to be recorded live in the studio, and therefore the BBC would have to produce something similar. In the event, all the Dalek voices were initially pre-recorded. A device called a ring modulator was developed by the BBC's Radiophonic Workshop and used to create the distinctive voices.

In their book, *The BBC Radiophonic Workshop: The First 25 Years*, Desmond Briscoe (who ran the Workshop for many years) and Roy Curtis-Bramwell explained that the voice of the Daleks was a direct descendent of that of a robot called Jones, who appeared in a BBC children's programme called *Sword from the Stars*. The man assigned to produce the voice of the Daleks was Brian Hodgson, one of the sound technicians working at the Workshop, who was for many years responsible for all *Doctor Who*'s special sound effects.

'The Jones robot was a very domesticated sort of robot and had an ordinary sort of voice, modulated at thirty cycles,' explained Hodgson. 'When we came to do the Daleks we remembered the Jones robot and combined him with the incredibly brilliant characterisation given to the voice by Peter Hawkins. Peter's voice was switched on and off electronically thirty times a second – and the Daleks spoke for the very first time. At first we were much concerned whether the Dalek voice would prove too grating and unpleasant for the children. We soon realised we had no need to worry: they took to the sound immediately.'

'The voice of the Daleks didn't come from me,' confirmed Hawkins. 'I think it was suggested that the Daleks should speak with uninflected voices so it had to be very flat. This posed its own problems because in the original days we thought this was going to be very dull. We got over that by speed and intensity. If something nasty happened to them, they tended to speed up their delivery and also got very much higher in pitch.

'I attended all the rehearsals and the Dalek operators got to know how I was going to play the voices for

Destiny of the Daleks (1979) 4 episodes
w. Terry Nation d. Ken Grieve

Paying an unexpected return visit to Skaro some centuries after the events of *Genesis of the Daleks*, the Doctor finds himself in the middle of a race between the robot Movellans and the Daleks to find Davros, whom both sides believe will give them the edge in a war between the races.

The Five Doctors (1983) 1 episode
w. Terrance Dicks d. Peter Moffatt

A Dalek makes a guest appearance to attack the first Doctor when he arrives on Gallifrey as a part of a plot to open the way to the tomb of Rassilon, giving eternal life to those who seek it.

Resurrection of the Daleks (1984)
2 episodes
w. Eric Saward d. Matthew Robinson

The Daleks set a time corridor as a trap to bring the Doctor to them so that they might use android replicas of him and his companions to assassinate the High Council on Gallifrey. The Daleks have also placed replicas in positions of power on Earth and want Davros to develop an antidote to a Movellan virus that affects only Daleks.

Revelation of the Daleks (1985)
2 episodes
w. Eric Saward d. Graeme Harper

Davros sets a trap for the Doctor on the planet Necros where he is creating a new breed of Daleks from the corpses that are cryogenically stored on that world.

Remembrance of the Daleks (1988)
4 episodes
w. Ben Aaronovitch d. Andrew Morgan

The Daleks head for Earth in 1963 to retrieve a powerful Gallifreyan weapon called the Hand of Omega, which the Doctor in his first incarnation had hidden. The Doctor is on hand to ensure that the Daleks and Davros do not obtain this powerful device and it instead destroys Skaro.

Doctor Who (1996)
90-minute TV Movie
w. Matthew Jacobs d. Geoffrey Sax

In a prologue the (unseen) Daleks have captured the Master and exterminate him for his crimes. The Doctor obtains the Master's remains to transport them to Gallifrey, but the Master is not as dead as he seems ...

The voice of the Daleks: Peter Hawkins

the various scenes. During rehearsals, I knew which Dalek was supposed to be talking because the operators rehearsed in only the bottom half of the Daleks, so you could see them. When we got into studio, I had a small monitor so that I could see the action, but the Daleks all looked the same – it became very difficult. Generally, the operators took their cues from me rather than vice versa.'

One of the ways that Barry and Martin got around the problem was by securing large numbers on their domes and placing rolls of sticky tape on their casings. At the time of actual recording, however, these aids were removed.

The Dalek team in the rehearsal rooms during rehearsals for *The Daleks' Master Plan*. Left to right: Gerald Taylor, John Scott Martin, Robert Jewell, Kevin Manser and Peter Hawkins.

Sydney Newman was not amused by Verity Lambert's inclusion of the Daleks in *Doctor Who*, as he explained in 1987: 'I remember seeing the show on the Saturday afternoon and I phoned Verity up immediately and I said "I want to see you in my office on Monday morning!"

'I really ripped into her and I said, "You've betrayed the whole concept – there were to be no damned bug-eyed monsters – and it's cheap, Verity, it's cheap science fiction!" She was protesting at the top of her voice but feeling guilty and she blurted out that these were actually human beings who were so far advanced that their bodies had atrophied. And of course the irony as the years went by was that it was the Daleks which made the series the rage that it did become.'

The head of the BBC's script department, Donald Wilson, also hated the story. 'He called David Whitaker and me into his office when he had read it,' recalled Lambert in 1996, 'and told us that it was absolutely dreadful. David and I were quite surprised because we rather liked it. He said "You can't possibly do this." But unfortunately – or fortunately as it turned out – we didn't have another serial ready so we absolutely had to do it. Donald was most unhappy about it and said that we had to write a two-part serial, all based in the spaceship, in order to bring us up to thirteen weeks so that if they wanted to cancel the show at that point they could. As it turned out, of course, the Daleks were a huge runaway success and we were one of the first BBC shows to get into the ratings. This little children's show got into the ratings which at that time had been dominated by ITV shows. It was amazing. Donald Wilson, to his credit, after the first few episodes of the Dalek story went out, and we had this national outcry, called me into his office and said "Well you clearly know more about this than I do so I won't bother to interfere with this any more."'

The success of the Daleks took everyone at the BBC by surprise, and, with the pressure to bring them back mounting, Lambert finally gave in and commissioned Nation in July 1964 to bring them back in a story which was to see them invade the Earth. The story was commissioned under the title *The Return of the Daleks* after having been known as, simply, *The Daleks (II)* for a time.

At the same time, the BBC had been receiving numerous requests from manufacturers and publishers to release toys and books based around the Daleks. The BBC did have an embryonic licensing arm, but this was pretty much a one-man operation, and there was not the time to devote to handling the massive interest that *Doctor Who* had generated.

The BBC therefore gave the job of handling all licences related to *Doctor Who* and the Daleks to an external company run by Australian Walter Tuckwell. Tuckwell agreed numerous licences for the creatures' use on items as diverse as wallpaper, crockery, fireworks, clothing and toys and he was also not averse to approaching manufacturers direct with ideas for Dalek-related products. He managed to generate an incredible amount of interest in the creatures and the show that had spawned them and, by Christmas of 1965, there were nearly one hundred different Dalek products available to buy.

It was in November 1964 that the Daleks returned to *Doctor Who* in a story now called *The Dalek Invasion of Earth*. Having been asked to resurrect the creatures after killing them off at the end of *The Mutants*, Nation resolved not to make the same mistake twice, and so decided to set *The Dalek Invasion of Earth* at a time before the Doctor encountered them on Skaro.

One of the earliest major publicity coups for *Doctor Who* took place when the Daleks went out on location filming around London for this story. Spencer Chapman, the designer allocated to *The Dalek Invasion of Earth*, knew that showing the Daleks on the streets was a requirement and realised that the small casters used on the Daleks' bases would not be efficient when on location. They were fine on smooth studio floors, but London's pavements and roads demanded something more rugged.

He therefore returned to one of Cusick's rejected ideas: that of sitting the operator on a small tricycle within the Dalek shell. The trikes were equipped with larger and more sturdy wheels and, to disguise the fact that the Dalek shells had to be raised off the ground to accommodate the tricycles, they were fitted with enlarged fenders around the base.

Nick Evans, one of the Dalek operators from that story, recalled: 'We had pedals like those on a bicycle inside the casing, and that took up a lot of room. They were even more cramped as a result.'

Evans also recalls an occasion on location when the Daleks were seen to be behaving in a somewhat suspicious manner. 'For *The Dalek Invasion of Earth* we were filming in London at Trafalgar Square and it was very cold. It was a bit of a business getting out of the Dalek machines and there was never anyone about to help you get out if you wanted to go for a pee. So at one point during the filming, there was this procession of Daleks that had found themselves a grating in Trafalgar Square and were queuing up to position themselves over it. It relieved the day, if I can put it like that.'

The Dalek operator who has played the creatures in more stories than any other is John Scott Martin. 'It's very odd being a Dalek,' he mused. 'If you are the right size, then it's very comfortable.

'You had to have about six hands: one to do the eyestalk, one to do the lights, one for the gun, another for the smoke canister underneath, yet another for the sink plunger. If you were related to an octopus then it helped.'

The Daleks invade Westminster. The Dalek Invasion of Earth.

Another operator, Peter Murphy (who also acted under the name Murphy Grumbar) commented in 1964, 'Being a Dalek is hard work. It's very hot inside under the studio lights and you can't wear more than a T-shirt and lightweight slacks. You have to pedal a machine like a child's tricycle and work four gadgets at the same time in a tiny space. It takes a long time to master a Dalek and even then they have a tendency to skid.

'On top of that, you have to learn every line in the script. A move in the wrong direction could be disastrous and you have to synchronise the Dalek's pre-recorded voice with the light on its head that flashes while it speaks.'

Although the basic shape of a Dalek remained the same throughout their many appearances over the years, numerous modifications were made. For *The Dalek Invasion of Earth,* as well as the changes to the wheels, Chapman arranged for disc-shaped antenna to be fitted to the back of the shoulder section, which was intended to explain how the Daleks received their motive power away from their metal city.

It wasn't long before the Daleks were back for a third assault on viewers. The story was initially called *Dr Who and the Daleks (III)* and was commissioned from Nation on 16 December 1964. Nation's story outline had the title *The Pursuers* and the final scripts were entitled *The Chase.*

Cusick was again allocated as designer and he arranged for the removal of the tricycles and rear disc added for *The Dalek Invasion of Earth.* However, to indicate some form of energy-collecting device, he had a series of 23 vertical slats attached to the upper metal belt around the shoulder section of each prop – 17 long ones and six shorter ones over the arm boxes at the front. Behind these slats was fixed a thin wire mesh. This version of the Dalek was to become the standard for almost all subsequent appearances and the Dalek props constructed up to that time were reused in each successive story. The next time any new casings were to be built was for *Planet of the Daleks* in 1973.

The Daleks were to appear once more during the period that William Hartnell was playing the Doctor, in an epic 12-part story called *The Daleks' Master Plan* which was co-written by Nation and former *Doctor Who* story editor Dennis Spooner. There was also a single episode 'trailer' for the story written by Nation with the episode title *Mission to the Unknown* (although, confusingly, the story title appears to have been *Dalek Cutaway*). This mammoth story was under discussion even as Nation was working on the scripts for *The Chase.*

The Daleks' Master Plan featured some scenes in which the Daleks were armed with flame-throwers rather

Davros was not content with ensuring the survival of the Kaled people, however. He also wanted power and immortality for himself. He recognised that, to survive, his creations would need to be utterly ruthless and single-minded, and so he bred these traits into his mutant creatures. He hoped that, through the Daleks, he would gain ultimate power, and intended that nothing would stop him. However, his creatures do not recognise his authority, regarding him as merely another inferior being.

After the Daleks apparently exterminated Davros, his life-support systems kept him alive for centuries until the Daleks returned to gain his help in breaking their logical stalemate with the android Movellans. When this plan failed, Davros was cryogenically frozen and returned to Earth. He was again 'rescued' by Daleks 90 years later in another attempt to help his creations in their war against the Movellans and narrowly escaped becoming the victim of first the Movellan anti-Dalek virus and secondly the destruction of the spaceship upon which he was working. He ended up on the planet Necros, where he created a trap for the Doctor, as well as developing more Dalek mutants. Daleks loyal to the Dalek Supreme were summoned by two Necrosians unhappy at Davros' actions and Davros was taken back to Skaro to stand trial. He somehow survived this and set himself up as the Dalek Emperor (although only his head was surviving by this point) and ended up destroying Skaro's sun (and Skaro with it) using the Hand of Omega – a Time Lord device otherwise known as a stellar manipulator. ➡

Top: Two assistants move a Dalek prop during studio recording for *The Chase* as Maureen O'Brien (Vicki), John Maxim (Frankenstein's Monster) and John Scott Martin (sitting in Dalek casing) look on. Bottom: A Dalek is buried in sand in a failed attempt to film it emerging. The scene was eventually achieved with a model. *The Chase.*

than their standard weaponry in order for them to burn a forest to the ground. This continued the theme of the Daleks being able to change their arm 'attachments', as had been seen previously in both *The Mutants* and *The Chase*.

When the step was taken to change the actor playing the Doctor from William Hartnell to Patrick Troughton, the Daleks smoothed the transition and gave the second Doctor his first battle.

In mid-1966, at the time that story editor Gerry Davis wanted to commission a Dalek story to introduce the

A sequence of stills showing a Dalek being destroyed, and a scene featuring a Dalek mutant during studio sessions for The Daleks' Master Plan.

new Doctor, Nation had no interest in writing the scripts himself and so granted permission for David Whitaker to script their appearance with the new Doctor. The scripts were commissioned as *The Destiny of Doctor Who* on 22 July 1966, and when they were seen by Sydney Newman, he requested on 7 October 1966 that the character of the Doctor be radically altered. This rewrite was carried out by Dennis Spooner, starting over the following weekend, as Whitaker was unable to do the work and rehearsals had already started. A part of the agreement for Spooner to do this was that he would receive no formal credit for his input.

Although the Daleks had been incredibly successful, the BBC had contrived to keep their method of operation secret for as long as they could. They wanted to create the impression that these really were alien creatures from outer space and many people assumed that the Dalek props were powered by motors or radio control or some other such mechanism. It wasn't until some pre-publicity for *The Power of the Daleks* in 1966 that the first photographs of a Dalek with its top off were published in one of the Sunday newspaper colour supplements, to the amazement of some and the knowledgeable smiles of others.

In May 1966, Nation had begun discussion with the BBC about the possibility of producing a pilot television film featuring the Daleks. The BBC was interested in the idea and Nation subsequently wrote a script called *Daleks – The Destroyers*, which was received by the BBC on 1 November. Unfortunately, discussions with the BBC came to a halt late in 1966 when it decided not to invest in the project (Nation had been suggesting a 50/50 split of the costs between his own film production company and the BBC) and also refused to assign all rights in the Daleks to Nation, although they were prepared to license Nation to use the Daleks in his own projects. After a further abortive attempt to sell the Dalek concept to America as a TV series early in 1967, Nation let the idea drop.

The Daleks' second and final battle with the second incarnation of the Doctor came in another story written by David Whitaker. Nation allowed Whitaker to script it on the basis that it was to be the final Dalek story. Whitaker's original outline, dated 4 January 1967, was called, simply, *Daleks*. The scripts for *The Evil of the Daleks*, as the story was retitled, were eventually commissioned on 24 January 1967.

In line with Nation's stipulation, *The Evil of the Daleks* ended with the destruction of the Dalek city on Skaro and there were no plans made to include the Daleks in further adventures. This tailing off of their appearances in *Doctor Who* can be linked to the rise and then decline of their popularity as a merchandisable product. As previously mentioned, Walter Tuckwell had done a phenomenal job of promoting the Daleks, and during 1965 and 1966 their popularity was at its height. Aside from the TV series itself, there was a stage play called *The Curse of the Daleks* written by Whitaker and staged over Christmas 1965, which featured the Daleks in an adventure of their own; there was a regular Dalek comic strip running in *TV Century 21* magazine; and there were also two cinema films released. The first, an adaptation of Nation's scripts for *The Mutants* called *Dr. Who and the Daleks*, was in 1965 and the second, a version of Nation's *The Dalek Invasion of Earth* called *Daleks' Invasion Earth 2150 A.D.*, was in 1966. The second film, although technically superior to the first, did not do as well at the box office, and sales and interest in all Dalek and *Doctor Who*-related merchandise was on the wane. Although no one was perhaps prepared to admit it, all the signs were that the Daleks had had their day and now it was time to move on to new pastures.

An approach was made to Nation in December 1967 by the BBC's Head of Copyright, John Henderson, suggesting a story in which the Daleks and the Cybermen join forces against the Doctor and also asking for permission to use the Daleks in successive seasons (at this time the sixth season would have been in the

The Daleks developed by Davros were able to operate on any terrain (the first test of Dalek armaments was carried out by Davros in the wastelands, and the Daleks were able to traverse the no man's land between the Kaled and Thal domes in order to destroy the Thals) but by the time of the Doctor's first encounter with them (from the Doctor's point of view) they were reliant on static electricity, picking up this energy from the floors of a metal city constructed for this purpose. They had also created complex equipment to monitor the corridors of their city and to alert them of movements at its perimeter. They were scientists, biologists and sculptors, able to analyse and synthesise drugs, grow food using artificial sunlight, and understand the properties of nuclear fission.

While they were confined to Skaro, the Daleks were of little threat to the rest of the universe, but eventually they developed space-travel and so the Dalek conquest of space began. Freed from the need to use static electricity once more, the Daleks developed different power sources for their motive and operational units and their weaponry with the effect that, while their guns were rendered inoperative by the power drain on Exxilon, the rest of their systems continued to function normally. They can operate underwater and under sand and their armour is made from bonded polycarbide.

The Daleks have a pathological hatred of anything that is not Dalek and will do anything and everything in their power to corrupt and control, and will destroy anything that stands in their way. They have exploited other life forms, such as the bestial Ogrons, the carnivorous Slyther and the lethal Varga plants, to act as their slaves and protectors. They can create mindless Robomen by wiping the minds of humans. They can bend life forms to their will by use of hypnotic devices, and, by using android technology, can create their own troops of loyal soldiers. They have also formed short-lived allegiances with ambitious humanoids such as Mavic Chen, the Master and Commander Lytton, all of whom the Daleks discarded when they were deemed of no further use to them. ➥

A classic moment from The Evil of the Daleks *is recreated in colour for the 1993 documentary,* Thirty Years in the TARDIS.

planning stages). Nation replied to the effect that he was happy for one or two Dalek stories to be made per season, but that he would like script approval, and also refused permission for a joint Dalek/Cybermen adventure. In the event, aside from a repeat showing of *The Evil of the Daleks* in 1968 to bridge the gap between seasons five and six, and a brief appearance at the conclusion of the Doctor's trial at the end of *The War Games,* the Daleks' next appearance proper was not until the start of the ninth season in 1972.

Producer Barry Letts and script editor Terrance Dicks had not seen the need to include the Daleks in their plans for the first few Jon Pertwee seasons. However, when comments started filtering down from the upper echelons of the BBC to the effect that it was about time the Daleks returned, combined with letters from viewers asking when the Daleks would appear, they started making plans to accordingly.

Nation was therefore approached by Letts and Dicks in April 1971 about writing a Dalek story, and was keen on the idea but was too busy to script it himself. Dicks therefore turned to writer Louis Marks, who already had a *Doctor Who* script in preparation called *The Ghost Hunters.*

Top: An unarmed Dalek enters as Valmar (Richard Hane) looks on and the Doctor (Patrick Troughton) confers with Quinn (Nicholas Hawtrey). *The Power of the Daleks.* Bottom: The Daleks — armed and dangerous! *The Power of the Daleks.*

Dicks instructed Marks to add the Daleks into his storyline as the main villain and, when this was done, the story's title underwent a title change to *Years of Doom* before finally becoming *Day of the Daleks* in July 1971.

There were only three complete Dalek props used in the making of *Day of the Daleks* and this was because they were all that the BBC had at the time.

Top: The Daleks in their control room. *Day of the Daleks.* Bottom: The Doctor (Jon Pertwee) encounters the Daleks in a posed publicity photograph for *Day of the Daleks.*

'When we went and looked in the BBC's storeroom where all the old props from the series were kept,' explained Paul Bernard, the director of *Day of the Daleks,* 'we could only find three-and-a-half Daleks. We refurbished three of them and I used that half-Dalek several times as a "blown-up" one. We simply didn't have the money to make any more.'

For *Day of the Daleks*, the Daleks were required to be seen on location, and to make them operate over rough terrain, wooden boards were laid down like tracks so that the Daleks could glide smoothly over them. This meant that Bernard had to ensure that the boards were never in shot, which limited his available camera angles.

Ricky Newby played a Dalek in *Day of the Daleks*. 'The first thing they asked me was, "Do you suffer from claustrophobia?" and, luckily, I didn't, so that was my first outing as a Dalek on *Doctor Who.*

'I thoroughly enjoyed it. One of the problems was that we never knew who was in charge of them – whether it was props or wardrobe. Sometimes we would be left in the Daleks while everyone else went to dinner and we struggled to get the tops off but we just couldn't do it. I asked people about this afterwards but the props people said it was wardrobe's responsibility to get us out and wardrobe said it was props. The result was that we were always late for our meals!

'It was difficult on location at times. For instance, there was a scene where we had to come out of a railway tunnel and it was a muddy field and so they laid down pieces of wood for us to roll along on without falling off.'

Cy Town, one of the Dalek operators for the following story to feature the creatures, *Frontier in Space*, also remembers problems with operating a Dalek on location. This was during the filming of a scene in which the Daleks come into view over the top ridge of a cliff. 'They had put down boards as usual because the Daleks couldn't move anywhere on location without boards being put down for them. However, because of our restricted vision, we couldn't see where the edge of this cliff was. There were prop men hanging on to the back of the casings to stop us from going too far forward. Directors used to like asking the Daleks to stop on their marks. What marks! We couldn't see the floor, let alone any marks on it!'

Martin recalls that they used to have a means of seeing the floor. 'At one point we had little lights inside the Dalek casings which we could put on and use to see markings on the studio floor when we were right

Top: The Dalek Emperor. *The Evil of the Daleks.* Bottom: Members of the production team on set during a break in recording for *The Evil of the Daleks.*

over them. These got phased out, however, because over time, the Daleks became worn and when the bulbs and batteries went, no one bothered to replace them.'

The Daleks made only a 'guest appearance' in *Frontier in Space*, appearing in the final episode, but this led directly into another Dalek story. Part of Letts' and Dicks' negotiation with Nation to allow *Day of the Daleks* to go ahead was that Nation would himself write the following Dalek story, which was initially called *Destination: Daleks* before being retitled *Planet of the Daleks*.

For the first time since *The Dalek Invasion of Earth*, four new casings were created for *Planet of the Daleks*. The basic difference in their construction (which was somewhat cruder) was that the lower body was made from plywood and not fibreglass. The hemispherical studs were attached to the outside of the base, rather than being pushed through from inside. The shoulder section again used no fibreglass. Instead, a thin sheet of metal was bent around a wooden frame to make the shape. The two 'arms' were simplified versions of the originals. As well as the four new casings, the three surviving sixties casings were again reused, and carried all the main action involving the creatures.

One further Dalek was seen in the story, the Dalek Supreme, and this was one of the props from the two Dalek films of the sixties, which was lent by Terry Nation to the BBC for their use.

Top: The Daleks and cloaked Spiridons in the Dalek city. *Planet of the Daleks.*
Bottom: The Supreme Dalek. *Planet of the Daleks.*

Following *Planet of the Daleks*, the creatures returned once more to battle the third Doctor. In *Death to the Daleks*, again scripted by Nation and initially called *The Exxilons*, only one of the new casings was reused, the bulk of the Dalek action being carried by the three sixties Daleks. They were all given a smart new colour scheme for this story: predominantly silver, with black being used for the lower body studs, the shoulder section, the upper metal belt and the neck mesh.

With a new Doctor in the form of Tom Baker taking over from Jon Pertwee, Letts and Dicks realised that including the Daleks in the line-up of the newcomer's first season would, as when Patrick Troughton took over the leading role, help to maintain audience loyalty. They therefore commissioned Terry Nation to produce a storyline that would reveal the Daleks' origins. This was delivered in early 1974 and called *Daleks – Genesis of Terror*. The production of this story was then carried forward by producer Philip Hinchcliffe and script editor Robert Holmes.

Something of the Daleks' early history had been revealed in their first ever story, *The Mutants*, back in 1963/4. The Doctor is at one point shown some etched tablets by the Thal woman Dyoni. They reveal that Skaro is the 12th planet in its solar system and that before a neutron war ravaged the planet, the Thals were warriors. Their cycle of mutation had gone full circle, leaving them as pacifists, whereas the Dals (the antecedents of the Daleks) had not completed their mutation and therefore needed the Dalek machines to travel around in.

In *Daleks – Genesis of Terror*, Nation decided to reinvent Dalek history and introduced viewers to Davros, the chief scientist of the people he now called Kaleds. This sort of reinvention was nothing new for Nation as he had already authorised an alternative version of the Daleks' creation in the *TV Century 21* comic strip (believed to have been written by David Whitaker), and had presented yet another variant in a short story written for a special *Radio Times* magazine to celebrate *Doctor Who*'s tenth anniversary in 1973.

Interviewed in 1989, Nation described how the idea of Davros had developed. 'the Daleks, when they have to make any kind of long speech, are immensely boring creatures,' he opined. 'You can't have a Dalek doing four or five sentences in a row, so I wanted someone to speak for the Daleks. This thing that was half man and half Dalek was a perfect example of this, and I made sure he was not killed in that one, because we had killed off the Daleks once. He became a very good plot piece, and anyway, any crazy old mad professor is wonderful to have around.'

The storyline for *Daleks – Genesis of Terror* described Davros as 'almost a machine himself' and stated that he was 'in a wheelchair'. The final scripts for the story, which by this time had been retitled *Genesis of the Daleks,* described Davros as follows:

The means of destruction at the Daleks' command are many, ranging from a variety of weapons that can be mounted on their individual casings to a Special Weapons Dalek, which is little more than a mobile tank with an awesomely powerful gun. They have developed the ability to fly and hover, can track foes through their heat patterns and have inbuilt alarm and warning systems to alert other Daleks of their plight if they are attacked.

None of this explains why the Doctor has managed to defeat them on so many occasions. It is the Doctor who is the Daleks' sworn enemy. Just the mention of his name sends them into a panic. On many occasions they have had the Doctor within their power only for him to escape having outwitted them once more. They have tried to use the Doctor's knowledge of their future defeats to secure victory; they have tried to use the Doctor's TARDIS as a means to ensure a total Dalek conquest; and they set their sights on the destruction of the Doctor's home planet of Gallifrey using a stellar manipulator.

Three photographs taken during location filming for *Day of the Daleks* showing the Daleks and Ogrons emerging from a disused railway tunnel.

DAVROS IS CONTAINED IN A SPECIALLY CONSTRUCTED SELF-POWERED WHEEL CHAIR. IT HAS SIMILARITIES TO THE BASE OF A DALEK. DAVROS HIMSELF IS A MASTERPIECE OF MECHANICAL ENGINEERING. HIS CHAIR IS A COMPLETE LIFE-SUPPORT SYSTEM FOR THE ANCIENT CREATURE. A THROAT MICROPHONE AND AMPLIFIER CREATE THE VOICE HE NO LONGER HAS. (ITS SOUND IS NOT UNLIKE THE VOICE OF A DALEK.) A MINIATURE H AND L MACHINE KEEPS HIS HEART AND LUNGS FUNCTIONING. A SINGLE LENS WIRED TO HIS FOREHEAD REPLACES HIS SIGHTLESS EYES. LITTLE OF HIS FACE CAN BE SEEN. TUBES AND ELECTRODES ATTACHED TO WHAT DOES SHOW. THE UPPER PART OF HIS BODY IS CONTAINED IN A HARNESS FROM WHICH GREAT COMPLEXES OF WIRES AND TUBES EMERGE.

THE ONLY REALLY HUMANOID FEATURE WE EVER SEE OF DAVROS IS AN ANCIENT WITHERED HAND THAT PLAYS ACROSS THE SWITCH PACKED SURFACE OF THE CONTROL PANEL THAT STRETCHES ACROSS THE FRONT OF THE CHAIR.

A Dalek enters the Exxilon city. *Death to the Daleks.*

Top: The Doctor (Jon Pertwee) and the Master (Roger Delgado) meet the Daleks. *Frontier in Space.* Bottom: Dalek operator Cy Town on location for *Frontier in Space.*

The final look of Davros was very Dalek-like. As Nation indicated, his wheelchair base was effectively the base of a Dalek, and, like the single eyestalk of the Dalek, Davros too 'saw' through an electronic eye fixed to his forehead.

To play the half-mutant Davros, the director of *Genesis of the Daleks,* David Maloney, cast Michael Wisher. Wisher had previously provided the Dalek voices for *Frontier in Space, Planet of the Daleks* and *Death to the Daleks.* 'Barry Letts phoned me up one day and said, "Hey, imitate a Dalek!" I stood at the other end of the phone and said, "You what?" and he said, "Go on, you know, 'Exterminate' and all that." So I croaked, "Exterminate!" in a Daleky voice and he said, "Great, get around here now, you're a Dalek."'

Peter Hawkins and David Graham had stopped playing the Dalek voices in the sixties. Graham's last story had been *The Daleks' Master Plan* while Hawkins' final story was *The Evil of the Daleks,* for which he was teamed with actor Roy Skelton. For *Day of the Daleks* the voices had been provided by Peter Gilbert and Oliver Messaline. With more Dalek stories on the way, Letts wanted someone who could do the voices effectively and Wisher fitted the bill admirably.

Maloney had worked with Wisher on *Planet of the Daleks* and knew that the actor would have little difficulty in producing the half-Dalek, half-human voice that the character of Davros required.

'Davros was just superb, everything fitted,' said Wisher. 'I rehearsed the part of Davros with a bag on my head. They tried the mask on me, you see, and I realised that it was like tunnel vision: I couldn't see a thing; so I always rehearsed in the same circumstances – with a paper bag and sitting in an old wooden wheelchair they got for me.

'Davros had all his vocal faculties, which were slightly assisted electronically. The character of Davros one must imagine as being about 150 years old. He has staved off death, and as each part of his body dies he builds some sort of machinery which will serve instead of it. His eyes are dead, so he must have a bionic eye fitted into his forehead, and one must assume that his own hearing is gone and that he has some sort of electronic device with which to hear. He is living in an iron lung and should have died years ago, but he won't die because the will is there to use every possible scientific means to remain and see this job through.'

Although this may have been Wisher's interpretation of Davros' origins, it is not his background as explained in the story. According to the plot, Davros was caught in a Thal attack on the scientific bunkers and was hideously disfigured as a result.

The mask for Davros was created by John Friedlander. 'Peter Day was the visual effects designer on that show,' explained

Top: A Dalek monitors Galloway (Duncan Lamont) and Hamilton (Julian Fox) as they begin their ascent of the power-draining beacon on Exxilon. *Death to the Daleks.* Bottom: Davros (Michael Wisher) and The Doctor (Tom Baker). *Genesis of the Daleks.*

A selection of photographs from *Destiny of the Daleks.* Top to bottom: two shots of Davros' chair undergoing refurbishment in the visual effects workshop; the original Davros mask; The Doctor (Tom Baker) and Davros (David Gooderson); Davros (David Gooderson) is discovered in the depths of the Kaled bunker.

Friedlander. 'He told me about Davros while I was between working on two shows and I had a little time free. They hadn't got an actor cast as Davros then so I did the mask purely on spec. Peter Day did the mobile base and the back, I did the head, the bits on the top and the hand.'

'The uniforms were sort of based on the German SS for this story,' said Barbara Kidd, the costume designer. 'There wasn't a lot left of Davros for me to do anything – only the waist to the neck.'

The three surviving sixties Dalek casings were reused in the story and were repainted a uniform gunmetal grey – aside from the studs and the neck mesh, which were black.

Genesis of the Daleks was a great success and yet the Daleks were not to reappear for a further four years, when Nation was commissioned to write a 'sequel' to *Genesis of the Daleks* called *Destiny of the Daleks.*

As had been discovered on *Day of the Daleks,* one problem with *Destiny of the Daleks* was a lack of Dalek props and insufficient budget to build more. The visual effects designer for *Destiny of the Daleks,* Peter Logan, was disappointed to find only seven very battered Dalek props in the BBC store. Two of these were too badly damaged to use, and one had to be cut up to make the moulds for some vacuum-formed Daleks that were required on location. This left only four Daleks available for use.

These four casings were repainted and repaired for the location filming, but on their return, Logan found that they were as damaged as they had been when first found in the store. They were repaired once more and then three of the props were requested by other BBC shows for guest appearances. They again were returned in a damaged state but this time there was no time to effect repairs before studio recording.

The vacuum-formed Daleks were created out of necessity as Logan had neither the time nor the money to build sufficient new Daleks for the location scenes where they converge on a spacecraft belonging to the robot Movellans (called Petrans in the original storyline) with the intention of blowing it up. Because these vacuum-formed props were very light and contained no wheels or other mechanisms, the actors inside the Daleks literally hoisted the casings up, and shuffled forward on their feet. This made the shells roll alarmingly from side to side which was very obvious in the final transmitted scenes.

Because time and money had been spent on the Daleks, there was not much remaining with which to repair and recreate Davros, who was returning in the story. An attempt was made to obtain Michael Wisher for the role. However he was on an overseas tour and was unavailable. Actor David Gooderson was cast instead. 'I tried to make Davros a bit more sympathetic,' he said. 'I always thought it a bit much that he was totally nasty. He is unpleasant, certainly, and has good reason to be so, especially with a face like his, but not quite *that* unpleasant. As an actor you sympathise with the character you're playing. You play him from that point of view. There's something very pathetic about this little man, this cripple. As a megalomaniac he's not particularly powerful, although he thinks he is.'

As a new actor was playing the part, Logan initially wanted to create a new mask for him to wear. However, on contacting John Friedlander he found that the cost was prohibitive and therefore had no choice but to use the original mask, which had been on display in one of the permanent *Doctor Who* exhibitions. 'It didn't quite fit,' said Gooderson. 'It had been on display and was a little worse for wear. It was like being a swimmer with goggles on – you can see dimly directly in front, but nothing at the side.'

Davros' chair also needed a major overhaul. Most of the switches on the control panel had been broken off and it needed a new seat but there was nothing that could not be repaired. Logan had one final shock with regards to Davros, and this was when he one day found the complex maze of wiring which formed a part of the headgear in a rubbish bin outside the visual effects workshop. Apparently a cleaner had mistaken it for rubbish

and had thrown it out. After this, Logan ensured that everything was locked away at the end of each day.

The Daleks were next due to appear in the 1983 season shortly after Peter Davison had taken over as the Doctor. In Davison's first season, transmitted in 1982, he had confronted the Cybermen, which had been redesigned and updated for the new eighties look and feel that John Nathan-Turner wanted for *Doctor Who*. The following year, it was decided to give the Daleks the same treatment, and so Nation was contacted by Nathan-Turner with regards to a script. Nation was again happy for the script editor, in this case Eric Saward, to be commissioned to write the story, with the proviso that Nation had script approval. Saward

was therefore commissioned on 13 March 1982 to start work on a project called *The Return,* which was intended as the big finale to the 20th season, bringing the Daleks and Davros back to *Doctor Who* in a climactic battle.

Because of industrial action at the BBC, production was disrupted on the final stories in the 20th season, and so *The Return* was put on hold. It was eventually decided to include the story in the 21st season, and so Saward reworked the scripts and the story was eventually transmitted under the title *Resurrection of the Daleks.* In the meantime, a single Dalek was included in *The Five Doctors.*

Wisher had been available to return as Davros had *The Return* been made as originally scheduled, but by the time *Resurrection of the Daleks* was in production, he was again out of the country. A third actor was therefore brought in to play Davros in *Resurrection of the Daleks.* Terry Molloy recalls that he was chosen to play the part by Matthew Robinson, the director of the story, because Robinson knew he was good at voices. 'I looked at the videos of the other Davroses and eventually said, "Yeah, no problem," and tried to get as close to the original as possible.

Top: A Dalek threatens the Doctor (Richard Hurndall) and Susan (Carole Ann Ford). *The Five Doctors.* Bottom: Davros (Terry Molloy). *Resurrection of the Daleks.*

'In *Resurrection of the Daleks* I wanted to see exactly how far Matthew wanted Davros to go in terms of mania and we arrived at the performance – which is nice because you're actually crafting something, not just throwing it together, because you want to be true to people's original conception of what Davros was, or is.

'Davros is great. One of the joys of being an actor is being able to play really evil baddies – Davros is as black as they come and there's very little grey in him at all. He's a totally cold, evil, ruthless person – and a total maniac – a sort of intergalactic Hitler.'

The mask for Davros was created by Stan Mitchell, an assistant at the BBC's Visual Effects Workshop. 'I was assigned to make the mask by Peter Wragg, the designer,' he explained. 'I wasn't familiar with the *Doctor Who* series at all and I wasn't familiar with the Davros character. I didn't realise how much importance was attached to him.

'The problem with the original mask was that it had become rather tatty and was beginning to disintegrate and so we had to make another. We also didn't have a mould to produce any more so it had to be re-modelled from scratch. I was therefore asked to design something for foam latex.

'I generally took a freer hand in the modelling of the thing than if I'd realised how important Davros was in the *Doctor Who* series. We started by getting Terry Molloy to come in so that we could take a face-cast and then mould it up in plaster to create a bust on which we could model the mask.

'I used videos quite a lot because the original mask was in a bit of a state and it was difficult to tell what the original shape had been. I can't say that I was too concerned with reproducing it exactly. I wasn't led to believe that it was that important.'

Once the mask had been created in foam latex, it was painted and prepared for use. With foam latex appliances, they are usually stuck to the artiste's face and then removed with a solvent at the end of the day, which tends to mean that the appliance doesn't survive the solvent. Therefore at least two appliances are made for each day's recording. 'In this case,' said Mitchell, 'because it was a fairly robust appliance, and the only delicate part was around the mouth and chin, we managed to get away with only two or three masks in total. The make-up artist was skilled enough to remove it each day without it sustaining too much damage.'

Top: Davros (Terry Molloy) in cryogenic storage. *Resurrection of the Daleks.* Bottom: Two shots of a Dalek falling from a warehouse on location for *Resurrection of the Daleks.*

The Daleks in *Resurrection of the Daleks* were mostly standard props that the BBC had in storage. Peter Wragg, the visual effects designer handling the story, eventually located two props which had been used in the permanent *Doctor Who* exhibitions at Blackpool and Longleat House.

'That gave us two working models,' said Wragg at the time. 'We needed four, and all we had for the others were a few bits and pieces from old Daleks. We were able to make up one from the pieces, but the last we had to build virtually from scratch.'

One modification made to the casings was to allow the dome section of two of the props to tilt open at an angle. This was to allow access to the 'creature' inside for a scene in which it is drugged and made subservient to Davros' will.

With *Resurrection of the Daleks*, Nathan-Turner and Saward continued the cycle of Davros-driven Dalek stories started with *Genesis of the Daleks*. In these, the Daleks themselves no longer held centre stage, and the plot revolved around Davros' schemes rather than the Daleks'.

The following story continued this idea, and in 1985 *Revelation of the Daleks* saw the Daleks and Davros return once more, although this time, the desire to include Davros stemmed from Nathan-Turner rather than from Nation. For this story, which was commissioned from Saward under the title *The End of the Road* on 27 March 1984, new Dalek casings were constructed for the first time since *Planet of the Daleks*. There were two factions of Dalek seen in this story: an attack force from the planet Skaro, loyal to the Dalek Supreme, for which existing Dalek props were refurbished and used, and a new force of Daleks created by Davros on the planet Necros, for which the new props were used.

These new casings were constructed from fibreglass and there were several differences between these and the existing Dalek casings. The base section studs were of a slightly smaller diameter and there was a greater gap than normal at the top and bottom of each panel. The shoulder section was shorter and also wider at the top and, in addition, the boxes to house the 'arms' were moulded in with the section, rather than being added afterwards. There were also seven small slats over the arm boxes rather than six.

The most striking difference, however, was the colour scheme. These new Daleks were painted predominantly cream, with just the lower body studs, the shoulder mesh, the neck mesh, the arm rod and the gun stick painted in gold.

Revelation of the Daleks also featured a 'glass' Dalek, a concept that had been introduced by David Whitaker in his 1964 novelisation of the first ever Dalek story. This Dalek was made from clear perspex by an outside contractor and had to be carefully polished to remove all trace of finger marks and dirt. Use was also made of a small, commercially available model Dalek created, built and marketed by model-maker Stuart Evans.

Davros was again played by Molloy for this story, and use was made of the same mask, costume and 'chair' as in his previous story. 'We still had the moulds,' said Mitchell, 'and they were taken out to Tom McLoughlin, one of the pioneers of the use of foam latex in this country, at Pinewood Studios where he was working, and he made the appliances for us.' For much of *Revelation of the Daleks*, only Davros' head was seen, and this was revealed to be some form of clone when the real Davros emerged at the story's conclusion with the hitherto unseen ability to fire a paralysing ray from his fingers and to hover in his Dalek-like base.

In Davros' and the Daleks' next appearance in *Doctor Who,* Davros' head appeared to be the only part of him remaining, and this was revealed to be housed in the casing of the Emperor Dalek.

Revelation of the Daleks. Top to bottom: Terry Molloy has his make-up checked; Davros (Terry Molloy) and Davros in the guise of the Great Healer; the Doctor (Colin Baker); the glass Dalek. Revelation of the Daleks.

The Dalek creatures themselves are not entirely helpless when removed from the confines of their machines. They have vestigial limbs with which they can operate the machines; they have eyes and they have some form of mouth which contains 'teeth'. They also speak the words that are heard outside the machine aloud, suggesting some form of vocal cords and the other physical characteristics associated with speech. The mutations have also taken different paths, resulting in different 'types' of Dalek mutant. The later creatures created by Davros have functional limbs and have mechanical prostheses grafted on to their bodies, while earlier mutations had only vestigial limbs and almost amoebic sensory organs. There was also a starfish-like mutation revealed as the creatures succumbed to the effects of the time destructor on Kembel, and the Doctor found a pink slimelike life form on the surface of Skaro at the time the Movellans arrived searching for Davros.

The Special Weapons Dalek. *Remembrance of the Daleks.*

This story was called *Remembrance of the Daleks*, commissioned under the title *Nemesis of the Doctor* on 30 October 1987 from writer Ben Aaronovitch, and featured the same two opposing Dalek factions as in *Revelation of the Daleks*. There was a generation controlled by Davros in his guise as the Dalek Emperor (referred to here as 'Imperial' Daleks) and an original group loyal to the Dalek Supreme.

Aaronovitch had not originally intended to use Davros in the story, but one of the BBC's visual effects assistants, Mike Tucker, suggested that the Daleks' creator be revealed as having been hidden inside the Dalek Emperor casing. Aaronovitch was happy to include this element in the scripts.

The Dalek Supreme's troops consisted of one sixties Dalek casing, plus four of the new 'Necrosian' Daleks created for the previous story, and repainted here in black and

The Imperial Daleks come under fire from the Special Weapons Dalek. Remembrance of the Daleks.

grey. For the Imperial Daleks, however, a totally new batch of casings were constructed. These were again painted in the cream and gold livery of Davros' forces from the previous story, with the addition of gold-coloured metallic foil on the shoulder slats, neck section and iris.

Because of advances in effects technology, the Dalek casings could now be created from new, flexible 'jelly' moulds and were somewhat simpler in design as a result. On the shoulder section, the vertical slats were moulded as a part of the section along with the arm boxes and the horizontal belts. As a result there was no wire mesh present behind the slats.

In another break from recent tradition rather than a rubber sucker, the end of the Daleks' arm stalk was tipped with a specially moulded cup incorporating a narrow slot which was designed to fit into the controls on the Dalek spacecraft. On the neck section, the traditional wire mesh was replaced with solid fibreglass which had slots cut in it to allow the operator to see out. The fibreglass and slots were then covered with a finely perforated metallic gold foil. The dome was designed so that it could rotate only about ten centimetres in either direction and would spring back automatically to the central position when released. The eyestalk was also redesigned and, like the dome, was spring-loaded so that it always returned to a pre-determined position when released by the operator. The base section was shaped as it had always been. However, the lower skirt around the base was moulded as a part of the body rather than being a flexible rubber strip added afterwards.

In an attempt to improve their mobility, the Daleks were fitted with three large 'balloon' tyres, which had the unfortunate effect of making the props wobble and bounce on location.

Cy Town, one of the Dalek operators for this story, remembers this. 'They had the innovative idea of replacing the casters with what can only be described as wheelbarrow wheels – large orange things. When we had casters we could move the Daleks in any direction we wanted simply by pushing with our knees, but with these wheelbarrow wheels, the back two were fixed in position, and we could have done with yet another hand to steer the Dalek in the right direction. They were really quite disastrous.'

'The wheelbarrow wheels also wobbled,' agreed Martin. 'The casters were very stable and we managed to glide along smoothly, but the larger wheels made the Daleks wobble from side to side and they looked simply awful.'

Not everything was deemed a backward step, however, and Town recalled that a major advance was in the operation of the head section: 'The designers had combined a number of operations into one place. On the handle that was used to turn the head around, there was the button to make the lights flash, and also a lever to make the eye stalk raise and lower. All this was designed to be operated by one hand, which was much better than the early days where the controls were all in different places inside the casing.'

Something that had always dogged the Daleks, and had even been picked up by popular newspaper cartoonists, was the creatures' apparent inability to climb a flight of stairs. The production team was aware of this and so, in *Remembrance of the Daleks*, a Dalek was finally shown doing just that. To achieve the scene, one of the Imperial Dalek casings was lifted up on a forklift truck, and the base supports were later removed from the picture using an electronic video process, and a red glow was placed around the base to further

ORIGINAL STORYLINE FOR *DALEKS – GENESIS OF TERROR* EPISODE ONE

The TARDIS is in limbo – it materialises in a garden where a Time Lord is waiting for Dr Who. He directs him to go to Skaro at a time before the Daleks have evolved to try to stop their creation. The Time Lord gives Dr Who a bracelet to transport him with Harry and Sarah to Skaro. They arrive in the middle of a war between the Kaleds and the Thals. Dr Who, Sarah and Harry see some action in a crater and move on towards the City Dome they can see in the distance. They discover that the weapons in use are a mixture of old and new and that the troops are very young. In a trench they endure a gas attack and Dr Who and Harry are captured by the Kaleds and taken to a Command Post. From there they are taken to Command HQ to be questioned by Ravon and later Gen. Greiner who tells them that the Kaleds are winning the war against the Thals and will soon wipe them out completely. Skaro is inhabited by Kaleds, Thals and Mutos (people suffering from radiation effects of old atomic wars). Meanwhile in the trench Sarah comes round alone and moves out the trench followed by an animal shape. At Command HQ, Greiner resumes his interrogation of Dr Who and Harry who puzzle him. Nyder enters requesting items from store, Greiner protests but Nyder mentions an order from Davros – a name that produces an instant reaction from Ravon and Greiner who become conciliatory. Nyder also questions Dr Who and Harry. Outside in the wastelands Sarah is searching for the Dr, sees a huge figure following her and runs in terror towards a faint light. She arrives at a ruin and peers through a hole to see Davros in a wheelchair attended by Gharman. They are obviously carrying out an experiment with a target, then out of the gloom glides a machine – a primitive Dalek which destroys the target to order, much to the satisfaction of Davros.

©Terry Nation 1975

The Daleks are prepared on location for Remembrance of the Daleks.

In *Remembrance of the Daleks*, the Daleks disproved the old adage that a Dalek could not climb stairs, as the Doctor (Sylvester McCoy) discovered to his horror.

mask the support.

In addition to the traditional Daleks, there have also been several other variants over the years. It became established in the sixties that the rank of a Dalek could be determined by its colour and so we were introduced to the Black Dalek, in charge of operations on Earth in the 21st century. Black Daleks, or Dalek Supremes, were also in charge of several assault missions in both *The Dalek Invasion of Earth* and *The Daleks' Master Plan.*

It was in the 1967 story *The Evil of the Daleks* that viewers first met the Dalek Emperor. In the camera script it was described as follows:

```
A VAST DALEK STANDING AT ONE END OF THE ROOM.

WHEN IT SPEAKS ITS VOICE MAKES THE ALIEN BUT
MELODIOUS SOUND OF DALEK VOICES SPEAKING AT ONCE ON
                    DIFFERENT LEVELS.
```

This massive creature was stationed on Skaro, the Daleks' home planet, and was connected to the Dalek city itself. It controlled all Dalek operations through its black-domed lieutenants and was itself immobile. Nation had conceived it as a larger version of the standard Dalek casing, but it was realised as a different form of Dalek altogether. The Dalek Emperor also appeared in *Remembrance of the Daleks* but this time (presumably at an earlier point in the Daleks' history) it was housed in a mobile casing, but with no traditional shoulder, neck or head section. Instead it had a massive domed head and, as previously noted, was actually Davros.

Another design of Dalek Supreme appeared in *Planet of the Daleks* with black and gold livery and this rank appeared again in the eighties stories *Resurrection of the Daleks* and *Remembrance of the Daleks* when it was painted in black and silver.

Although the Daleks have seen several modifications to their 'sucker' and 'gun' arms over the years – like, for example, a claw being fitted, or various pieces of technical equipment – in *Remembrance of the Daleks* viewers saw for the first time one of the Daleks' war forces in the form of the Special Weapons Dalek.

This was described in the rehearsal scripts as:

```
A LARGE FLOATING WEAPONS PLATFORM.

THE PLATFORM CARRIES A LARGE HOWITZER LIKE WEAPON ON ITS BACK
                    (PAINTBOX)
```

Although the description was not of a Dalek, it was realised as a standard Dalek lower base with a tank-like upper half. It was constructed from a variety of different materials – including the top of a plastic dustbin –and was initially painted in cream and gold before being 'dirtied down' to give the impression that it had served in many battles.

Remembrance of the Daleks was the last time that the Daleks made an appearance on screen in *Doctor Who* (although their voices were heard in a pre-credits sequence for the 1996 *Doctor Who* TV movie condemning the Master to extermination), but it is certain that wherever the Doctor travels, his arch enemies will not be far behind … plotting … and planning the downfall and ultimate extermination of the Doctor himself.

The Dalek Emperor Casing which housed the remains of Davros, as used in *Remembrance of the Daleks.*

CHAPTER 10

THE LEGEND CONTINUES

From the Daleks to the Cheetah People, during its 26-year run on BBC television *Doctor Who* featured around 200 different alien monsters, races, robots and other assorted nasties. It is hard to think of the show without remembering the monsters – indeed, for a six year period from *Spearhead from Space* in 1970 until *The Seeds of Doom* at the very start of 1976, every story featured a monster of some description.

Even after the show finished as a regular BBC production in 1989, the legacy of *Doctor Who*'s monsters persisted, and, although the 1996 television movie did not feature any monsters *per se*, concentrating instead on the eternal battle between the Doctor and the Master, it did include a mention – and voices – of the Daleks at the very start, and a horrific computer-generated snake creature.

In the scenes of the snake entering through the mouth into the body of a hapless medic called Bruce, and subsequently moulding it to the Master's own needs, the TV movie *Doctor Who* echoed the themes of bodily corruption which had made shows like *The Tomb of the Cybermen*, *The Ark In Space* and *Kinda* as suspenseful and exciting as they undoubtedly were at the time of their first transmission. Unfortunately, this horrific impact was often cited by well-meaning adults as being a subject of great concern when it came to the impressionable minds of the children tuning in.

Whenever *Doctor Who* presented a story or a scene specifically designed to frighten, there always seemed to be a level of concern, whether expressed by politicians or by 'public interest' groups like Mary Whitehouse's National Viewers' and Listeners' Association, that it was not a good thing to scare children – and therefore, as *Doctor Who* was scary, the show itself was not a good thing.

In 1965, one newspaper, the *Daily Mail*, went so far as to speak to a Harley Street psychiatrist named Dr Ellis Stungo in relation to the release of the cinema film *Dr. Who and the Daleks*.

Dr Stungo was quoted as saying: 'These horrible things are enough to upset a stable child let alone one who is not so well balanced. Even adults are likely to be disturbed by them.

'These relentless monsters with absolutely no feelings, bent on destruction, are bound to give children nightmares.

'In these days of space travel, when nothing is impossible, these things could well have a highly detrimental effect on a child's mind.'

One presumes that the 'things' of which Dr Stungo was speaking were the Daleks, although this was not made clear in the article.

The Master Snake. *Doctor Who*.

In 1977, when the BBC arts programme *The Lively Arts* decided to feature the *Doctor Who* phenomenon in an edition called *Whose Doctor Who*, the producers decided to solicit the views of an educational psychologist as to the impact *Doctor Who* and its monsters could have on young minds. John Miller's assessment was as far from Dr Stungo's as was possible.

'There is a tendency,' said Miller, 'even among intelligent people like teachers, doctors, the clergy – people who ought to know better – to pretend that all the nasty things in life come from outside. I have no doubt that a television programme can have a disturbing effect on a child. But I think it's very naive to attribute this purely to the television programme, because an image cannot affect you *per se* unless it latches on to something that is already inside you.

'I think that what we all tend to deny in our technological society is that human nature has a dark, hidden side, a mysterious, frightening aspect which monsters, or representations of various sorts, activate.

'What *Doctor Who* does in a caricature way in the programme describes very much what I feel I'm doing as a psychologist (this may sound quite ludicrous!) I have, supposedly, a lot of wonderful technological knowledge, like Doctor Who's supposed to have. But I know that ultimately what will enable me to help a child, or a family, is just being honest, sincere, receptive.'

Speaking from a personal point of view, I was one of the many who had nightmares after watching *Doctor Who*. There was a period in the late sixties when I was literally too frightened to watch. I remember myself as a six-year-old lurking in the hallway listening to the soundtrack of *The Ice Warriors* while my younger brother – at only three years old – stayed in the room watching and told me what happened afterwards. I also remember watching parts of *The Invasion* – most notably the scenes in which Jamie, Zoe and Isobel encounter an insane Cyberman in the sewers under London – through the crack in the door because I was too scared to actually be in the same room as the silver giants.

Despite all these shocks and scares – also provided, perhaps I should add, by seventies programmes like *Ace of Wands*, *The Tomorrow People* and the occasional late-night horror film on BBC2 – I did not grow up to be a twisted mass murderer.

Doctor Who has always been, and will always be, simply entertainment. The monsters are crucially important in this as they provide a focus for the show, something for the Doctor to battle against. They are a vital part of the *Doctor Who* mythos and are one of the reasons that the show is still fondly remembered today.

The Daleks, surely one of the greatest creations of the sixties, have gone on to earn their own entry in the Oxford English Dictionary, and the inspirational children of *Doctor Who*, its concepts and its monsters, can be found in television programmes and films across the world.

Doctor Who would not have been *Doctor Who* without the monsters.

Long may they be remembered.

CHAPTER 11

A-Z OF MONSTERS

This is a selective listing of many of the alien races, creatures and robotic menaces that the Doctor has met in his travels which could be described as 'monsters'. For these purposes I have taken the term 'monster' to include all non-humanoid creatures (whatever their motives or dispositions, and whether they originate from an alien planet or from Earth, although I have not included animals like cats and dogs), certain robotic or mechanical creations (but not computers), and also those humanoid creatures whose appearances differ sufficiently from those of ordinary human beings to give them a monstrous quality. Humans or humanoid characters whose appearances differ only slightly from those of human beings (e.g. the Moroks and the Xerons from *The Space Museum*, George Cranleigh from *Black Orchid*), have not been included.

Only those *Doctor Who* adventures transmitted on BBC television as a part of the ongoing *Doctor Who* series – including the 1996 television movie – have been included in the creation of this list. Assorted programmes, films, spin-offs and presentations within other shows, including *K-9 And Company*, *Shada*, *Dimensions in Time*, and also the various extended or re-edited versions of stories released on video and original video, audio and literary works, whatever their provision, have not been used as source material.

The list includes all actors and actresses who played the listed monsters, whether as standard speaking roles, stunt performers or as stand-ins. Where certain monsters temporarily (or permanently) took the form of human or humanoid beings, the human artistes are listed. Where a human or humanoid changes into a monster, the artistes are only listed where a full change took place (for example, Bromley is listed as becoming a full Primord whereas Private Wyatt is not, the Doctor did not turn into a full Androgum in *The Two Doctors* and the Doctor, the Master, Ace and Midge did not turn into full Cheetah People in *Survival*).

AGGEDOR

Created by Brian Hayles
The Curse of Peladon (1972)
The Monster of Peladon (1974)
Nick Hobbs

Sacred beast of the planet Peladon. Worshipped as a myth, yet the Doctor discovered that one of the creatures was still alive. This creature was killed by Eckersley, a traitorous mining engineer.

ALIENS

Created by David Whitaker
The Ambassadors of Death (1970)
Captain: Peter Noel Cook
Ambassadors: Ric Felgate, Steve Peters, Neville Simons
Voice: Peter Halliday

An alien race undertook a peaceful exchange with Earth and sent three alien ambassadors to Earth in place of three human astronauts. The aliens had, in fact, been duped by the xenophobic General Carrington, who was determined to provoke a war against them.

ALPHA CENTAURI

Created by Brian Hayles
The Curse of Peladon (1972)
The Monster of Peladon (1974)
Body: Stuart Fell
Voice: Ysanne Churchman

A hermaphrodite hexapod, Alpha Centauri was ambassador in residence on the planet Peladon after deciding to stay following the acceptance of the planet into the Galactic Federation. See page 47.

ANDROGUMS

Created by Robert Holmes
The Two Doctors (1985)
Chessene O'The Franzine Grig: Jacqueline Pearce
Shockeye O'The Quawncing Grig: John Stratton
Dead Androgum: Jay McGrath

A race of creatures used by Professor Joinson Dastari for his genetic experiments. The Androgums were voracious gourmands and Dastari was trying to turn them into a more civilized and cultured life form.

ANIMUS

Created by Bill Strutton
The Web Planet (1965)
Voice: Catherine Fleming
The Animus was a parasitic creature which exuded a web to drain the life from its host planets. The Doctor defeated it on the planet Vortis, where it had taken control of the *Zarbi*, native ant creatures, and used them to terrorise the intelligent but peaceful *Menoptra*.

ANTI-MATTER MONSTER

Created by Louis Marks
Planet of Evil (1975)
Monster: Mike Lee Lane
Professor Sorenson: Frederick Jaeger
Sorenson Monsters: Ray Knight, Douglas Stark
Double for Sorenson: Terry Walsh

A creature which emerged from its own universe to try to retrieve anti-matter taken from the planet Zeta Minor by Professor Sorenson while on a Morestran survey mission. Sorenson became infected with anti-matter and transformed into anti-man before being replicated into multiple versions of the same creature. Sorenson was 'cured' when the Doctor returned the anti-matter to the anti-matter universe.

ARCTURUS

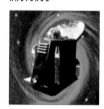

Created by Brian Hayles
The Curse of Peladon (1972)
Peter Murphy Grumbar
Voice: Terry Bale

Representative of the Arcturans on the planet Peladon. Arcturus was secretly behind a plot to prevent Peladon from joining the Galactic Federation.

ARGOLINS

Created by David Fisher
The Leisure Hive (1980)
Pangol: David Haig
Mena: Adrienne Corri
Morix: Laurence Payne
Vargos: Martin Fisk
Baby Pangol: Alys Dyer
Guides: Roy Montague, Derek Suthern, Maurice Connor, Douglas Stark, Annette Peters, Jenny Roberts, Ken Sedd, Mary Rennie, Mike Reynell

Pangol Body Parts: Tim Oldroyd, Reg Woods, Douglas Roe

Peaceful inhabitants of the radioactive planet Argolis. The Argolins ran the Leisure Hive, an intergalactic entertainment complex, which was rapidly losing money. The Argolin race was sterile, and Pangol was the first of a new strain of Argolin, born from the tachyon recreation generator. He hoped to clone himself to continue his race.

ARIDIANS

Created by Terry Nation
The Chase (1965)
Malsan: Ian Thompson
Prondyn: Al Raymond
Rynian: Hywel Bennett
Aridian: Brian Proudfoot

Peaceful, somewhat fishlike inhabitants from the hot and sandy planet Aridius, which was visited by the Doctor and his companions for a holiday.

AUTONS

Created by Robert Holmes
Spearhead from Space (1970) AAA
Terror of the Autons (1971) EEE
Channing: Hugh Burden (AAA)
Major General Scobie: Hamilton Dyce (AAA)
Hospital Porters: Victor Crocksford, Roy Brent (AAA)
Secretary: Constance Carling (AAA)
Auton in Forest: Ivan Orton (AAA)
Commissionaire: Ronald Mayer (AAA)
Display Mannequins: Dennis Hayward, Roger Houghton, Tom Segal, Keith Simon, Kenneth Lindford, Roger Minnis (AAA)
Auton Replica: Walter Goodman (AAA)
Autons at Factory: Hein Viljoen, Barry Ashton, Bob Williman, Arnold Chazen, Cy Town, Keith Ashley (AAA)
Leader: Pat Gorman (EEE)
Leader's Voice: Haydn Jones (EEE)
Policemen: Terry Walsh, Dinny Powell (EEE)
Troll Doll: Tommy Reynolds (EEE)
Daffodil Men: Bob Blaine, Les Clark, Ian Elliott, Nick Hobbs, Charles Pickess, Mike Stevens, Tom O'Leary (EEE)
Auton in Safe: Tom O'Leary (EEE)

Anything made of plastic can become an Auton when the *Nestene Consciousness* animates it. Auton forms include: window mannequins, waxwork dummies, daffodils, a telephone cord, policemen, an armchair and a troll doll. See page 42.

AXOS

Created by Bob Baker and Dave Martin
The Claws of Axos (1971)
Men: Bernard Holley, Roger Minnis, Geoff Righty, Steve King, David Aldridge
Woman: Patricia Gordino, Sue Crossland
Boy: John Hicks
Girl: Debbie Lee London

Glob: Douglas Roe, Clive Rogers
Rolling Glob: Eden Fox, Stuart Myers
Globby: Clinton Morris, Douglas Roe
Monsters: Marc Boyle, Jack Cooper, Derek Martin,
Peter Holmes, Clinton Morris, Steve Smart, Stuart Fell, Reg
Harding, Steve Emmerson, Nick Hobbs
Voice of Axos: Bernard Holley

Axos was a parasitic entity which drained the life from planets it
visited. It was able to create extensions of itself in the form of the
planet's native inhabitants, and gained trust in order for it to
spread enough of itself around the planet for feeding to
commence on a global scale. The parasite manifested itself as
an organic spacecraft, golden-skinned humanoid creatures,
tentacled monsters and as a powerful energy-transforming
mineral called Axonite. The Doctor trapped Axos in a time loop,
from which it could not escape.

BANDRILS

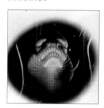

Created by Glen McCoy
Timelash (1985)
Ambassador's Voice: Martin Gower

The Bandrils were the former allies of the planet Karfel but
became enemies when the dictatorial *Borad* gained power on
Karfel. Eventually the Bandrils launched a missile at Karfel, but
luckily the Doctor was on hand to deflect it while the Karfelons
attempted to establish diplomatic negotiations once more. With
the *Borad* out of the way, peace seemed inevitable.

BEAUS

Created by Terry Nation
The Daleks' Master Plan (1965/6)
Gerry Vidal

A delegate of the *Dalek* alliance, introduced by *Zephon*. He
escaped from Kembel to warn his own people of the Daleks'
plans of conquest.

BELL PLANTS

Created by John Flanagan and Andrew McCulloch
Meglos (1980)

One of the aggressive native vegetable lifeforms on the planet
Tigella.

BIO-MECHANOID

Created by Ian Briggs

Dragonfire (1987)
Leslie Meadows

The Bio-Mechanoid was a biomorph, a genetically engineered
being designed to keep and protect a power crystal. It was
hidden in the ice caverns on the planet Svartos and was hunted
by the evil Kane to power his spacecraft and allow him to seek
retribution against his own people.

BOK

Created by Robert Sloman and Barry Letts
The Dæmons (1971)
Stanley Mason

Bok was a stone gargoyle that resided in the crypt under the
church in the village of Devil's End. Using the ancient psionic
power of the *Dæmons*, the Master brought the gargoyle to life in
order to terrorize the villagers and to do his bidding. Bok was
eventually de-animated when the Dæmon Azal destroyed himself.

BORAD

Created by Glen McCoy
Timelash (1985)
Robert Ashby

The Borad was the dictatorial leader of the planet Karfel. Once a
scientist named Magellan, he had become a half-Karfelon, half-
Morlox mutant following a failed experiment with the gas
mustakozene-80. He planned to rule Karfel and the neighbouring
planets, and also to transform the Doctor's companion Peri into
a mutant like himself so that she could become his bride. The
Doctor defeated the Borad and sent him back in time through
the Karfelons' Timelash device, where he ended up on Earth, in
Loch Ness in the 11th Century.

BRAIN

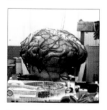

Created by Pip and Jane Baker
Time and the Rani (1987)
Voice: Peter Tuddenham, Jacki Webb

In order to achieve her aim of creating a time manipulator, the
Rani constructed a giant organic brain into which she fed the
combined knowledge of geniuses kidnapped from across time
and space. The brain was eventually destroyed when the Rani's
plans were thwarted by the Doctor.

CELATION

Created by Dennis Spooner
The Daleks' Master Plan (1965/6)
Terence Woodfield

A delegate of the *Dalek* alliance, introduced by *Zephon*. With
Malpha, Celation planned to overthrow Chen but ultimately left
Kembel to warn his own people of the Daleks' plans of conquest.

CHAMELEONS

Created by Malcolm Hulke and David Ellis
The Faceless Ones (1967)
Captain Blade: Donald Pickering, Terence Denville
Director: Bernard Kay
Jamie: Frazer Hines
Michelle Leuppi: Anneke Wills
Jenkins: Christopher Tranchell
Meadows: George Selway
Nurse Pinto: Madalene Nicol
Double for Nurse Pinto: Elisabeth Smith
Spencer: Victor Winding
Airport Personnel in Plane: John Evans, Ann Gaibriel,
Tony Lang, Steve Pokol, Audrey Searle, Audrey Stewart
Chameleons: Robin Dawson, Barry Du Pres, Pat Leclerc,
Roy Pearce

The Chameleons were a tragic race of aliens who had lost their
own identities in a catastrophe on their home planet. As a result
they headed for Earth and, posing as a travel company, stole the
identities of the young humans who were travelling on their aircraft.
The Doctor uncovered their plan and agreed to help them find
another solution to their problem, once all the kidnapped
humans were revived and returned.

CHEETAH PEOPLE

Created by Rona Munro
Survival (1989)
Karra: Lisa Bowerman
Double for Karra: Wayne Michaels, Damon Jeffrey
Cheetahs: Emma Durrell, Susan Goode, Damon Jeffrey,
Samantha Leverette, Leslie Meadows, Basil Patton, Lee Towsey,
Adel Jackson

The Cheetah people inhabited a planet that was rapidly
approaching destruction. The planet exerted a strange influence
over those who visited it, ultimately transforming them into
cheetahs. The Master had become ensnared by the planet and
drew the Doctor and Ace to him. Ace started to change, but the
Doctor managed to break the Master's influence allowing the
Doctor and Ace to return to the TARDIS. See page 71.

CHIMERONS

Created by Malcolm Kohll
Delta and the Bannermen (1987)
Delta: Belinda Mayne
Chima: Tim Scott
Chimeron Princess age 6 months: Jessica McGough
Chimeron Princess age 4: Amy Osborn
Chimeron Princess age 9: Laura Collins
Chimeron Princess age 12: Carley Joseph
Chimerons: Russell Brook, Ian McClaren

The Chimerons were a dying race, all but wiped out thanks to the
crusade of Gavrok and his Bannermen. The final Chimeron
Queen, Delta, fled to Earth carrying with her the last remaining egg
from which would hatch a Chimeron Princess. The Doctor helped

A-Z MONSTERS

Delta escape from Gavrok and the new Princess grow to maturity.

CHINESE DRAGON

Created by Don Houghton
The Mind of Evil (1971)
unknown

A Chinese dragon was conjured by Captain Chin Lee using power from the Keller Machine to cause the American delegate to a peace conference, Senator Allcott, to have a near-fatal heart attack.

CHUMBLIES

Created by William Emms
Galaxy 4 (1965)
Jimmy Kaye, Angelo Muscat, Pepi Poupee, Tommy Reynolds, William Shearer

The Chumblies were the robot slaves of the *Rills,* whom the Doctor met on a doomed planet in Galaxy 4. They were named by the Doctor's companion Vicki after she noted their curious bobbing movement.

CITY

Created by Terry Nation
Death to the Daleks (1974)

On the planet Exxilon, the natives constructed a fabulous 'living' city which ran itself and extended its roots deep into the ground. The city eventually decided that its creators were not worthy to live in it and so banished them to the outside where the race reverted to savagery. The city drained power from the rest of the planet using a flashing beacon, and was eventually destroyed when the beacon was blown up by a group of humans trying to escape from the planet with the cure to a space plague.

CLEANING ROBOTS

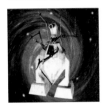 

Created by Stephen Gallagher [6G]; Stephen Wyatt [7E]
Terminus (1983) 6G
Paradise Towers (1987) 7E

When a plague ship docked at Terminus Centre, after those infected with the lazar disease had departed, the ship was cleaned and decontaminated by cleaning robots [6G]. The apartment complex of Paradise Towers was kept clean by several cleaning robots which roamed the hallways and lurked in the swimming pool. When *Kroagnon* took control of them, they started to kill the inhabitants [7E].

CLOCKWORK SOLDIERS

Created by Peter Ling
The Mind Robber (1968)
Paul Alexander, Ian Hines, Richard Ireson

The Clockwork Soldiers were servants of the Master of the Land of Fiction.

CONTROL

Created by Marc Platt
Ghost Light (1989)
Sharon Duce

The control creature in the angel-like being *Light's* attempt to catalogue all life. In reaction to its enforced emprisonment by *Josiah Smith*, Control rapidly developed from an inarticulate shambling creature into a beautiful young lady. Josiah Smith regressed into what Control had been, while Control herself became part of a new team to carry on with Light's work once the angel had been dispersed.

CRYONS

Created by Paula Moore
Attack of the Cybermen (1985)
Flast: Faith Brown
Rost: Sarah Berger
Threst: Esther Freud
Varne: Sarah Greene
Cryons: Tricia Clarke, Maggie Lynton, Irela Williams

The Cryons were the original inhabitants of the planet Telos, sent into exile deep below ground when the *Cybermen* arrived to build their tombs. The Cryons can live only in sub-zero temperatures and are experts in refrigeration equipment. Eventually the Cryons hit back and helped the Doctor and a group of humans destroy the Cybermen's frozen army on Telos.

CYBERMATS

Created by Kit Pedler and Gerry Davis
The Tomb of the Cybermen (1967) MM
The Wheel in Space (1968) SS
Revenge of the Cybermen (1975) 4D

Small, rodent-like robot slaves of the *Cybermen.* They were used to attack when there was no way for the Cybermen to be there themselves. They have been known to home in on the brainwaves of humans [MM], emit a killing wave of energy [SS] and inject a virulent poison through a bite [4D]. See page 23.

CYBERMEN

Created by Kit Pedler
The Tenth Planet (1966) DD
The Moonbase (1967) HH
The Tomb of the Cybermen (1967) MM
The Wheel in Space (1968) SS
The Invasion (1968) VV
The War Games (1969) ZZ
Carnival of Monsters (1973) PPP
Revenge of the Cybermen (1975) 4D
Earthshock (1982) 6B
The Five Doctors (1983) 6K
Attack of the Cybermen (1985) 6T
Silver Nemesis (1988) 7K
Gern: Gregg Palmer (DD)
Jarl: Reg Whitehead (DD)
Krail: Reg Whitehead (DD)
Krang: Harry Brooks (DD)
Shav: Gregg Palmer (DD)
Talon: Harry Brooks (DD)
Tarn: Sonny Willis (HH)
Cyberleader: Christopher Robbie (4D), David Banks (6B, 6K, 6T, 7K)
Cyberlieutenant: Mark Hardy (6B, 6K, 7K), Brian Orrell (6T)
Cyberscout: William Kenton (6K)
Cybercontroller: Michael Kilgarriff (MM, 6T)
Cybermen: John Haines, John Knott, Bruce Wells, John Slater (DD); John Clifford, Ronald Lee, John Levene, Barry Noble, John Wills (John Maxim), Reg Whitehead, Peter Greene, Keith Goodman, Bernard Reid, Terry Wallis, Decland Cuffe, Derek Chafer (HH); Hans De Vries, Tony Harwood, John Hogan, Richard Kerley, Ronald Lee, Charles Pemberton, Kenneth Seeger, Reg Whitehead (MM); Jerry Holmes, Gordon Stothard, Tony Harwood (SS); Ralph Carrigan, Derek Chafer, Terence Denville, Charles Finch, Pat Gorman, Richard King, John Spradbury, Peter Thornton (VV); Roy Pearce (ZZ); Terence Denville (PPP); Pat Gorman, Tony Lord, Melville Jones (4D); David Bache, Norman Bradley, Graham Cole, Peter Gates-Fleming , Steve Ismay, Jeff Wayne (6B); Mark Bassenger, Norman Bradley, Graham Cole, Gilbert Gillan, Emyr Morris Jones, Myrddin Jones, Ian Marshall-Fisher, Richard Naylor, Alan Riches, Mark Whincup, Lloyd Williams, Lee Woods, Stuart Fell (6K); John Ainley, Pat Gorman, Thomas Lucy, Ian Marshall-Fisher, Roger Pope, Ken Barker (6T); Paul Barrass, Danny Boyd, Tony Carlton, Bill Malin, Scott Mitchell, Brian Orrell, Paul Heasman (7K)
Voices: Roy Skelton (DD, SS); Peter Hawkins (DD, HH, MM, SS); Peter Halliday (VV)
Cyber-Director Voice: Peter Halliday (VV)

Originally from the planet Mondas, the Cybermen started out quite similar to humans, but they developed the science of Cybernetics to a great degree and started replacing their own body parts and organs with machines. They also altered their brains, removing all trace of emotion, leaving a coldly logical creature with a strong instinct to survive. The Cybermen have attempted to invade Earth on several occasions [DD, HH, SS, VV, 6B, 6T] and the Doctor has also encountered them in their frozen tombs on Telos [MM, 6T], trying to blow up the planet Voga, a rich source of gold, which is lethal to the Cybermen [4D], in the Death Zone on Gallifrey [6K] and attempting to gain control of *Nemesis* [7K]. See page 23.

DÆMONS

Created by Robert Sloman

The Dæmons (1971)
Azal: Stephen Thorne

Azal was the last of the Dæmons, an ancient race of godlike creatures who gave knowledge to less-developed worlds to see how they would cope. Earth was one such experiment, and the last Dæmon needed to pass on his power. The Doctor refused this power but the Master embraced it. The Doctor's companion's attempted self-sacrifice turned Azal's power back on himself and he was destroyed.

DALEKS

Created by Terry Nation
The Mutants aka *The Daleks* (1963/4) B
The Dalek Invasion of Earth (1964) K
The Space Museum (1965) Q
The Chase (1965) R
Dalek Cutaway (1965) T/A
The Daleks' Master Plan (1965/6) V
The Power of the Daleks (1966) EE
The Evil of the Daleks (1967) LL
The War Games (1969) ZZ
The Mind of Evil (1971) FFF
Day of the Daleks (1972) KKK
Frontier in Space (1973) QQQ
Planet of the Daleks (1973) SSS
Death to the Daleks (1974) XXX
Genesis of the Daleks (1975) 4E
Destiny of the Daleks (1979) 5J
The Five Doctors (1983) 6K
Resurrection of the Daleks (1984) 6P
Revelation of the Daleks (1985) 6Z
Remembrance of the Daleks (1988) 7H
Doctor Who (1996)
Operators: Peter Murphy Grumbar (B, K, Q, EE, LL, KKK, QQQ, SSS, XXX); Robert Jewell (B, K, R, T/A, V, EE, LL, ZZ); Kevin Manser (B, K, R, T/A, V, EE); Michael Summerton (B); Gerald Taylor (B, K, R, T/A, V, EE, LL); Nick Evans (K, EE); Ken Tyllson (K, LL); John Scott Martin (R, T/A, V, EE, LL, KKK, QQQ, SSS, XXX, 4E, 6K, 6P, 6Z, 7H); Ricky Newby (KKK); Cy Town (QQQ, SSS, XXX, 4E, 5J, 6P, 6Z, 7H); Keith Ashley (4E), Toby Byrne (5J, 6P, 6Z); Mike Mungarvan (5J); Tony Starr (5J, 6P, 6Z, 7H); Norman Bacon (7H); David Harrison (7H); Hugh Spight (7H); Nigel Wild (7H)
Dalek Supreme Operator: Tony Starr (SSS)
Emperor: Terry Molloy (7H)
Voices: David Graham (B, K, R, T/A, V); Peter Hawkins (B, K, Q, R, T/A, V, EE, LL); Roy Skelton (LL, SSS, 4E, 5J, 6K, 6Z, 7H); Oliver Gilbert, Peter Messaline (KKK); Michael Wisher (QQQ, SSS, XXX, 4E); David Gooderson (5J); Royce Mills (6P, 6Z, 7H); Brian Miller (6P, 7H); John Leeson (7H).
Emperor Dalek voice: Peter Hawkins (LL)
The Daleks were the most evil of all the creatures the Doctor encountered over the years. The Doctor has met them many times, including in their metal city on Skaro [B] when he thought he had destroyed them after their power supply was deactivated. However, they returned in Earth's future to invade and conquer the planet in an attempt to replace the core with a motive device and thus pilot the planet around the cosmos [K]. Since this time, the Doctor encountered the Daleks in many different situations: chasing him across time and space [R], plotting to control the solar system and its empire with its so called guardian as their ally [T/A, V], as a group of stranded Daleks trying to take over a far-flung Earth colony [EE], in a different version of Earth's future as they try to ensure that their conquest of the planet happens [KKK], planning an attack on the galaxy with an invisible army [SSS], attempting to win a battle against the robotic Movellans [5J, 6P] and battling against their own kind as *Davros* split the race into two factions, one loyal to himself and the others loyal to the Dalek Emperor on Skaro [7H]. See page 79.

DAVROS

Created by Terry Nation
Genesis of the Daleks (1975) 4E
Destiny of the Daleks (1979) 5J
Resurrection of the Daleks (1984) 6P
Revelation of the Daleks (1985) 6Z
Remembrance of the Daleks (1988) 7H
Michael Wisher (4E); David Gooderson (5J); Terry Molloy (6P, 6Z, 7H)

Davros was the head of the Kaled Scientific Elite on Skaro, working to try to win the war against the Thals. He developed the *Dalek* as a means to ensure the survival of the Kaled race. See page 88.

DESTROYER, THE

Created by Ben Aaronovitch
Battlefield (1989)
Marek Anton

The Destroyer was an ancient demon summoned by Morgaine the witch to destroy the Earth. Before the creature was able to break its silver bonds, Brigadier Lethbridge-Stewart of UNIT, temporarily out of retirement, killed it with a silver bullet. See page 68.

DINOSAURS

Doctor Who and the Silurians (1970) BBB
Carnival of Monsters (1973) PPP
Invasion of the Dinosaurs (1974) WWW
The Mark of the Rani (1985) 6X

The Doctor has encountered dinosaurs on several occasions. An allosaurus was used by the *Silurians* under Wenley Moor as a 'guard dog' [BBB]; a plesiosaur was terrorizing the crew of the SS Bernice trapped inside Vorg's miniscope [PPP]; numerous dinosaurs, including a brontosaurus, a stegosaurus, a pterodactyl and a tyrannosaurus, were transported to London by misguided scientists hoping to turn back time [WWW]; the Rani had collected the embryos of several dinosaurs during her travels and a tyrannosaurus came to life and grew when she and the Master became trapped in her TARDIS [6X].

DRACONIANS

Created by Malcolm Hulke
Frontier in Space (1973)
Emperor: John Woodnutt
Prince: Peter Birrel
First Secretary: Lawrence Davidson

Messenger: Ian Frost
Space Pilot: Roy Pattison
Captain: Bill Wilde
Emperor's Guards: Stewart Myers, Rodney Cardiff, Richard King, Steve Tierney, Ken Wade
Guards: Laurence Held, Leslie Bates
Draconians: Bill Burridge, Andy Devine, Terry Sartain, Bill Matthews, Ray Millar, Kevin Moran

The Draconians were a noble and honourable race who, in the 26th century, established a diplomatic peace with Earth in exchange for trading and other rights. This treaty was in danger of being destroyed when the Master, working for the *Daleks*, attempted to start a war between Earth and Draconia. The Draconians operated a dynastic system of government and were ruled by an Emperor who sat in the palace on their home world. The Doctor was made a noble of Draconia by the 51st Emperor. See page 48.

DRACULA, COUNT

The Chase (1965)
Malcolm Rogers

A life-size robot of the famous bloodsucking count was met by the Doctor in a haunted house – part of the Festival of Ghana – in 1996.

DRAHVINS

Created by William Emms and Verity Lambert (BBC)
Galaxy 4 (1965)
Maaga: Stephanie Bidmead
One: Marina Martin
Two: Susanna Carroll
Three: Lyn Ashley
Dead Clone: Lyn Ashley

The Drahvins were a race of female warriors who reduced their males to breeding stock. The ruling females created unintelligent cloned slaves which were not named and were not allowed to develop full personalities, existing simply to serve their commander. The Drahvins were ruthless and cunning and would stop at nothing to achieve their aims.

DRASHIGS

Created by Robert Holmes
Carnival of Monsters (1973)

The Drashigs were a giant caterpillar-like life form from one of Grundle's satellites. They were blind and hunted by scent alone. However once they had the scent of their prey, they would not stop until they had caught it. A colony of Drashigs were trapped on Vorg's miniscope and were inadvertently released on Inter Minor following the disruption of the scope's systems by the Doctor. The creatures were killed by the showman Vorg's quick reflexes and use of the Inter Minorians' eradicator weapon.

DRATHRO

Created by Robert Holmes
The Trial of a Time Lord (1986)
Voice: Roger Brierley
Operator: Paul McGuinness

Drathro was the L3 robot guardian of some mysterious 'secrets' – in reality information from the Matrix which had been stolen from the Time Lords by beings from Andromeda. It was powered by a black light converter on the planet Ravolox (formerly Earth), but shifted from its original position by the Time Lords to try to hide the existence of the 'secrets'). Drathro and the 'secrets' were destroyed when the converter was blown up.

ERGON

Created by Johnny Byrne
Arc of Infinity (1983)
Malcolm Harvey

The Ergon was a creature created by *Omega* to do his bidding on Earth while Omega was himself trapped in the antimatter universe.

'EXCELLENCY'

Created by Philip Martin
The Trial of a Time Lord (1986)
Deep Roy

A delegate from Possicar on the planet Thoros-Beta to negotiate trading terms with the *Mentor* Lord Kiv.

EXXILONS

Created by Terry Nation
Death to the Daleks (1974)
Bellal: Arnold Yarrow
Gotal: Roy Heymann
High Priest: Mostyn Evans
Exxilon Messenger: Tex Fuller
Exxilons: Leslie Bates, Bob Blaine, Derek Chafer, Steve Ismay, Kevin Moran, Dennis Plenty, Michael Reynel, David Rolfe, Terry Sartain, Marc Boyle, Max Faulkner, Roy Pearce, Terry Denville, Nigel Wynder, Terry Walsh

Once a proud spacefaring race, the Exxilons degenerated once their own a living *city* decided it no longer needed them and banished them. The Exxilons split into two factions, one who worshipped the city as a god and another who wanted to destroy it.

EYE-PLANTS

Created by Terry Nation
Planet of the Daleks (1973)

Native plantlife on the planet Spiridon. The plants became agitated when a *Dalek* was near and were used by the Thal party as an early-warning system.

FENDAHL

Created by Chris Boucher
Image of the Fendahl (1977)
Fendahl Core: Wanda Ventham

The Fendahl was a gestalt entity described as being death incarnate. It fed on death and caused the destruction of Mars before the Time Lords trapped it in a time loop. One of its relics – a skull – was discovered on Earth, and a chain of ancestry brought it back to existence in the 20th century. The Doctor managed to stop it, and destroyed the relic so that the Fendahl could no longer be summoned.

FENDAHLEEN

Created by Chris Boucher
Image of the Fendahl (1977)

The Fendahleen were the snakelike servants of the *Fendahl* core. The 12 acolytes of the Fendahl were converted into Fendahleen when the Fendahl manifested on Earth.

FENRIC

Created by Ian Briggs
The Curse of Fenric (1989)
Judson: Dinsdale Landen
Sorin: Tomek Bork

Fenric was an evil entity from the dawn of time with which the Doctor had battled since the third century. The Doctor carved bones into chess pieces and challenged Fenric to solve a puzzle, with the result that Fenric became trapped in the shadow dimensions. A flask containing Fenric's essence was brought to England by Vikings in the ninth century and the descendants of those Vikings became Fenric's pawns: its wolves. Ace was a part of this ongoing battle but the Doctor ultimately prevented Fenric's return with the help of the Ancient One, a *Haemovore*, who destroyed Fenric's host body and himself with a lethal poison gas.

FIRE FLY

Created by Pip and Jane Baker
Time and the Rani (1987)

A type of deadly fire fly was used by the Rani to punish the *Lakertyians* within their pleasure dome.

FISH PEOPLE

Created by Geoffrey Orme
The Underwater Menace (1967)
Full Fish People: Cathy Ash, Mary McMillen, Judy Nicholls, Tony Starr
Half Fish People: Derek Calder, Nigel Clayton, Alex Donald, Perin Lewis, Tony Starr

The insane Professor Zaroff was self-styled ruler of the undersea city of Atlantis. Any mariner unlucky enough to cross Zaroff's path was converted into a Fish Person by injection and surgery. These creatures then lived underwater and harvested food and seaweed from the sea in order to feed the human population of Atlantis.

FOAMASI

Created by David Fisher
The Leisure Hive (1980)
David Bulbeck, David Korff, Andrew Lane, James Muir

The Foamasi were a race of reptiles resistant to the effects of radiation. During a 20-minute war between the *Argolin* people and the Foamasi, the planet Argolis was turned into a radioactive wasteland and the Argolins were made sterile. As a result of the war, the Argolins built a leisure hive on their planet, dedicated to developing cross-cultural understanding. The West Lodge, a group of Foamasi citizens, made an offer to the Argolin leaders to buy the planet, which they secretly intended to use as a venue for their illegal activities. However, the Foamasi government became aware of the plans and sent representatives to Argolis to stop the sale.

FRANKENSTEIN'S MONSTER

The Chase (1965)
John Maxim

A robot of Baron Frankenstein's famous fictional monster was encountered by the Doctor in a funfair at the Festival of Ghana in 1996.

FUNGOIDS

Created by Terry Nation
The Chase (1965)
Jack Pitt, John Scott Martin, Ken Tyllson
Ambulatory fungus life form on the planet Mechanus.

GARM, THE

Created by Stephen Gallagher
Terminus (1983)
R. J. Bell

The Garm was a mysterious dog-faced alien present on the plague-treatment space station Terminus Centre, who carried and escorted those suffering from the lazar disease to the radiation chambers for treatment. The Garm was enslaved by the Vanir, who ran the station and, in exchange for helping prevent a catastrophic explosion, the Doctor freed the Garm to help the Vanir on his own terms.

GASTROPODS

Created by Anthony Steven
The Twin Dilemma (1984)
Mestor: Edwin Richfield
Gastropods: Ridgewell Hawkes, Steve Wickham

The Gastropods were thought to have died out until Mestor and his compatriots invaded the planet Joconda, enslaved its population and used the planet as a breeding and distribution point for Mestor's eggs.

GEARON

Created by Terry Nation
The Daleks' Master Plan (1965/6)
Jack Pitt

One of the alliance members involved in the *Daleks'* plan to conquer the solar system. Gearon was killed by Mavic Chen when he and the other delegates tried to depose Chen from the alliance.

GELL GUARDS

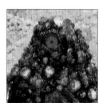

Created by Bob Baker and Dave Martin
The Three Doctors (1972/3)
Peter Murphy Grumbar, Ricky Newby, John Scott Martin, Cy Town

Amorphous blobs of matter created by Omega to bring the Doctor from Earth to his anti-matter universe.

GIANT ANTS

Created by Louis Marks
Planet of Giants (1964)

The Doctor and his companions encountered a number of dead giant ants when they became miniaturised on Earth.

GIANT BATS

Created by Robert Holmes
The Caves of Androzani (1984)

Denizens of the deep caves on Androzani Minor. The milk from the queen bat was the only known antidote to spectrox toxaemia.

GIANT BEE

Created by Louis Marks
Planet of Giants (1964)

The Doctor and his companions encountered a dead giant bee when they became miniaturised on Earth.

GIANT CAT

Created by Louis Marks
Planet of Giants (1964)

The Doctor and his companions encountered a giant cat when they became miniaturised on Earth.

GIANT EARTHWORM

Created by Louis Marks
Planet of Giants (1964)

The Doctor and his companions encountered a dead giant earthworm when they became miniaturised on Earth.

GIANT FLY

Created by Louis Marks [J]; Robert Sloman and Barry Letts [TTT]; Philip Martin [6V]

Planet of Giants (1964) J
The Green Death (1973) TTT
Vengeance on Varos (1985) 6V

The Doctor and his companions encountered a giant fly when they became miniaturised on Earth [J]. The *giant maggots* hatched into venom-spraying giant flies [TTT]. A small gee-jee fly was made to appear giant sized when the Doctor and his friends entered the 'purple zone' in the punishment dome on Varos [6V].

GIANT MAGGOTS

Created by Robert Sloman and Barry Letts
The Green Death (1973)

Maggots were grown to giant size by pollution from the Global Chemicals factory in Wales. The maggots had a venomous bite which turned the victim bright green during a slow painful death.

GIANT RATS

Created by Robert Holmes
The Talons of Weng-Chiang (1977)
Stuart Fell

Created by the experiments of Magnus Greel in the late 19th Century. Leela was attacked by a giant rat in London's sewers.

GIANT SPIDERS

Created by Robert Sloman and Barry Letts
Planet of the Spiders (1974)
Queen's Voice: Kismet Delgado
Lupton's Spider Voice: Ysanne Churchman
Spider Voices: Ysanne Churchman, Kismet Delgado, Maureen Morris
Voice of The Great One: Maureen Morris
Puppeteer: Barry Smith

When an Earth colony ship arrived on the planet Metebelis 3, as well as the humans, on board were spiders which found their way into the mountains. There, bathed in the blue radiation they developed sentience and grew to giant size. They were ruled by the Great One, a massive mutant spider with an insane desire to grow in power and to rule the universe. The Great One and the rest of the spiders were destroyed when the Great One obtained the final crystal to complete her web of power. The resultant feedback blew up the caves and the mountain in which the spiders lived.

GODS OF RAGNAROK, THE

Created by Stephen Wyatt
The Greatest Show in the Galaxy (1989)
Dad/God: David Ashford
Mum/God: Janet Hargreaves
Girl: Kathryn Ludlow
Girl God: Lorne McCulloch
Voice of Girl God: Alan Waring

The Gods of Ragnarok had corrupted the Psychic Circus on the planet Segonax and were using it to provide the constant entertainment which they craved. Anyone who failed to entertain them was killed. The Doctor confronted and defeated them by turning their own power against them.

GREAT INTELLIGENCE

Created by Mervyn Haisman and Henry Lincoln
The Abominable Snowmen (1966) NN
The Web of Fear (1967) QQ
Voice: Woolf Morris (NN); Jack Watling, Ralph Watson (QQ)

The Great Intelligence was a formless entity from space which twice tried to establish a bridgehead on Earth using its robot *Yeti*.

GREY LADY

The Chase (1965)
Roslyn de Winter

A robot effigy of a ghostly wailing lady was seen by the Doctor in a haunted house – part of the Festival of Ghana in 1996 – while he was trying to escape from the *Daleks*.

GUNDAN ROBOTS

Created by Stephen Gallagher
Warriors' Gate (1981)
Robert Vowles, John Blackman, Derek Chafer, Maurice Connor, George Gordon, Pat Gorman, Chris Michelle, Brian Moorhead, Carl More, Tony Pryor, Terry Sartain

The Gundan robots were created by the humanoid slaves of the Tharils. They were designed to enter the Tharils' Gateway and destroy the creatures before guarding the Gateway against their return.

HAEMOVORES

Created by Ian Briggs
The Curse of Fenric (1989)
Jean: Joann Kenny

Phyllis: Joanne Bell
Wrens: Marianne Bergin, Mandy Demetrious, Sheryl Leigh Fraser, Claudia Lyster, Nicola Maddock, Suzi Mollett, Jane Perry, Roslyn Riley, Kate Shury, Wendy Spear
Drowned Soldier: John van der Pool
The Ancient One: Raymond Trickett
Haemovores: Ian Collins, Jennifer Crome, Ian Elliott, Perry Evans, Ann Graham, Raymond Martin, Jacqui Nolan, Tony Ryan, Graham Stagg, Cy Town, Tip Tipping, Paul Heasman, Sam Kent Smith, Joe Kent Smith, Alan Marshall, Graham Brown

The Haemovores were a race of bloodsucking monsters from Earth's future which were summoned back in time by *Fenric* in its ongoing battle against the Doctor. Their victims could also become vampire-like creatures. The Ancient One came from a world further in the future and could destroy the lesser Haemovores by thought. Ultimately the Ancient One refused to carry out Fenric's orders to carry a deadly pollutant into the sea and instead killed itself and Fenric's then current host body using the pollutant. See page 73.

HORDA

Created by Chris Boucher
The Face of Evil (1977)

Small, vicious creatures native to an alien world upon which a group of humanoid colonists crash-landed. Under the influence of a schizophrenic computer, Xoanon, the humanoids split into two factions, one of which, calling themselves the Sevateem, used the Horda as a form of trial by ordeal.

HUSKS

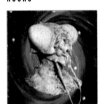

Created by Marc Platt
Ghost Light (1989)
Keith Harvie, Jack Talbot

The living shed skins of *Light's* survey being, *Josiah Smith*.

ICE WARRIORS

Created by Brian Hayles
The Ice Warriors (1967) OO
The Seeds of Death (1969) XX
The War Games (1969) ZZ
The Curse of Peladon (1972) MMM
The Monster of Peladon (1974) YYY
Varga: Bernard Bresslaw (OO)
Turoc: Sonny Caldinez (OO)
Isbur: Michael Attwell (OO)
Rintan: Tony Harwood (OO)
Zondal: Roger Jones (OO)
Slaar: Alan Bennion (XX)
Izlyr: Alan Bennion (MMM)
Ssorg: Sonny Caldinez (MMM)
Azaxyr: Alan Bennion (YYY)
Sskel: Sonny Caldinez (YYY)
Ice Warriors: Sonny Caldinez, Tony Harwood, Steve Peters (XX); Tony Harwood (ZZ); David Cleeve, Terence Denville, Alan

Lenoir, Kevin Moran (YYY)

The Ice Warriors originated from Mars and were a militaristic race of creatures, prepared to die for causes they saw as for the greater Martian good. The Warriors have on two occasions [OO, XX] tried to conquer the Earth to make it their home – Mars was a dead and dying world – and have also been involved in the Galactic Federation, both as a force for good [MMM], and as one for evil [YYY], when a faction of Warriors were plotting with enemies in Galaxy 5 to prolong a bitter war. They were also among those enemies shown by the Doctor as a part of his defence during his first trial by the Time Lords [ZZ]. See page 35.

ICE SOLDIERS

Created by Terry Nation
The Keys of Marinus (1964)
Michael Allaby, Alan James, Peter Stenson, Anthony Verner

Guardians of one of the keys to the Conscience Machine on Marinus. The Ice Soldiers were frozen in blocks of ice along with the key, so that, in order to obtain the key, the Soldiers would be released as well.

ID CREATURES

Created by Chris Boucher
The Face of Evil (1977)
Tom Baker

Invisible monsters summoned by the schizophrenic computer Xoanon. They became visible when fired upon.

JAGAROTH

Created by David Fisher
City of Death (1979)
Scaroth: Julian Glover, Richard Sheekey
Voices: Peter Halliday, Tom Chadbon

The final Jagaroth spacecraft exploded upon take-off from a prehistoric Earth, the power from the blast bringing life to the planet. Unfortunately Scaroth, the ship's pilot, was splintered in time and the different aspects of himself all worked towards the end of travelling back in time to prevent the explosion from happening in the first place.

JOCONDANS

Created by Anthony Steven
The Twin Dilemma (1984)
Noma: Barry Stanton

Drak: Oliver Smith
Chamberlain: Seymour Green
Guards: Mark Bassenger, Graham Cole, Leslie Conrad, Mike Mungarvan, David Ransley, Robert Smythe, John Wilson

Feathered inhabitants of Joconda which was taken over by the *Gastropod* Mestor.

HANDY MAN, THE

Created by Graeme Curry
The Happiness Patrol (1988)
David John Pope

A robot constructed from sweet confections, built by Gilbert M to act as executioner for Helen A, the matriarchal ruler of Terra Alpha, where unhappiness was punishable by death. Gilbert had brought the bones of the Kandy Man in a suitcase to Terra Alpha from the planet Vasilip and constructed the robot's body in the Kandy Kitchen. The Kandy Man was destroyed when the *Pipe People* flooded a pipe – through which the Kandy Man was attempting to escape – with strawberry fondant surprise, dissolving the creature. See page 66.

HASTRIANS

Created by Bob Baker and Dave Martin
The Hand of Fear (1976)
Eldrad: Judith Paris, Stephen Thorne
King Rokon: Roy Skelton
Technic Oban: Peter Roy
Zazzka: Roy Pattison

The planet Kastria was devastated by Eldrad, who was sentenced to obliteration for his crimes. The obliteration failed, and pieces of Eldrad's silicone-based body fell to Earth, to be found by the Doctor's assistant Sarah. Returning to Kastria intent on ruling, Eldrad discovered that his race were no more as they had destroyed themselves rather than risk Eldrad's return as their leader.

KITLINGS

Created by Rona Munro
Survival (1989)

The Kitlings were natives of the *Cheetah People's* planet and looked somewhat like adult Earth cats. They were used by the natives to travel to Earth in order to obtain victims for the hunt. The Master also used the Kitlings as his eyes on Earth as he attempted to track down and entrap the Doctor.

KOQUILLION

Created by David Whitaker
The Rescue (1965)
Ray Barrett

Koquillion was a disguise adopted by the murderer Bennett to prevent the young Vicki from discovering the truth about the death of her father when their ship crashed on the planet Dido.

KRAALS

Created by Terry Nation
The Android Invasion (1975)
Styggron: Martin Friend
Chedaki: Roy Skelton
Chargehand: Stuart Fell

Natives of the planet Oseidon, the Kraals intended to invade the Earth using android duplicates and then to release a virus to wipe out all life, leaving the planet for the Kraals to take over.

KROAGNON

Created by Stephen Wyatt
Paradise Towers (1987)
Voice: Richard Briers
Kroagnon/Chief Caretaker: Richard Briers

The Great Architect of an apartment complex called Paradise Towers. Kroagnon so loved his building that he built himself into it and then proceeded to use *robot cleaners* to kill all the occupants who were cluttering it up. Kroagnon finally took over the body of Paradise Towers' Chief Caretaker.

KROLL

Created by Robert Holmes
The Power of Kroll (1978/9)

Kroll was a god worshipped by the green-skinned Swampies on the third moon of Delta Magna. In reality, Kroll was a squidlike creature grown to giant size when it ingested the Swampies' holy relic – in truth a segment of the Key to Time. When the segment was retrieved by the Doctor and Romana, Kroll was transformed into hundreds of small squid.

KRONOS

Created by Robert Sloman
The Time Monster (1972)
Marc Boyle
Face: Ingrid Bower

Kronos was a Chronovore – literally a devourer of time. The

Master summoned the creature with the hope of controlling it using power from an ancient Atlantean crystal. However, Kronos turned out to be uncontrollable.

KROTONS

Created by Robert Holmes
The Krotons (1968/9)
Operators: Robert Grant, Robert La Bassiere (Robert Grant), Miles Northover
Voices: Roy Skelton, Patrick Tull

The warlike Krotons were a crystalline life form. A group of the creatures had crash-landed on the planet of the Gonds, and waited until the natives had developed sufficient mental energy to reactivate them so that they could leave the planet. The Doctor and his companion Zoe eventually provided the required energy and the Krotons re-formed from a crystalline slurry. The Doctor destroyed them by introducing sulphuric acid into their life-support system, which dissolved them. See page 19.

KRYNOID

Created by Robert Banks Stewart
The Seeds of Doom (1976)
Krynoid/ Charles Winlett (stage 1 Antarctica): John Gleeson
Krynoid/ Arnold Keeler (stage 1 England): Mark Jones
Krynoid (stage 2): Keith Ashley, Ronald Gough
Voice: Mark Jones

The Krynoid was an alien form of plant life which destroyed all animal life on the planets upon which it germinated. Two Krynoid pods were discovered in the Antarctic and one was obtained by an obsessive botanist who promptly decided to grow his own Krynoid. Soon Earth was in danger as the plant grew bigger than a house and prepared to germinate. It was destroyed by a missile attack.

LAKERTYANS

Created by Pip and Jane Baker
Time and the Rani (1987)
Ikona: Mark Greenstreet
Beyus: Donald Pickering
Faroon: Wanda Ventham
Lanisha: John Segal
Sarn: Karen Clegg
Lakertyans: Haydn Andrews, Joseph Arland, Philip Babut, Amanda Jane Beard, June Bishop, Suzanne Britten, Darrell Brook, Russell Brook, Christine Charlesworth, Tricia Clarke, Paul Cottingham, Josh Elwell, Peter Fenton, Debbie Lamb, Mandy Lesley, Micky Max, Christopher Mosque, Mike Mungarvan, Russ Murray, Oscar Peck, Chris Rainbow, Helena Richards, Penny Rigden, Steve Rome, Sara Wishart, Andrew Woodman, Amanda Gray

The Lakertyans were a peaceful race of reptilian humanoids whose planet was invaded by the Rani during her attempt to construct a time manipulator.

LARVAE GUN

Created by Bill Strutton
The Web Planet (1965)
Jack Pitt, Hugh Lund

Mobile venom-spitting weapons used by the *Animus*-controlled *Zarbi* to keep the *Menoptra* enslaved. Also known as a Venom Gun or Venom Grub.

LIGHT

Created by Marc Platt
Ghost Light (1989)
John Hallam

Light was an angel-like being of unknown origin, an intergalactic cataloguer of species who came to Earth to survey life there. While Light slept in his spaceship, *Josiah Smith* was sent out to adapt and to carry out the survey while *Control* stayed within the ship in an unchanged state. When Light was awakened by the Doctor's companion Ace and the neanderthal Nimrod, he had become unbalanced and realized that evolution meant he would never complete his work. He therefore decided to destroy all life on Earth. The Doctor convinced Light that everything changed and evolved, including himself, and that his catalogue would never be complete. Light, unable to deal with this information, dispersed himself following the departure of his spaceship containing the now dominant Control, Josiah Smith, insane explorer Redvers Fenn-Cooper and Nimrod.

LUKOSER, THE

Created by Philip Martin
The Trial of a Time Lord (1986)
Thomas Branch

The Lukoser was a part-man, part-wolf hybrid created from Dorf, the former equerry of King Yrcanos, by Crozier during his attempts to find a means of transplanting the *Mentor* Lord Kiv's brain into another body.

MACRA

Created by Ian Stuart Black
The Macra Terror (1966)
Control Voice: Denis Goacher
Operator: Robert Jewell

The Macra were a race of parasitic giant crabs which infiltrated a human colony on a distant planet and enslaved the inhabitants of a holiday camp to mine the gas they needed to survive.

MAGMA CREATURE

Created by Robert Holmes
The Caves of Androzani (1984)
Colin Taylor

A fearsome creature which roamed the lower levels of the caverns and tunnels beneath the surface of the planet Androzani Minor.

MAGNETON

Created by Terry Nation
The Mutants aka *The Daleks* (1963/4)

One of the native inhabitants of Skaro, the Magneton was a creature composed of a soft metal which generated electricity. The Thals used the creatures to power their flashlights.

MAGS

Created by Stephen Wyatt
The Greatest Show in the Galaxy (1988/9)
Jessica Martin

Mags was a female werewolf from the planet Vulpana, captured by Captain Cook and brought to the planet Segonax.

MALPHA

Created by Terry Nation
Dalek Cutaway (1965) T/A
The Daleks' Master Plan (1965/6) V
Robert Cartland (T/A); Brian Mosley (V)

One of the alliance members at the *Dalek* conference. With *Celation*, Malpha planned to overthrow Mavic Chen. He escaped to warn his own people of the Daleks' plans.

MALUS, THE

Created by Eric Pringle
The Awakening (1984)

The Malus was an alien entity which arrived on Earth on a probe from the planet Hakol. The creature fed on fear and used psychic projections to intensify the feelings in those around it. It tried to re-create a battle from the English civil war in the town of Little Hodcombe in 1984 by taking over the mind of Sir George Hutchinson.

MANDRAGORA

Created by Louis Marks
The Masque of Mandragora (1976)
Voice: Peter Tuddenham

The Mandragora Helix was a spiral of energy with an intelligence at its centre. It 'hitched a lift' with the TARDIS to 15th-century Earth – where a brotherhood of Mandragora-worshippers gained true power through the entity's influence. The Doctor rendered the Mandragora energy on Earth harmless by draining it into the ground.

MANDRELS

Created by Bob Baker
Nightmare of Eden (1979)
Robert Goodman, David Korff, James Muir, Jan Murzynowski, Derek Suthern

The Mandrels were a form of mud-monster from the planet Eden, which, when killed, rapidly decomposed into the addictive drug vraxoin. See page 53.

MARA

Created by Christopher Bailey
Kinda (1982) 5Y
Snakedance (1983) 6D
Dukkha: Jeffrey Stewart (5Y)
Anatta: Anna Wing (5Y)
Anicca: Roger Milner (5Y)
Snake: Stephen Calcutt (5Y)
Tegan: Janet Fielding (5Y, 6D)
Aris: Adrian Mills (5Y)
Lon: Martin Clunes (6D)

The Mara was a demonic creature from 'the inside' – a different dimension, access to which can be gained through dreams. On the planet Deva Loka the Mara possessed first Tegan and then one of the native Kinda, Aris [5Y]. The Mara was first brought into being on the planet Manussa when the Sumarans created a crystal which allowed mental energy to take physical form. This crystal became a holy relic and the Mara tried to re-create itself during a ceremony to celebrate the 500th anniversary of its banishment. Although Tegan was again possessed, along with Lon, son of the local Federator, the Doctor was on hand to prevent the Mara from gaining physical form [6D].

MARSHMEN

Created by Andrew Smith
Full Circle (1980)
Barney Lawrence, Steve Kelly, Stephen Calcutt, Graham Cole,
Keith Guest, James Jackson, Stephen Watson
Marshchild: Norman Bacon

The Marshmen emerged from the swamps on the planet Alzarius during Mistfall and were one of the life forms in the planet's evolutionary cycle. See page 62.

MARSH SPIDERS

Created by Andrew Smith
Full Circle (1980)

The Marsh Spiders were one of the life forms in the evolutionary cycle on the planet Alzarius.

MASTER-SNAKE

Created by Matthew Jacobs
Doctor Who (1996)

The Master had been exterminated by the *Daleks*, but had requested that the Doctor return his remains to Gallifrey. However, the Master was not dead, and manifested himself as a glistening snake-like creature, first attacking the TARDIS and forcing it to materialise on Earth, and then to physically enter and possess the body of Bruce, a medic.

MECHANOIDS

Created by Terry Nation
The Chase (1965)
Operators: Peter Murphy Grumbar, Jack Pitt, John Scott Martin
Voices: David Graham

The Mechanoids were human-built robots sent to prepare a planet for Earth colonisation. The colony ships never arrived and so the Mechanoids maintained a specially-built city in readiness. See page 14.

MEDUSA

The Mind Robber (1967)
Sue Pulford

One of the mythical creatures summoned by the Master of the Land of Fiction to try to transform the Doctor and his companions into fictional characters.

MEGARA

Created by David Fisher
The Stones of Blood (1977)
Operators: Angie Passmore, John Thirtle
Voices: Gerald Cross, David McAlister

The Megara were two justice machines trapped on board a ship in hyperspace by the criminal Cessair of Diplos. When released, they tried the Doctor for the crime of releasing them without proper authority, but the Doctor revealed to them that Vivien Fay (who had been posing as the Cailleach – a mythical Druidic creature) was, in fact, Cessair.

MEGLOS

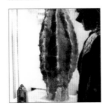

Created by John Flanagan and Andrew McCulloch
Meglos (1980)
Tom Baker, Christopher Owen

Meglos was a xerophyte – an intelligent cactus creature – and the last of his people, the Zolfa-Thurans. Meglos could also change his shape to another form and impersonated both an Earthling and the Doctor in an attempt to obtain a dodecahedron of power from the planet Tigella in order to power a devastating weapon with which he first intended to destroy Tigella, and then to control the universe. Thanks to the Doctor, when the weapon was operated, it destroyed Zolfa-Thura and Meglos along with it.

MELKUR

Created by Johnny Byrne
The Keeper of Traken (1981) 5T
Time-Flight (1982) 6C
Graham Cole

Melkur was the name given by the people of the Traken Union to the calcified statues of evil beings which visited their planet. They looked after these creatures and tended to them. The Master arrived on Traken, and his TARDIS took the form of a Melkur operated from within by the evil Time Lord. He was seeking the power of the bioelectronic source on Traken in order to try to save himself after he had reached the last of his incarnations [5T]. A phantom Melkur

was used by the Master to try to prevent Tegan and Nyssa from entering an inner sanctum on prehistoric earth [6C].

MENOPTRA

Created by Bill Strutton
The Web Planet (1965)
Captain Hilio: Martin Jarvis
Hlynia: Jocelyn Birdsall
Hrhoonda: Arthur Blake
Hrostar: Arne Gordon
Prapillus: Jolyon Booth
Vrestin: Roslyn De Winter
Slave Menoptra: Ken McGarvie

The Menoptra were one of the native life forms on the planet Vortis before the *Animus* arrived and forced them off-world. They were an advanced and noble butterfly people with large wings.

MENTORS

Created by Philip Martin
Vengeance on Varos (1985) 6V
The Trial of a Time Lord (1986) 7B
Sil: Nabil Shaban (6V, 7B)
Kiv: Christopher Ryan (7B)
Mentors: Richard Henry, Philip Rostant (7B)

The Mentors were a race of maggot-like creatures native to Thoros-Beta who were obsessed with finance and power. One of their number, Sil, tried to bully the inhabitants of Varos into accepting a low price for their zeiton 7 ore [6V], and was also present when the brain of the Mentor leader, Lord Kiv grew too big for his cranium and had to be transplanted. The scientist Crozier perfected another technique whereby the memories and personality could be implanted into another body, and the Doctor's assistant Peri apparently became the host [7B]. See page 64.

MIND PARASITE

Created by Don Houghton
The Mind of Evil (1971)

The Master, under the guise of Professor Emil Keller, installed an alien mind parasite in a prison for violent offenders. The parasite drained the evil impulses from the convicts' brains leaving them totally pacified. When the machine had absorbed enough evil, however, it took on a life of its own and started to attack and kill anyone who got in its way.

MINOTAUR

Created by Peter Ling
The Mind Robber (1968) UU
The Time Monster (1972) OOO
Richard Ireson (UU)
Dave Prowse, Terry Walsh (OOO)

The mythical Cretan beast. It was summoned by the Master of the Land of Fiction to attack the Doctor and his companion Zoe [UU] and also was discovered by the Doctor in the labyrinth of ancient Atlantis [OOO].

MIRE BEAST

Created by Terry Nation
The Chase (1965)
Jack Pitt

Native octopus-like creature which lived on the planet Aridius.

MOGARIANS

Created by Pip and Jane Baker
The Trial of a Time Lord (1986)
Atza: Sam Howard
Ortezo: Leon Davis

Creatures from the planet Mogar that do not breathe oxygen. Mogar was being mined by Earth for metal and some of the Mogarians were angry about this. Atza and Ortezo were two such Mogarians and intended to hold a space liner to ransom to force Earth to withdraw. Unfortunately, the liner they chose was also being overrun by *Vervoids* and the two Mogarians died during the various conspiracies that were afoot.

MONOIDS

Created by Paul Erickson and Lesley Scott
The Ark (1966)
First: Edmund Coulter
Second: Frank George
One: Edmund Coulter
Two: Ralph Carrigan
Three: Frank George
Four: John Caesar
Monoids: Bernard Barnsley, Eric Blackburn, Denis Marlow, Bill Richards, Chris Webb, Raymond Byrom
Voices: John Halstead, Roy Skelton

The Monoids were unspeaking servants to a spacecraft of humans en route to a new Earth. The trip took 700 years and in that time – aided by a cold virus accidentally introduced by the Doctor's companion Dodo – the Monoids took over the ship, enslaved the humans and gained the power of speech. On arrival on the planet Refusis II, the Monoids and humans were eventually forced to work together and treat each other as equals by the invisible *Refusians*.

MORBIUS

Created by Terrance Dicks
The Brain of Morbius (1976)
Headless Monster Body: Alan Crisp

Monster: Stuart Fell
Voice: Michael Spice

Morbius was a renegade Time Lord, tracked down and presumed destroyed by his own people. Doctor Solon, however, preserved Morbius' brain and constructed a new patchwork body in which to house it. The brain and the body were destroyed when they plummeted over a cliff. See page 51.

MORLOX

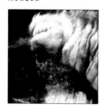

Created by Glen McCoy
Timelash (1985)

Hideous snake-like creatures living in tunnels under the surface of the planet Karfel. The *Borad* was part man, part Morlox.

MORPHO

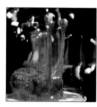

Created by Terry Nation
The Keys of Marinus (1964)
Voice: Heron Carvic

Morpho was a collective of disembodied brains which had enslaved a community on Marinus by creating the hypnotic illusion of luxury.

MOVELLANS

Created by Terry Nation
Destiny of the Daleks (1979)
Commander Sharrell: Peter Straker
Lan: Tony Osoba
Agella: Suzanne Danielle
Guard: Cassandra
Movellans: Bruce Callender, Inga Daly, Wilson M George, Chrissi Hewett, Ken Kajadhar, Jules, Tawny Sands

A race of robots which successfully waged a war against the *Daleks*. The Movellans were totally logical and discovered that this placed them in stalemate with the Daleks, whose battle computers also offered logical moves. They therefore arrived on Skaro at the same time as the Daleks to try to recover *Davros* whom both sides believed would help win the war. They later developed an anti-Dalek virus which all but wiped out the creatures from Skaro and led to the Movellans winning the war.

MR SIN

Created by Robert Holmes
The Talons of Weng-Chiang (1976)
Deep Roy

Mr Sin looked like a normal ventriloquist's doll but was in fact an android creature containing the brain of a pig created by Magnus Greel in the 30th century.

MUMMIES

Created by Lewis Griefer
Pyramids of Mars (1976)
Nick Burnell, Melvyn Bedford, Kevin Selway
Golden Mummies: Nick Burnell, Kevin Selway

The mummies were servicer robots controlled by Sutekh the *Osiran* in order to construct a rocket to destroy a pyramid on Mars which was holding him prisoner on Earth. See page 52.

MUTANTS [DALEK]

Created by Terry Nation (4E), Eric Saward (6Z)
Genesis of the Daleks (1975) 4E
Revelation of the Daleks (1985) 6Z
Thing: Dod Watson (4E)
Mutant: Ken Barker (6Z)
Head of Arthur Stengos/Dalek: Alec Linstead (6Z)

Davros used humans and animals in his experiments to find suitable material with which to create *Daleks*. Those creatures which survived, including a partially glimpsed 'thing', were kept in caves around the Kaled base on Skaro [4E]. The Doctor and Peri were attacked by a mutant, the result of one of Davros' experiments, on their way across ground to Tranquil Repose, a mortuary facility on the planet Necros [6Z].

MUTANTS

Created by Peter Grimwade
Mawdryn Undead (1983)
Mawdryn: David Collings
Mutants: Peter Walmsley, Brian Darnley, David Cole, Ian Craig, Mitchell Horner, Michael Leader, Richard Olley

Mawdryn and seven of his colleagues were condemned to endless mutation by the elders of their planet. They lived on a spacecraft which, every 70 years, came close to a planet where they could attempt to find help. The only thing they wished for was death, and they wanted the Doctor to sacrifice his remaining regenerations to help them to die.

MUTANTS [SOLONIAN]

Created by Bob Baker and Dave Martin
The Mutants (1972) NNN

Frontier in Space (1973) QQQ
The Brain of Morbius (1976) 4K
Ky: Garrick Hagon (NNN)
Old Man: Sydney Johnson (NNN)
Bodyguard: Steven Ismay (NNN)
Mutants: John Scott Martin, Laurie Goode, Bill Gosling, Nick Thompson Hill, Mike Mungarvan, Ricky Newby, Eddie Sommer, Mike Torres (NNN)
Mutant: John Scott Martin (QQQ)
Kriz: John Scott Martin (4K)

The natives of the planet Solos underwent a radical mutation as a part of their evolutionary cycle. From humanoids they progressed into hideous insectoid mutant creatures before entering a pupal stage from which they emerged as beautiful and powerful super-beings [NNN]. Jo was terrified by them and saw one when subjected to the Master's fear-inducing device [QQQ]. One of the mutant stage Solonians crash-landed on the planet Karn, where Dr Solon's assistant, Condo, cut off its head [4K].

MUTATIONS

Created by Terry Nation
The Mutants aka The Daleks (1963/4)

The planet Skaro, as well as a petrified forest and the Dalek city, featured a lake of mutations where the horrific remnants of the neutronic war between the Daleks and the Thals lived. See also *Mutos*.

MUTES

Created by Bob Baker and Dave Martin
The Armageddon Factor (1979)
Stephen Calcutt, Mike Braben, James Haswell, Ridgewell Hawkes, Danny Rae, Eddie Whiting, Derek Suthern, Michael Gordon-Browne

The Mutes were the silent servants of the Shadow, who was endeavouring to gain the Key to Time for the Black Guardian.

MUTOS

Created by Terry Nation
Genesis of the Daleks (1975)
Sevrin: Stephen Yardley
Gerrill: Jeremy Chandler
Mutos: Stephen Calcutt, John Deleiu, James Muir, Roger Salter, Terry Walsh, Michael Crane, John Sowerbutt

The Mutos were mutated Kaleds, the results of the use of chemical weapons during the Kaled – Thal war on Skaro. They were banished into the wasteland – due to a desire to keep the Kaled race 'pure' – where some survived. See also *Mutations*.

MYRKA

Created by Johnny Byrne
Warriors of the Deep (1984)
Back: John Asquith
Front: William Perrie

The Myrka was a massive sea-creature used by the *Silurians* and *Sea Devils* to attack a Sea Base. It carried a fatal electrical charge such that anyone who attempted to touch it was killed instantly. The Doctor destroyed it with a high intensity ultraviolet light.

NAVARINOS

Created by Malcolm Kholl
Delta and the Bannermen (1987)
Murray: Johnny Dennis

The Navarinos were a fun-loving race who organized intergalactic trips to selected periods of Earth's history. Murray was the Navarino driver for a tour on which the Doctor and Mel had won a place. (NB: It has been assumed that not all the passengers on the tour were Navarinos and so only the driver, Murray, who was definitely a Navarino, has been listed in the above cast list.)

NEMESIS

Created by Kevin Clarke
Silver Nemesis (1988)
Fiona Walker

The Nemesis statue was created by Lady Peinforte in 1638 from the 'living' metal validium, which fell to Earth in that year. The Doctor was on hand to launch the statue into space after separating from it a bow and arrow made from the same substance. In 1988, the statue returned to Earth, where it was coveted by several groups: some neo-Nazis, the *Cybermen*, Lady Peinforte (who had time-travelled from the past) and the Doctor. The statue revealed that it knew more of the Doctor's origins than had previously been revealed, but was programmed by the Doctor to again leave Earth and destroy the Cybermen's fleet in space.

NESTENE CONSCIOUSNESS

Created by Robert Holmes
Spearhead from Space (1970)
Terror of the Autons (1971)

The Nestene Consciousness was a gestalt being with a natural form similar to an octopus. The Nestenes had no bodies of their own but did dsiplay an affinity for plastic, and could place a portion of themselves into items made from plastic in order to animate them. These plastic facsimiles were called *Autons*. They first came to Earth in a shower of plastic meteorites, but the Doctor defeated their plans of conquest [AAA] before the Master again summoned them to Earth. They were thrown back into space when the Doctor convinced the Master that the creatures would never let him rule. [EEE] See page 42.

NIMON

Created by Anthony Read
The Horns of Nimon (1979/80)
Robin Sherringham, Bob Appleby, Trevor St John Hacker
Voices: Clifford Norgate

The Nimon were a species of bull-headed humanoids who crossed the galaxy like locusts, sucking the life out of planets before migrating to the next. Their victims included the planet Crinoth, and the planet Skonnos was next in line. The Doctor managed to destroy their power complex on Skonnos, leaving the Nimon trapped on Crinoth.

OGRI

Created by David Fisher
The Stones of Blood (1978)

The Ogri were a species of silicone life from the planet Ogros which fed on globulin, a protein found in human blood.

OGRON EATER, THE

Created by Malcolm Hulke
Frontier in Space (1973)
David Bradburn

On the *Ogrons*' planet an amorphous creature which inhabited the caves was worshipped as a god by the Ogrons. Given the chance, the Ogron-Eater would devour its worshippers.

OGRONS

Created by Louis Marks
Day of the Daleks (1972) KKK
Carnival of Monsters (1973) PPP
Frontier in Space (1973) QQQ
Maurice Bush, David Joyce, Rick Lester, Frank Menzies, Geoffrey Todd, Bruce Wells (KKK); Rick Lester (PPP); Stephen Thorne, Michael Kilgarriff, Rick Lester, Maurice Bush, Steve Kelly, Maurice Purvis, Geoffrey Todd, Bruce Wells, Chris Stevens (QQQ)

A powerful ape-like life form from a distant planet. The Ogrons

were used by the *Daleks* as slaves due to their powerful strength and lack of intelligence.

OMEGA

Created by Bob Baker and Dave Martin
The Three Doctors (1972/3) RRR
Arc of Infinity (1983) 6E
Stephen Thorne (RRR), Ian Collier, Peter Davison (6E)

Omega was a Gallifreyan solar engineer who travelled into the heart of a black hole in order to detonate a device which would supply his people with unlimited power. Although the Gallifreyans believed that Omega had perished, he had in fact survived in a universe of anti-matter. Over time he shaped this universe using only his will and plotted to return to take his revenge against those whom he felt had abandoned him to his fate. The Doctor eventually destroyed Omega on Earth.

OMEGA'S CHAMPION

Created by Bob Baker and Dave Martin
The Three Doctors (1972/3)
Alan Chuntz

To prove his supremacy, the trapped Gallifreyan solar engineer *Omega* challenged the Doctor to a battle against his dark side, represented by a troll-like creature.

OPTERA

Created by Bill Strutton
The Web Planet (1965)
Hetra: Ian Thompson
Nemini: Barbara Joss
Optera: Jane Bowman, Len Russell

The Optera were the wingless underground cousins to the *Menoptra* on the planet Vortis. They assisted the Doctor's companion Ian to enter the heart of the parasitic *Animus* in order to destroy it.

OSIRANS

Created by Lewis Griefer and Robert Holmes
Pyramids of Mars (1975)
Sutekh: Gabriel Woolf
Voice of Horus: Gabriel Woolf

Sutekh was one of the ancient Egyptian gods, in truth an alien Osiran who left death and destruction in his path. He was captured by his brother Horus, and rendered immobile in a pyramid on Earth, controlled from a pyramid on Mars. Using his mental

energy, Sutekh enslaved an unwary archaeologist and used him to construct a rocket intended to destroy the pyramid on Mars and release Sutekh. This plan failed, but the Doctor was forced to travel to Mars and destroy the power source. Sutekh was released, but the Doctor trapped him in a time corridor and aged the Osiran to death.

PIPE PEOPLE

Created by Graeme Curry
The Happiness Patrol (1988)
Wences: Phillip Neve
Wulfric: Ryan Freedman
Pipe People: Bilent Hassan, Charles Martin, Steven Martin, Lee Pearse

These creatures lived in the pipes and underground tunnels on the planet Terra Alpha. They had been driven underground by human colonists and worked to oppose the schemes of Helen A.

PLANETARIANS

Created by Terry Nation
Dalek Cutaway (1965)
Johnny Clayton, Pat Gorman, Sam Mansaray, Len Russell

Unnamed delegates of the Dalek Alliance on Kembel. In *The Daleks' Master Plan* these creatures are named: *Beaus, Sentreal, Warrien* and *Gearon*. It is not known which actor played which creature in *Dalek Cutaway*.

PLASMATONS

Created by Peter Grimwade
Time Flight (1982)
Steve Fideli, Paul Heasman, Martin Grant, Chris Holmes, Graham Jarvis, Giles Melville, Mykel Mills, Nigel Tisdall
Snake Creature Puppeteer: Richard Gregory

The Plasmatons were creatures constructed from proteins in the air by the mysterious oriental mystic Kalid – the Master in disguise – in order to trap and bring others to him. One of these entities was in the form of a two-headed snake-like creature conjured to threaten the Doctor.

POLYPHASE AVITRON

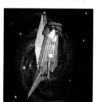

Created by Douglas Adams
The Pirate Planet (1978)

The Polyphase Avitron was a robot parrot owned by the Captain of the planet-destroying ship *Zanak*. It was destroyed by K-9.

PRIMORDS

Created by Don Houghton
Inferno (1970)
Director Stahlmann: Olaf Pooley
Platoon Under-Leader Benton: John Levene
Bromley: Ian Fairbairn
Primords: Dave Carter, Pat Gorman, Walter Henry, Philip Ryan, Peter Thompson

When exposed to a green liquid seeping from a deep-drilling shaft, humans transformed into subhuman ape-like creatures which needed heat to survive.

QUARKS

Created by Mervyn Haisman and Henry Lincoln
The Dominators (1968) TT
The War Games (1969) ZZ
John Hicks, Gary Smith, Freddie Wilson (TT); Freddie Wilson (ZZ)
Voices: Sheila Grant (TT)

The Quarks were the robot servants of the Dominators who tried to convert the planet Dulkis into a radioactive power source for the Dominators' space fleet [TT]. They were also among those enemies shown by the Doctor as a part of his defence during his first trial by the Time Lords [ZZ].

RAAK, THE

Created by Philip Martin
The Trial of a Time Lord (1986)
Russell West

A monster created by Crozier on Thoros-Beta. It was used to operate tidal control machinery and was killed by the Doctor in self defence.

RASTON WARRIOR ROBOT

Created by Terrance Dicks
The Five Doctors (1983)
Keith Hodiak

A powerful and fast-as-light killer robot discovered by the Doctor in the Death Zone on Gallifrey. The robot wiped out an entire squadron of armed *Cybermen* with little effort.

REFUSIANS

Created by Paul Erickson and Lesley Scott
The Ark (1966)
Voice: Richard Beale

The Refusians were the invisible inhabitants of Refusis II to which the last survivors of humanity travelled when Earth was destroyed. The humans had been enslaved by the reptilian *Monoids* but the Refusians forced them to settle their differences when they arrived on Refusis II to start a new life.

RILLS

Created by William Emms
Galaxy 4 (1965)
Peter Holmes, Bill Lodge, Brian Madge, David Brewster
Voices: Robert Cartland

The Rills were hideously ugly warthog-like creatures which had been involved in a space battle with a group of *Drahvins*. Both ships crashed on a nearby planet which was on the verge of destruction. The peaceful Rills tried to help the warlike Drahvins but they refused assistance and instead tried to destroy the Rills. With the aid of their robot helpers, the *Chumblies*, and the Doctor, the Rills escaped the dying planet, but the Drahvins perished.

ROBOT

Created by Terrance Dicks
Robot (1974/5)
Michael Kilgarriff
Robot Hands: John East

Professor Kettlewell created his 'experimental prototype robot K-1' as a means to help mankind, but a political pressure group, the Scientific Reform Society, intended to use it to blackmail the world. The robot ended up killing Kettlewell and growing to giant size before it was destroyed by a metal-eating virus.

ROBOT BUS CONDUCTOR

Created by Stephen Wyatt
The Greatest Show in the Galaxy (1988/9)
Dean Hollingsworth

This robot tried to kill Ace when she investigated a derelict tour-bus once owned by Kingpin, founder of the Psychic Circus on the planet Segonax.

ROBOT, L1 SERVICER

Created by Robert Holmes
The Trial of a Time Lord (1986)
Mike Ellis

A robot used by *Drathro* on the surface of the planet Ravolox.

ROBOT, MINING

Created by Malcolm Hulke
Colony in Space (1971)
John Scott Martin

A robot used for digging and taking soil and mineral samples from a planet's surface, used by the Interplanetary Mining Corporation (IMC). They also equipped one of the robots with claws and used it to terrorise any colonists who stood in the way of IMC's exploitation of a world.

ROBOTS

Created by Chris Boucher
The Robots of Death (1977)
D84: Gregory De Polnay
SV7: Miles Fothergill
Robots: Mark Blackwell Baker, Peter Langtry, John Bleasdale, Richard Seager, Mark Cooper, Jeremy Ranchev

On a sandminer combing a planet for mineral ore, the slave robots were being altered by a robot-loving human called Taren Capel. The robots started to kill off the human crew and when the Doctor and Leela arrived, they were accused of the crimes until the real killers revealed themselves.

RUTAN

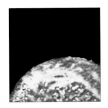

Created by Robert Holmes (story written by Terrance Dicks)
Horror of Fang Rock (1977)
Reuben: Colin Douglas
Voice: Colin Douglas

The Rutans were the sworn enemies of the *Sontarans*. In basic appearance, the Rutans were similar to jellyfish but could change their appearance at will to blend in with their surroundings. They were electrically charged and could kill using a powerful electric shock.

SAND MONSTER

Created by David Whitaker
The Rescue (1964)
Tom Sheridan

The sand monster was a pet looked after by Vicki on the planet Dido. It was harmless, yet was killed by Barbara when she thought Vicki was in danger from it.

SCREAMERS

Created by Terry Nation
The Daleks' Master Plan (1965/6)

Bloodsucking bat creatures with six-foot wingspans from the planet Desperus.

SEA DEVILS

Created by Malcolm Hulke
The Sea Devils (1972) LLL
Frontier in Space (1973) QQQ
Warriors of the Deep (1984) 6L
Leader: Peter Forbes-Robertson (LLL);
Sea Devils: Marc Boyle, Peter Brace, Alan Chuntz, Jack Cooper, Stuart Fell, Pat Gorman, Bill Horrigan, Mike Horsburgh, Steve Ismay, Brian Nolan, Frank Seton, Mike Stevens, Terry Walsh, Derek Ware, Geoffrey Witherick (LLL); Pat Gorman (QQQ); Mike Braben, Steve Kelly, Dave Ould, Jules Walters, Chris Wolfe, Christopher Farries (6L)
Sauvix: Christopher Farries (6L)

The Sea Devils were underwater cousins to the *Silurians*. They were revived from hibernation by workmen on an abandoned sea fort, and then contacted by the Master to help him dominate the world [LLL]. Jo was frightened of them and saw one when subjected to the Master's fear-inducing device [QQQ]. A troop of Sea Devil Warriors was revived by the *Silurians* in order to attack a Sea Base and start a global war [6L]. See page 46.

SENSORITES

Created by Peter R Newman
The Sensorites (1964)
First Sensorite: Ken Tyllsen
Second Sensorite: Joe Greig
Third Sensorite (Administrator): Peter Glaze
Fourth Sensorite (Engineer): Arthur Newall
First Elder: Eric Francis
Second Elder: Bartlett Mullins
First Scientist: Ken Tyllsen
Second Scientist: Joe Greig
Warrior: Joe Greig
Sensorites: Gerry Martin, Anthony Rogers

The Sensorites were the peaceful inhabitants of the Sense-Sphere and were fearful of humans as they blamed them for a plague that was killing their people. The Doctor revealed the true culprits to be a group of insane human astronauts who were poisoning the Sense-Sphere's water supply with deadly nightshade.

SENTREAL

Created by Terry Nation
The Daleks' Master Plan (1965/6)
Ian East or Brian Edwards (casting uncertain)

One of the alliance members involved in the *Daleks'* plan to conquer the solar system. Sentreal escaped to warn his own people about the Daleks.

SERVO ROBOT

Created by David Whitaker
The Wheel in Space (1968)
Freddie Foote

The Servo Robot was running the otherwise crewless space rocket the *Silver Carrier,* which had been hijacked by the *Cybermen* as a part of their plan to invade Earth.

SHRIVENZALES

Created by Robert Holmes
The Ribos Operation (1978)
Stuart Fell, Nick Wilkinson

These creatures roamed the passages and catacombs below the city of Shur on the planet Ribos. They were used as 'guard dogs' to protect the royal jewel room.

SILURIANS

Created by Malcolm Hulke
Doctor Who and the Silurians (1970) BBB
Warriors of the Deep (1984) 6L
Old Silurian: Dave Carter (BBB)
Young Silurian: Nigel Johns (BBB)
Scientist: Pat Gorman (BBB)
Voices: Peter Halliday, Paul Barton (BBB)
Silurians: Paul Barton, Simon Cain, Dave Carter, Pat Gorman, John Churchill (BBB)
Icthar: Norman Comer (6L)
Scibus: Stuart Blake (6L)
Tarpok: Vincent Brimble (6L)

The Silurians were a race of intelligent, civilised reptiles who inhabited the Earth possibly around the Eocene period of history. Their scientists predicted that a meteor would strike the Earth and so the Silurians went into hibernation. The meteor did not strike and the Silurians slept on until they were roused by the construction of a nuclear research base in caves under Wenley Moor [BBB]. Later, a group of three Silurians tried to initiate a global war amongst humanity, leaving the planet for the reptiles to take over [6L]. See page 45.

SKARASEN, THE

Created by Robert Banks Stewart
Terror of the Zygons (1975)

Cyborg 'pet' of the *Zygons.* They fed off its lactic fluids and used it to attack oil rigs off the coast of Scotland. It lived in Loch Ness where it remained when the Zygon spacecraft was destroyed.

SLYTHER, THE

Created by Terry Nation
The Dalek Invasion of Earth (1964)
Nick Evans

A carnivourous alien life form kept as a 'pet' and 'guard dog' by the Black *Dalek.* It fell to its death down a pit shaft at the Daleks' mine workings in Bedfordshire.

SMITH, JOSIAH SAMUEL

Created by Marc Platt
Ghost Light (1989)
Ian Hogg

A part of the angel-like being *Light's* team on Earth. Smith was to carry out the survey and, as such, rapidly adapted into whatever life form would allow the work to progress the most efficiently. As he adapted, Smith shed his old non-human forms as living husks, but he also developed the thirst for power and freedom from his master, Light, and determined to bring down the English monarchy by having Queen Victoria assassinated. As *Control* rapidly adapted, and Light was destroyed, Smith regressed to a base state as Control took charge of Light's ongoing survey.

SONTARANS

Created by Robert Holmes
The Time Warrior (1973/4) UUU
The Sontaran Experiment (1975) 4B
The Invasion of Time (1978) 4Z
The Two Doctors (1985) 6W
Commander Linx: Kevin Lindsay (UUU)
Field-Major Styre: Kevin Lindsay (4B)
Double for Field-Major Styre: Stuart Fell (4B)
Marshal: Kevin Lindsay (4B)
Commander Stor: Derek Deadman (4Z)
Sontarans: Stuart Fell, Martyn Richards, Norman Rochester (4Z)
Group Marshal Stike: Clinton Greyn (6W)
Major Varl: Tim Raynham (6W)

A ruthless clone race of warriors. They were militaristic and expert at all forms of war. The Doctor encountered one of their number on Earth in the Middle Ages [UUU], and later met another on Earth in the far future [4B]. The creatures attempted to invade Gallifrey [4Z] and also, with the aid of a scientist named Dastari, tried to discover the Time Lords' secret of time travel [6W]. See page 55.

SPIRIDONS

Created by Terry Nation
Planet of the Daleks (1973)
Wester: Roy Skelton
Spiridons: David Billa, Gary Dean, Terence Denville, Ronald Gough, Kevin Moran, Kelly Varney, Geoffrey Witherick
Voices: Michael Wisher, Roy Skelton

The invisible Spiridons found themselves enslaved by the *Daleks* when they arrived on their planet seeking the secret of invisibility for themselves. One of the Spiridons, Wester, helped Jo, and later sacrificed his own life in order to prevent the Daleks releasing a virus that would wipe out all unprotected life on the planet. The Spiridons became visible at the moment of their death.

STIGORAX

Created by Graeme Curry
The Happiness Patrol (1988)
Howl: Graeme Curry

Helen A, the tyrannical ruler of Terra Alpha, had a dog-like stigorax called 'Fifi' as a pet. They were described by the Doctor as ruthless, intelligent predators.

TERILEPTILS

Created by Eric Saward
The Visitation (1982) 5X
Time-Flight (1982) 6C
Michael Leader, Michael Melia, David Summer (5X)
Phantom: Chris Bradshaw (6C)

The Terileptils came from a distant planet. The Doctor met them on Earth when a criminal who had escaped from the prison planet of Raaga with three fellows crashed there in the 17th century. The Doctor tried to help the aliens, but they ended up being killed in a fire started in Pudding Lane, London, in the year 1666 [5X]. A phantom Terileptil was used by the Master to try to prevent Tegan and Nyssa from entering an inner sanctum [6C].

TETRAPS

Created by Pip and Jane Baker
Time and the Rani (1987)
Urak: Richard Gauntlett
Tetraps: Mark Carroll, Lea Derek, Ian Durrant, Paul Goddard, Andrew James, Ricardo Mulhall, Paul Page-Hanson

The batlike Tetraps were slaves of the Rani when she attempted to use the planet Lakertya as a base for her experiments to create the alloy loyhargil. Ultimately the Tetraps turned on her and took her back to their planet.

THARILS

Created by Stephen Gallagher
Warriors' Gate (1981)
Biroc: David Weston
Lazlo: Jeremy Gittins
Female Tharil: Erika Spotswood
Tharils: Carl Bohun, Laurie Goode, Michael Gordon-Browne,
Andy Hart, James Muir, Joe Santo

The time-sensitive Tharils were used by unscrupulous traders to navigate the time winds and see ships through safely. This state of affairs had come about because the Tharils had mistreated humankind in the past, and the humans had sent *Gundan* robots to wipe them out. A Tharil named Biroc sought to set matters straight and rescued his fellows from slavery. The Doctor's companion Romana remained with the Tharils in E-Space to help them in their quest for freedom.

TRACTATORS

Created by Christopher H Bidmead
Frontios (1984)
The Gravis: John Gillett
Tractators: William Bowen, George Campbell, Hedi Khursandi,
Michael Malcolm, Stephen Speed

The Tractators were a race of grub-like burrowing insects which could control gravity. When a Gravis appears – an intelligent Tractator – they operate as a hive mind and systematically destroy any other life on the planet, eventually turning the planet into a travelling craft for their use. If the Gravis is separated from the other Tractators, they return to their normal docile state. As well as the planet Frontios, they had also attacked Trion in the distant past.

TRANTIS

Created by Terry Nation
Dalek Cutaway (1965) T/A
The Daleks' Master Plan (1965/6) V
Ronald Rich (T/A); Roy Evans (V)

Trantis was the sole attendee from the outer galaxies at the Intergalactic Conference of Andromeda and was also a member of the *Dalek* alliance. The Daleks used Trantis as a test subject for their time destructor weapon and, when the weapon failed, they exterminated him anyway.

TYTHONIAN

Created by David Fisher
The Creature from the Pit (1979)

The planet of Tythonus was rich in mineral wealth, but low in vegetation and so a Tythonian ambassador called Erato travelled to the neighbouring planet of Chloris on which exactly the opposite balance occurred. Unfortunately, Lady Adrasta wanted to maintain her monopoly of metal on Chloris and so had Erato thrown into a pit where she sacrificed those who opposed her. Erato, however, had sent a distress message and the Tythonians launched a neutron star at Chloris in retaliation. The Doctor helped Erato prevent the neutron star from destroying Chloris.

UNICORN

Created by Peter Ling
The Mind Robber (1968)
Goldy

One of the fictional creatures summoned by the Master of the Land of Fiction to attack the Doctor, Zoe and Jamie.

URBANKANS

Created by Terence Dudley
Four to Doomsday (1982)
Monarch: Stratford Johns
Enlightenment: Annie Lambert
Persuasion: Paul Shelley

The Urbankans were a race of frog-like creatures from the planet Urbanka. One of their number, Monarch, was insane and believed himself to be God. He caused the destruction of Urbanka by stripping it of all its mineral wealth and planned to do the same to Earth. This was to achieve faster-than-light travel so that he could go back in time and meet himself: the creator. Monarch intended to destroy humanity with a poison, produced by the Urbankans, which shrank matter. In the end he succumbed to the poison himself.

USURIANS

Created by Robert Holmes
The Sun Makers (1977)
The Collector: Henry Woolf

The Collector was an Usurian who ran the Company on the planet Pluto. The Usurians were magnificent accountants and taxed everything on the planet to ensure that profits were maximised. When the Doctor introduced a two per cent growth tax into their computers, the Collector could not cope with making a loss and reverted to his true form – a seaweed-like creature.

UXARIANS

Created by Malcolm Hulke
Colony in Space (1971)
The Guardian: Norman Atkyns
Priests: Roy Heymann, Stanley Mason, Antonia Moss
Primitives: Pat Gorman, Stewart Anderson, Derek Chafer,
Les Clark, Emmett Hennessy, John McGrath, Alan Peters,
Gregory Powell, Walter Turner, Mike Stephens, Terry Walsh,
Dinny Powell, Alf Joint, Mike Horsburgh, Valentino Musetti

Remnants of the once-powerful civilisation on the planet Uxarius. The Guardian looked after the doomsday weapon with which the Master hoped to rule the universe. The Priests had lost the power of sight through living underground, and worshipped the Guardian. The telepathic Primitives had also degenerated and were living as scavengers in peace with a group of human colonists.

VAMPIRES

Created by Terrance Dicks
State of Decay (1980)
Aukon (Anthony O'Connor): Emrys James
Camilla (Lauren MacMillan): Rachel Davies
Zargo (Miles Sharkey): William Lindsay

The Time Lords fought a long battle against the Great Vampires and they were believed dead until the Doctor encountered one in E-Space. The creature had corrupted three space travellers and turned them into vampires who needed blood with which to arise. The Doctor managed to destroy the Great Vampire and Aukon, Camilla and Zargo crumbled to dust as their master died.

VARDANS

Created by David Weir, Graham Williams and Anthony Read
The Invasion of Time (1978)
Vardan Leader: Stan McGowan
Vardans: Tom Kelly, Julian Hudson

The Vardans planned an invasion of the Time Lords' planet Gallifrey and used the Doctor to open a way for them. The Vardans could transmit themselves as energy waves and the Doctor was secretly working with them in order to discover the location of their home planet and place it in a time loop. What the Doctor did not realise was that once the path to Gallifrey was clear, the Vardans' masters, the *Sontarans*, would arrive, intent on stealing the Time Lords' matrix of knowledge.

VARGA PLANTS

Created by Terry Nation
Dalek Cutaway (1965) T/A
The Daleks' Master Plan (1966) V
Jeff Garvey: Barry Jackson (T/A)
Gordon Lowery: Jeremy Young (T/A)
Roy Reeves, Tony Starr, Leslie Weekes

The Varga plants lived on the planet Kembel and protected a *Dalek* city from discovery. If pricked by a Varga thorn, a human would gradually turn into a Varga plant himself. This fate befell Jeff Garvey and Gordon Lowery, two of Space Security Service agent Marc Cory's team investigating the planet.

VEGA NEXOS

Created by Brian Hayles
The Monster of Peladon (1974)
Gerald Taylor

One of a race of mining creatures working on Peladon. Vega Nexos was killed by the 'spirit of *Aggedor*' – in truth a heat ray – while demonstrating a sonic lance.

VERVOIDS

Created by Pip and Jane Baker
The Trial of a Time Lord (1986)
Peppi Borza, Bob Appleby, Paul Hillier, Jerry Manley,
William Perrie, Gess Whitfield
Mutant (Ruth Baxter): Barbara Ward

The Vervoids were plants bred by Professor Lasky, which were being transported on a luxury liner when they were allowed to 'hatch'. They were carnivorous and intelligent and devastated the passengers before the Doctor stopped them using burning vionesium – a magnesium-like substance – to make them wither and die.

VIRUS

Created by Bob Baker and Dave Martin
The Invisible Enemy (1977)
Nucleus: John Scott Martin
Nucleus Voice: John Leeson

The Virus was a space-borne entity which attacked a space shuttle and took over the crew. It then spread to Titan base before becoming lodged in the Doctor's mind. Using equipment from the TARDIS the Virus was inadvertently grown to giant size and attempted to breed and spawn on Titan before it was destroyed

in an explosion.

VISIANS

Created by Terry Nation
The Daleks' Master Plan (1965/6)
Francis Whilley

The Visians were an invisible four-toed, eight-foot-tall life form from the planet Mira. They became visible when fired upon.

VOGANS

Created by Gerry Davis
Revenge of the Cybermen (1975)
Magrik: Michael Wisher
Vorus: David Collings
Sheprah: Brian Grellis
Tyrum: Kevin Stoney
Vogans: David Billa, David Sulkin, Cy Town, Leslie Weekes,
Terry Walsh, Alan Chuntz, Roy Caesar, Harry Fielder,
Barry Summerford
Voice: Michael Wisher

A race of creatures living under the surface of the planet Voga in fear of the *Cybermen*. They planned to destroy a Cyberman spacecraft by using a human double-agent to lure the Cybermen to Voga.

VOORDS

Created by Terry Nation
The Keys of Marinus (1964)
Yartek: Stephen Dartnell
Voords: Martin Cort, Peter Stenson, Gordon Wales

Black rubber-clad creatures immune to the effects of the pacifying influence of the Conscience of Marinus. Their leader, Yartek, led them in an attack on Arbitan, Keeper of the Conscience, in an attempt to control the planet. See page 12.

WAR MACHINES

Created by Ian Stuart Black
The War Machines (1966)
Gerald Taylor

Computerised killing machines controlled by the super-computer WOTAN.

WARRIEN

Created by Terry Nation

The Daleks' Master Plan (1965/6)
Ian East or Brian Edwards (casting uncertain)

One of the alliance involved in the *Daleks'* plan to conquer the solar system. Warrien escaped to warn his own people about the Daleks.

WEED CREATURES

Created by Victor Pemberton
Fury from the Deep (1967)

The weed creatures initially manifested as a parasitic seaweed which took control of its human victims through a sting. The weed could exhale a poisonous gas and a suffocating foam. The creatures were sensitive to sound and were killed by the amplified sound of the screams of the Doctor's companion Victoria.

WHITE ROBOTS

Created by Peter Ling and Derrick Sherwin
The Mind Robber (1968)
John Atterbury, Ralph Carrigan, Bill Weisener, Terry Wright

Robot servants of the Master of the Land of Fiction. The white robots captured Jamie and Zoe during the Master's attempts to fictionalise them.

WIRRN

Created by Robert Holmes from an idea by John Lucarotti
The Ark in Space (1975)
Stuart Fell, Nick Hobbs
Wirrn Grub: Stuart Fell

The Wirrn were a spacefaring race of insects which used other species as the hosts for their eggs. When the eggs hatched, the Wirrn pupae could infect other life forms and convert them into Wirrn, the adult creature retaining the knowledge and intelligence of the original host body. They were encountered by humankind in Andromeda.

WOLF WEEDS

Created by David Fisher
The Creature from the Pit (1979)

A vegetable life form native to Chloris. The Wolf Weeds were ambulatory balls of vegetable matter that could be trained to attack and immobilise on the command of the Huntsman.

WOOD BEAST

Created by David Fisher
The Androids of Tara (1978)

Ray Lavender

A furry bear-like creature which lived in the woods surrounding Castle Gracht on the planet Tara.

XERAPHIN

Created by Peter Grimwade
Time-Flight (1982)
Anithon: Hugh Hayes
Zarak: Andre Winterton

The Xeraphin of Xeriphas travelled to Earth but, on their arrival, found that they were suffering from radiation sickness. They collected themselves into a single entity to wait for the sickness to pass, but at the point of their rebirth, the Master interfered and caused the death of the new Xeraphin. The Master then contacted the core and caused it to split into a good side and a bad side, the latter attempting to create more evil Xeraphin and take over the universe.

YETI

Created by Mervyn Haisman and Henry Lincoln
The Abominable Snowmen (1966) NN
The Web of Fear (1967) QQ
The War Games (1969) ZZ
The Five Doctors (1983) 6K
Tony Harwood, John Hogan, Richard Kerley, Reg Whitehead (NN); Roger Jacombs, Jeremy King, John Levene, John Lord, Gordon Stothard, Colin Warman (QQ); John Levene (ZZ); Lee Woods (6K)

The Yeti were the robot servants of the formless *Great Intelligence*. They were controlled through mobile silver spheres which could be reprogrammed. They were armed with deadly web guns [QQ] and used to carry out the Intelligence's plans on Earth. A Yeti was used as an example of the evils fought by the Doctor during his trial by the Time Lords [ZZ] and a lone Yeti attacked the Doctor and the Brigadier in the Death Zone on Gallifrey [6K]. See page 17.

ZARBI

Created by Bill Strutton
The Web Planet (1965)
Robert Jewell, Kevin Manser, John Scott Martin, Gerald Taylor

The Zarbi were a race of peaceful giant ants which roamed the planet Vortis. When the *Animus* arrived, it took control of the Zarbi and bent them to its purpose: the oppression of the intelligent life form, the *Menoptra*. With the Animus defeated, the Zarbi returned to their former way of life. See page 13.

ZEPHON

Created by Terry Nation
The Daleks' Master Plan (1965/6)
Julian Sherrier

Master of the fifth galaxy and member of the *Dalek* alliance. The Doctor disguised himself as Zephon in order to infiltrate the Daleks' conference on Kembel. Zephon was killed by the Daleks.

ZOMBIES

Created by Terry Nation
Death to the Daleks (1974)
Steve Ismay, Terry Walsh

In order to protect itself from attack, the 'living' *city* built on the planet Exxilon grew zombie-like antibodies to repel the Doctor, Bellal and two *Daleks* which had penetrated the city's outer defences. Once formed, the zombies forced the Daleks to retreat as they were impervious to the Dalek's weapons.

ZYGONS

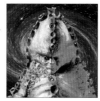

Created by Robert Banks Stewart
Terror of the Zygons (1975)
Broton: John Woodnutt
Zygons: Keith Ashley, Ronald Gough
Zygon Voices: Lilias Walker, Robert Russell

A spacecraft containing a group of Zygons arrived on Earth after their home planet was destroyed by solar flares. They hid at the bottom of Loch Ness in Scotland, and planned to take over the world. They fed off the lactic fluids of the cyborg *Skarasen*. They had the ability to re-form their appearance into that of humans by copying a human's body pattern. This allowed them to operate amongst humankind in order to de-stabilise the government. The majority were destroyed when their ship exploded after the Doctor caused it to self-destruct, and their leader Broton was later shot by the Brigadier.

ORIGINAL MONSTER DESIGNS

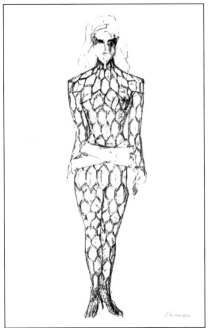

Above, left to right: Fish Person (design by Sandra Reid), Chimeron (by Richard Croft), Light (by Ken Trew)

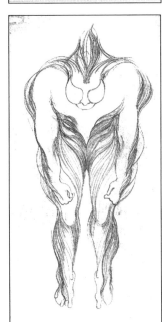
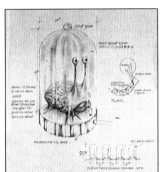

Above, clockwise: Gastropod (by Pat Godfrey), Morpho Brain (by Raymond P Cusick), Quark (by Martin Baugh), Vega Nexos (by Barbara Kidd).

INDEX

INDEX

Italicised numerals represent pictorial references